RECOLLECTIONS OF A TEJANO LIFE

Number Thirty-Nine,
Jack and Doris Smothers Series in Texas History, Life, and Culture

RECOLLECTIONS OF A TEJANO LIFE

Antonio Menchaca in Texas History

EDITED BY TIMOTHY MATOVINA AND
JESÚS F. DE LA TEJA
WITH THE COLLABORATION OF JUSTIN POCHÉ

UNIVERSITY OF TEXAS PRESS
Austin

First edition, 2013
First paperback edition, 2014

Requests for permission to reproduce material
from this work should be sent to:
Permissions
University of Texas Press
P.O. Box 7819
Austin, TX 78713-7819
http://utpress.utexas.edu/index.php/rp-form

⊚ The paper used in this book meets the minimum requirements
of ANSI/NISO Z39.48–1992 (R1997) (Permanence of Paper).

Library of Congress Cataloging-in-Publication Data
Menchaca, Antonio, 1800–1879.
Recollections of a Tejano life : Antonio Menchaca in Texas
history / edited by Timothy Matovina and Jesús F. de la Teja ;
with the collaboration of Justin Poché. — First edition.
pages   cm. — (Jack and Doris Smothers series in Texas
history, life, and culture ; number thirty-nine)
Includes bibliographical references and index.
ISBN 978-0-292-74865-1 (cloth : alkaline paper)
ISBN 978-1-4773-0217-0 (paperback)
1. Menchaca, Antonio, 1800–1879.   2. Mexican Americans—Texas—
Biography.   3. Soldiers—Texas—Biography.   4. Texas—History—
Revolution, 1835–1836—Personal narratives.   5. Texas—History—To
1846—Sources.   6. Texas—History—1846–1950—Sources.   7. San Antonio
(Tex.)—History—19th century—Sources.   I. Matovina, Timothy M.,
1955-   II. Teja, Jesús F. de la, 1956-   III. Poché, Justin D.   IV. Title.
F389.M396   2013
976.4′03092—dc23   [B]   2012047275

doi:10.7560/748651

CONTENTS

PREFACE

Our purpose in writing this volume is to provide the first complete and annotated publication of the reminiscences of nineteenth-century San Antonio native and San Jacinto veteran José Antonio Menchaca. The original manuscript for the first half of the reminiscences is no longer extant, though the material it contains has been published twice and is known to a number of historians and readers of Texas history. But to date many researchers are not even aware of the existence of the second half, as it has been available only in manuscript form at the Briscoe Center for American History at the University of Texas at Austin. The somewhat deteriorated condition of that original manuscript, a recording of Menchaca's reminiscences toward the end of his seventy-nine years with the collaboration of an Anglo-American scribe, and the fact that variant versions of the first half of the reminiscences were published are just some of the challenges we faced in presenting Menchaca's testimony in a manner that is both as faithful as possible to his recollections while also helpful for modern readers. Thus a brief overview of the recording and publication history of Menchaca's reminiscences and the strategic choices we made in reproducing them is in order.

A portion of Menchaca's recollections was first published in serialized form in the San Antonio weekly the *Passing Show* in 1907 and was reprinted in 1937 by Frederick C. Chabot in a publication of the Yanaguana Society, a local history group of which Chabot was one of the founders. The latter edition has long been the only cited version of the known portion of Menchaca's text, which is usually referred to as his memoirs since the *Passing Show* titled the work "The Memoirs of Captain Menchaca" and Chabot followed suit in his Yanaguana Society edition by titling the book *Memoirs*. For the published first part of Menchaca's recollections, the title is not out of place, since the narrative focuses on events he relates covering the years from 1807 to 1836 in which he directly or indirectly participated. But the second, previously unpublished part of the manuscript includes a number of observations and the recounting of legends that do not fit under the category of memoirs. Therefore, since the scope of Menchaca's narrative is broader than the people and events with which he was personally associated and covers a wide range of topics, it seems more appropriate to refer to the manuscript as his reminiscences.

The preparation of Menchaca's reminiscences for publication posed numerous challenges. First, there was the matter of the widely unknown version of the first half of the original manuscript. Until today the first half of Menchaca's work as it appeared in the version prepared by Chabot and published by the Yanaguana Society of San Antonio in 1937, *Memoirs*, was the only one widely available. It proved difficult to track down the version of this part first published in the *Passing Show*, in which the reminiscences were serialized between 22 June and 27 July 1907. Fortunately, we located a complete run in the Texana Collection of the San Antonio Public Library in clippings form. Second, there are differences between the *Passing Show* and Yanaguana Society versions, but no guidance exists as to which conforms more closely to the original document. Likewise, there is no guidance on the relationship between the unpublished second part, which begins mid-sentence, and the twice-published first part, since we do not know how much, if any, material may be missing. Third, there is the matter of how much Menchaca's collaborator, who actually wrote down his reminiscences, may have interjected himself. In particular, the reminiscences bounce between first- and third-person narrative. And, fourth, there is the matter of the draft nature of the document as a whole. Neither James P. Newcomb of the *Passing Show*, responsible for the first published version, nor Chabot, responsible for the Yanaguana Society version, attempted to produce a smooth edition that corrected the grammatical, orthographic, and factual problems in the original first half of the reminiscences, and the second-half manuscript is a very rough draft.

In the edited version of Menchaca's reminiscences presented here we attempt to give the modern reader a useable reconstruction that informs while preserving to the extent possible Menchaca's original intent. It is obvious on comparing the two available versions that Newcomb either was incapable of proofreading (he died a few months after the *Passing Show* version appeared) or lacked editorial control to proofread what appeared in the weekly installments. Chabot, however, appears to have gone beyond merely restoring what was missing in the *Passing Show* when he prepared the Yanaguana Society version. Thus for this volume we have selected the earlier, *Passing Show* version, which is presumably closer to the original manuscript, as the governing document for the first part, but for this edition we have also restored a notable two-paragraph section from the Chabot version that appears to have been omitted from the *Passing Show* (along with a number of other phrases that appear to have been omitted from the *Passing Show* but that make the text more intelligible). We have marked these restorations by underlining the text and placing it within brackets in part 1 of the unedited version of the reminiscences; in the edited version we have simply made these editorial changes without explanatory notation.

Because the unpublished second part of the original, handwritten manuscript sustained some damage over the years, we have extrapolated the missing material as much as possible in the edited version, while using ellipses within brackets in the unedited version to indicate the gaps. Furthermore, while we have resolved grammatical, orthographic, and continuity issues in the edited version, we have presented the unedited narrative in a form that remains as close to the original as possible, including a number of underlined phrases. Therefore, we have forgone the use of *sic*, since the intent is to present the document as is. The result is that for the unedited version the first part is a literal transcription of the *Passing Show* version with the two paragraphs and other phrase insertions from the Chabot version added, while the second part is presented as a reproduction in type of the original handwritten manuscript, with the exception of the pagination and spacing.

Shifts from first- to third-person narrative in the reminiscences and sometimes-confusing references to the various parties involved in the action required standardization. Throughout the edited version of the reminiscences, wherever Menchaca refers to himself we have placed the reference in the first person to avoid confusion. As he employs the terms *American* and *Mexican* in a haphazard and sometimes anachronistic fashion, we have used the terms *republican* and *royalist* early in the first part to distinguish between those fighting for and against Mexican independence. Later in the edited reminiscences, where appropriate, we use the term *Tejanos* for the Hispanic population of Texas to distinguish them from Mexicans from elsewhere. We have retained the term *American* where it clearly refers to Anglo-American individuals, but we have changed it to *Texan* where the circumstances refer to both Anglo-Texans and Tejanos or to the pro–Texas independence forces and government.

We have checked Menchaca's statements of fact against the historical record, and in the edited version we have corrected names, places, and events either in the text or in the explanatory notes. To reduce the volume of material in the citations, except where a note cites works in full for explanatory purposes, we have briefly cited references to works consulted and listed them in full in the bibliography. We refer in the notes to instances in which Menchaca's collaborator may have interjected himself. Consequently, we offer the reader a version that has been edited to make it readable and intelligible, with grammar and orthography made consistent according to current usage.

This project began with the call that Frank de la Teja put out to a group of colleagues and friends to assemble biographical essays on a number of Tejano leaders from the Mexican statehood and Texas War of Independence period for a conference to be held at Texas State University–San Marcos in October 2006. Among those responding to the call was Timothy Matovina, who wrote an essay on Antonio Menchaca that became part of the book that resulted from the conference, *Tejano Leadership in Mexican and Revolutionary Texas*. Subsequently we collaborated to compose a revised introductory essay that broadens the contribution on Menchaca that appeared in that book. We also prepared transcriptions for an edited version of Menchaca's reminiscences, a task for which Frank took on the leading role. Finally, we did additional investigative work to clear up numerous issues and undertook to edit the Menchaca manuscript into a seamless whole.

The editors would like to thank Justin Poché for doing initial transcription work and primary research, including investigations in the collections at the DeGolyer Library supported by a Clements Center–DeGolyer Library Research Travel Grant from the Clements Center for Southwest Studies at Southern Methodist University. Thanks also to the staffs at the Daughters of the Republic of Texas Library and the Briscoe Center for American History and to Frank Faulkner of the San Antonio Public Library for their assistance in tracking down numerous odds and ends that allowed us to piece much of the story together. We also wish to thank Gloria Thomas for her thorough work as copyeditor, which significantly improved the final product. And we are most grateful to Paula Brach of Notre Dame's Cushwa Center for the Study of American Catholicism, who effectively secured permissions and prints of photo illustrations for this volume.

INTRODUCTION

Antonio Menchaca in Texas History

Aboisterous crowd paraded through the streets of San Antonio to the city's Alamo Plaza on the morning of 2 March 1859. Led by a band of musicians and members of the Alamo Rifles volunteer militia, the entourage included military officers, the San Antonio Fire Association, the mayor and other local officials, teachers and schoolchildren, community members, and about twenty persons with badges identifying them as the "veterans of '36," all gathered to celebrate the twenty-third anniversary of Texas independence. Prominent on the speaker's platform erected for the occasion were two San Antonio Tejanos: José Antonio Navarro, one of the two Texas-born signers of the Texas Declaration of Independence, and José Antonio Menchaca, a veteran of the Texas Revolution renowned for his valor at the decisive battle of San Jacinto. According to a local newspaper report of this event, the speaker for the occasion, I. L. Hewitt, "was repeatedly applauded in a very enthusiastic manner, and especially in his allusions to the two venerable patriots on the platform, Col. Navarro and Capt. Manchaca [*sic*]."[1]

Hewitt extolled Navarro as a signer of the Declaration of Independence, a participant in the ill-fated 1841 Texan Santa Fe Expedition, and subsequently a prisoner in Mexico who refused President Antonio López de Santa Anna's offer of clemency if he would renounce his loyalty to Texas. Then the orator exalted "Capt. Antonio Manchaca, he who today bears the Lone Star flag,—Mexican born[2]—'Twas he who fought shoulder to

---

1. *San Antonio Herald*, 5 March 1859, pp. 3–4.

2. The use of *Mexican born* made Menchaca an outsider—a partner in the struggle, perhaps, but one who had to reject his own people. Of course, Menchaca, Navarro, and other Tejanos who participated in the struggle on the Texan side were the only Texas-born participants.

shoulder with the Texans at the battle of San Jacinto—True and faithful to our country then, may he long live to enjoy the fruition of his patriotism."[3]

Yet amazingly, in this same speech, with both Menchaca and Navarro seated behind him on the dais, Hewitt claimed Texas's winning of independence from Mexico demonstrated that "no enemy however countless in their numbers can force the bold Anglo Saxon to yield to a tyrant's decrees—independent in thought and action, his political freedom he claims as his birthright." This seeming contradiction reflects a common contention in ceremonial rhetoric around the Alamo and celebrations of Texas independence: the fight for Texas independence inevitably transformed its participants from people of various nations and backgrounds into true Texans and true Americans.

Depictions of Menchaca focusing primarily on his military exploits and his "American" loyalties continued beyond his own lifetime. In the introduction to the partial publication of Menchaca's reminiscences in the San Antonio weekly the *Passing Show*, his longtime acquaintance James P. Newcomb avowed that the Tejano's "sympathies carried him into the ranks of the Americans." Newcomb even went so far as to describe Menchaca's physical characteristics as bearing "the marks of a long line of Castilian ancestors," rhetorically severing Menchaca from both his Tejano loyalties and his Mexican heritage. Similarly, the obituary of Menchaca published in the *San Antonio Express* declared that he was "born a Mexican" but that "when the Texas war for independence came on, Don Antonio was found upon the side of our people, a contestant for that liberty and those privileges of citizenship which are bequeathed to the American." Claims such as these reveal a larger pattern regarding some Tejanos and others deemed loyal to the Texas or U.S. causes. James Crisp notes similar rhetorical commentaries regarding nineteenth-century Tejanos like José Antonio Navarro, whose patriotism led Anglo-Americans to claim that he was "not of the abject race of Mexicans," but was rather "a Corsican of good birth," that is, a European. In more contemporary times, Edward Linenthal shows that public ceremonies at the Alamo continue to mediate a message of "patriotic conversion" whereby through courage in battle those of diverse backgrounds leave behind their ancestral heritage to become Texans and Americans.[4]

---

3. Quotations from Hewitt's speech in this and the following paragraph are taken from the copy of his presentation in the *San Antonio Herald*, 5 March 1859, p. 4. The speech was also printed in the *San Antonio Daily Herald*, 9 March 1859, p. 2.

4. James P. Newcomb, introduction to *Memoirs*, by Antonio Menchaca, ed. Frederick C. Chabot, 11; *San Antonio Express*, 2 November 1879, p. 4; *Northern Standard*

Though Menchaca's reminiscences contain a section on the Texas Revolution that is disproportionate in length to other subjects treated, the focus on his status as a veteran of the Texas Revolution is further amplified in Frederick C. Chabot's 1937 publication. Like the *Passing Show* version, Chabot's does not include the nonmilitary portion of the reminiscences (perhaps because he was unaware of them) and ends the narrative at the battle of San Jacinto.[5] Whatever the reason for Chabot's omission, of the four leading nineteenth-century San Antonio Tejano figures known to have left behind their recollections—Juan Seguín, José Antonio Navarro, José María Rodríguez, and Menchaca—the latter's reminiscences were the only ones to remain unpublished in their entirety until now.[6] Indeed, many researchers are unaware of the existence of the unpublished portion of Menchaca's reminiscences and its recollections and musings on the events, social life, people, physical structures, and legends that shaped San Antonio's history.

Menchaca's reminiscences reveal some essential considerations about nineteenth-century Tejano biography: how Tejanos like Menchaca perceived themselves and wanted to be remembered, their views of Tejano character, and their understanding of the Tejano legacy during the tumultuous century of change that in Menchaca's own lifetime had seen them pass from being part of Spain to being part of Mexico, the Republic of Texas, the United States, the Confederate States of America, and then the United States again. A critical reading of the reminiscences shows that, un-

---

(Clarksville), 6 March 1845, as cited in James Ernest Crisp, "Anglo-Texan Attitudes toward the Mexican, 1821–1845," 402; Edward Tabor Linenthal, *Sacred Ground: Americans and Their Battlefields*, 61–62.

5. A fuller treatment of the manuscript's genesis and the *Passing Show* and Chabot publications is given below, in the body of this essay.

6. Juan N. Seguín, *Personal Memoirs of John N. Seguín from the Year 1834 to the Retreat of General Woll from the City of San Antonio in 1842*; José Antonio Navarro, *Apuntes históricos interesantes de San Antonio de Béxar escritos por el C. Dn. José Antonio Navarro, en noviembre de 1853. Y publicados por varios de sus amigos*; J[osé] M[aría] Rodríguez, *Rodríguez Memoirs of Early Texas*. Seguín's memoirs are reprinted in both edited and unedited versions in *A Revolution Remembered: The Memoirs and Selected Correspondence of Juan N. Seguín*, ed. Jesús F. de la Teja, 2nd ed., 71–122. Navarro's "historical commentaries" were first published in various installments of the English-language San Antonio press during the 1850s and then published privately in a Spanish-language version in San Antonio in 1869; a facsimile and an English translation of the 1869 Spanish publication of the *Apuntes* is in José Antonio Navarro, *Defending Mexican Valor in Texas: José Antonio Navarro's Historical Writings, 1853-1857*, ed. David R. McDonald and Timothy Matovina.

like contemporaries such as Newcomb or the orator Hewitt, Menchaca saw neither his military service nor the Texas victory over Mexico as an eradication of the Tejano past and a transmogrification of Tejano patriots into Anglo-Texans or Anglo-Americans. Though the reminiscences encompass a number of hyperbolic statements and inaccurate details and as a historical record must be read with a hermeneutic of caution, they clearly illuminate that a critical study of Menchaca cannot be complete without careful attention to how he narrated his own life and times during his twilight years.[7] Coupled with other available primary documents on Menchaca's life, his reminiscences are not solely another source for the events they narrate, but, more importantly, a firsthand account of the perceptions, biases, and mindset of nineteenth-century Tejanos like Menchaca as they looked back over the span of their lives.

FAMILY

José Antonio Menchaca was a fourth-generation Tejano, the son of Juan Mariano Menchaca and María de la Luz Guerra. According to the parish baptismal register, Father Gavino Valdez baptized the eight-day-old José Antonio on 17 January 1800.[8] Although in the years before his death in 1879 he would claim descent from the wrong first settlers of San Antonio, he was nevertheless correct that his ancestors were among the town's founders.

7. By the 1870s enough was known about early Texas history that Menchaca's "faulty" recollection of events could be singled out. For instance, in the 27 March 1871 issue of the *Indianola Weekly Bulletin*, the editor, probably newspaperman and historian John Henry Brown, attempted to correct comments attributed to Menchaca by the editor of the *Goliad Guard* regarding the founding dates for San Antonio and Goliad. While Brown himself got the dates wrong, his general observation that Menchaca was prone to spinning a yarn was coupled with respect for Menchaca's patriotic and generous character: "Our old friend, Manchaca [*sic*], has always been a big-hearted patriot, but knows far more about fighting Indians and game cocks than about history, anterior to his personal recollections—which are rich and racy. Once upon a time—a dark day in Texas—when we had been sixty hours traveling without food, the noble-hearted Manchaca [*sic*] gave us a portion of all he had for his wife and children, his supply being about one gallon of corn. And during the intervening period of nearly thirty years, he has ever, and ever shall, occupy a green place in our memory" (p. 2).

8. Entry 450, San Fernando Cathedral Baptisms, book 5, San Fernando Cathedral Archives, Archdiocese of San Antonio Chancery (hereafter SF followed by the type of register and book number).

It is a shame that Antonio apparently was unaware of his family's colorful roots in his beloved San Antonio. Both of his maternal great-grandfathers were soldiers in the city's earliest days. Antonio Guerra was one of the men Governor Martín de Alarcón recruited in Monclova for his 1718 expedition to found a settlement on the San Antonio River, and between 1718 and sometime in the 1740s Guerra served in the presidio company there. Whether he was married before or after he came to San Antonio is not clear, but he and his wife, Catarina Jiménez Menchaca, had at least four children during his enlistment. Having made his life in San Antonio, Guerra lived out his retirement among his children and grandchildren, passing away in the spring of 1759.[9]

Among Antonio and Catarina's children was Antonio's grandfather, José Joaquín Guerra, who was baptized in San Antonio on 19 February 1735 and buried there on 19 April 1790. Little is known of Joaquín, who for at least part of his adult life made a living as one of the civilian assistants at Mission San Antonio de Valero. On the few occasions that he appears in the town's and mission's sacramental records, he is listed as a "mestizo," a "mulato," or, as in his burial record, a "coyote." Likewise, his wife, María Guadalupe de Ávila, who had at least twelve children with him between 1763 and 1781, is recorded as a "mestiza" or a "mulata" in the sacramental records. That the children of soldiers who appear in the records as *españoles* (Spaniards) were later identified as being of mixed blood is not surprising, for in the eastern frontier provinces of New Spain, of which Texas was a part, there was a tendency to equate military service with pure Spanish blood.[10] The

9. Autos sobre diferentes noticias que se han participado a su Exa. de las entradas que en estos dominios hacen los franceses por la parte de Coahuila y providencias dadas para evitárselas y fundación de la misión en la provincia de los Texas, 1715, Provincias Internas, vol. 181, Archivo General de la Nación, Mexico City, Mexico (hereafter PI); Autos sobre las providencias dadas por su ex., al gobernador de la provincia de Texas para la pacificación de los Indios Apaches y sus aliados, 1731, PI vol. 32; Autos a consulta de dn. Thoribio de Urrutia Capn. del Presidio de Sn. Antonio de Vejar en la Provincia de Texas, sobre aumento de soldados, y otras providencias que pide, para contener los insultos que hacen los Indios Apaches; sobre que también instó D. Joseph de Urrutia su Pe. difunto, PI vol. 32; Testamentary Proceedings for Joseph Urrutia, Bexar, 27 February 1741, Bexar Archives, Briscoe Center for American History, University of Texas at Austin (hereafter these archives are cited as BA); entry 89, SF Marriages, book 4a; entry 224, SF Burials, book 4b.

10. Unnumbered entry for 19 February 1735, entries 73, 135, 209, 287, 385, 497, 653, 790, 1042, 1274, 1368, 1550, SF Baptisms, book 4; entry 1368, SF Burials, book 10; criminal case against Roque, Anselmo, Francisco, and Mateo, Indians of Mission Valero, for the

magic that an officer could perform with a pen on behalf of his soldiers, improving their *calidad* (quality) to that of Spaniards, generally did not extend to their children after they moved out on their own or even to themselves following their retirement.[11]

Antonio's grandmother, María Guadalupe de Ávila, was the daughter of Antonio's other great-grandfather, Felipe de Ávila, who came from Saltillo, Mexico, and entered military service in San Antonio in 1722. An enlisted man, Ávila has the distinction of having been involved in a 1730 homicide that led to the oldest recorded criminal investigation in San Antonio's history. According to the testimony, Ávila found his wife, Ildefonsa (or Aldonza) Rincón, naked in bed with Nicolás Pasqual, and there was an altercation during which Pasqual stabbed Ávila, who was saved by his brother-in-law and next-door neighbor, Sebastián Rincón. A few weeks later there was a second confrontation during which Ávila shot Pasqual dead. Found not guilty of murder, he was nevertheless ordered transferred to Presidio del Río Grande, and he then disappears from the record. His family remained in San Antonio, where his sons went on to serve in the presidio and acquire property and his daughter María Guadalupe married Joaquín Guerra.[12]

---

murder of Miguel Leal, 11 August 1778, BA. In northeastern New Spain, including Texas, *mestizo* and *coyote* were interchangeable terms denoting an individual of mixed Spanish-Indian blood. Elsewhere in New Spain, the term *coyote* denoted someone of mestizo-Indian parentage. A *mulato* was the offspring of a Spanish-black union. The label *español* was itself often compounded with the adjectives *americano* for individuals born in the New World and *europeo* for those born in Europe. Moreover, one need not be from Spain to be an *español*, as the term was commonly applied to anyone of European blood.

11. On the role of race in frontier military society, see Jesús F. de la Teja, "Why Urbano and María Trinidad Can't Get Married: Social Relations in Late Colonial San Antonio." See also De la Teja, *San Antonio de Béxar: A Community on New Spain's Northern Frontier*, 24–28.

12. Autos a consulta hecha del Pe. Fr. Joseph González, Misionero del Presidio de San Antonio Balero Contra el Capitán Don Nicolás Flores por los motivos que expresa, PI vol. 32; Causa criminal hecha pr. muerte de Nicolás Pasqual contra Felipe de Ávila, Trinidad, 12 April 1730, PI vol. 32; Donación de un solar a Aldonza Rincón y otro a Blas de Ávila, 29 July 1765, Land Grants, Spanish Archives, Bexar County Clerk's Office, San Antonio, microfilm roll 64 (hereafter BCSA); Donación de un solar a Juan Bautista de Ávila, 22 March 1774, BCSA Land Grants, microfilm roll 64; Census list of Villa, 31 December 1792, Nacogdoches Archives Transcripts, Briscoe Center for American History, University of Texas at Austin (hereafter these transcripts are cited as NAT); Blas de Ávila, vecino del presidio de S. Antonio de Béxar, sobre haberle quitado por el gober-

Among the dozen children born to María Guadalupe Ávila and Joaquín Guerra between 1763 and 1785 was María de la Luz Guerra, Antonio's mother. Luz's marriage to Mariano Menchaca produced ten children, of whom Antonio was the sixth. Like the other children of early soldiers, Luz appears in the documents as being of mixed blood. Baptismal and census records list her variously as a "mestiza," "mulata," "loba," or "coyote," and all but the last two of her children are similarly identified in the baptismal registers as "mestizos," "coyotes," "lobos," or "tresalvas."[13] Sometime between 1820 and 1830 she became widowed, and, as Antonio relates, she lived into the 1840s.[14]

At the time of his death sometime in the 1820s, when he was in his mid- to late sixties, Antonio's father, Mariano Menchaca, had achieved a measure of prosperity. Having opted not to follow his father into military service as other Bexareños (residents of the San Antonio de Béxar area) did in the last decades of Spanish rule, Mariano rounded up horses and cattle as opportunities arose and otherwise hired out for agricultural work. The last Spanish colonial census of San Antonio, taken in 1820, lists Mariano as a resident of the *barrio del sur*, that is, the town's south ward, which extended south from what are today Dolorosa and Market Streets between San Pedro Creek and the San Antonio River. It also indicates that he was a *labrador*, or landholding farmer. Taking Antonio at his word that the family was in San Antonio in 1813 when Joaquín Arredondo entered the city following the battle of Medina, Mariano appears to have been one of the many residents of the city who avoided becoming entangled in the bloody rebellion against Spanish rule. Mariano was also one of those individuals who experienced gradual "whitening" over time, early records recording his status as a "coyote" or "mestizo," but later records referring to him as an "español."[15]

---

nador un pedazo de tierra para mercenarla al cura. Año de 1778, Archivo de Gobierno, Saltillo Legajo 5 expediente 303, in Spanish Materials from Various Sources, vol. 840, no. 4, Briscoe Center for American History, University of Texas at Austin; Padrón de las familias y almas que hay en esta Villa de San Fernando de Austria [*sic*], fecho en 31 December 1796, BA.

13. A *lobo* was an individual of Indian and mulatto parentage, while the meaning of the word *tresalva* is lost.

14. Entries 73, 135, 209, 287, 385, 497, 653, 790, 1042, 1274, 1425, 1542, 1677, SF Baptisms, book 4, and entries 55, 228, 310, 450, 585, 731, 830, 995, SF Baptisms, book 5; Padrón general, Béxar año de 1790, BA; Padrón de las almas que existen, 31 December 1792, NAT; Padrón de las almas que hay en esta villa, 31 December 1793, BA.

15. Cuaderno en que se sientan las partidas de el derecho que pagan los que cogen reses orejanas y caballerías mesteñas correspondientes al predicho año. 31 December

Mariano had come to San Antonio in 1759 with his family after his father's retirement from the military. Antonio's paternal grandfather, Marcos Menchaca, kept his family moving during his military career, when he was stationed at the presidios of Sacramento, Santa Rosa, Río Grande, San Xavier, and San Sabá. As his petition for land in San Antonio listed the San Xavier and San Sabá presidios as his last postings before retirement, it is almost certain that he was present at the *Norteños'* destruction of Mission San Sabá—and may have participated in the failed campaign against them in 1759.[16] As someone with a large family, veteran status, and an interest in stock raising, he obtained in 1762 a grant for land west of San Pedro Creek, where he lived out his remaining years. By the time he passed away sometime in the early to mid-1770s, he had secured his family's well-being for years to come. Governor Domingo Cabello's comprehensive census of 1778 included María Josefa Cadena, Marcos's widow, as the head of a household that still included four of their children as well as a servant. The family's property included a *jacal* (shack) and three market-garden plots,[17] along with three mares, two horses, three yoke of oxen, and sixty head of cattle. Josefa, who also worked as a midwife, outlived her husband by about thirty years, long enough to be present at the birth of her grandson José Antonio, future hero of Texas independence, in 1800.[18]

1784, BA; Cuaderno en que se sientan las partidas de el dro. que pagan los que cogen reses orejanas y caballerías mesteñas en el discurso de el predicho año. 31 December 1785, BA; Petition of José Mariano Menchaca, 10 March 1792, BA; Padrón de las almas 31 December 1793, BA; Census, barrio del sur, 1820, BA.

16. Following years of effort, the Franciscan missionaries at San Antonio were successful in obtaining permission and government support for a mission inside Lipan Apache country. In 1757 a presidio and mission were constructed near present-day Menard, but by March 1758 the mission had been unable to attract any Apaches to settle down. On the other hand, those tribes hostile to the Lipan Apaches, including Comanche, Wichita, and Caddo groups, collectively referred to as the Nations of the North, or *Norteños*, viewed the mission as part of a Spanish alliance with their mortal enemy. On 16 March 1758, they destroyed the mission, killing two missionaries and a number of assistants. After a two-day siege of the nearby presidio, the Indians withdrew. It took over a year to organize a punitive campaign against the *Norteños*, which resulted in a Spanish defeat at present-day Spanish Fort, Texas, in early October 1759. The best narrative treatment of the episode remains Robert S. Weddle, *The San Sabá Mission: Spanish Pivot in Texas*.

17. The term used in the census is *huerta*, which refers to a large garden dedicated to growing vegetables and fruit for market.

18. Petición para un solar presentada por Marcos Menchaca, 20 December 1760, BCSA

Ancestors of José Antonio Menchaca

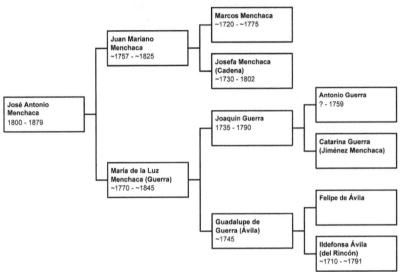

FIGURE 1
Family tree of José Antonio Menchaca. Chart by Jesús F. de la Teja.

Little is known about Antonio's early years and his family life in general, save for his recollections of the battles for Mexican independence from Spain fought in or near San Antonio during his youth, which will be treated below. In 1826 he married Teresa Ramón, a descendant of a military leader stationed at San Antonio during the early eighteenth century. As in the case of other prominent San Antonio families, the Menchacas' social circle was not limited to their fellow Tejanos. One of their daughters, Antonia Manuela, married French émigré Jean Batiste Ducuron LaCoste, while another, María Antonia, married Maximilian Neuendorff. The very proper Neuendorff's letter seeking "Antoñita's" hand in marriage is pre-

Land Grants, microfilm roll 66; SF Confirmations, book 4b; Libro de cuentas de los soldados del Real Presidio de Nuestra Señora del Pilar de los Adaes destacados en este de San Antonio de Béxar donde consta lo que cada uno va devengando por tercios, y se le subministra diariamente por su capitán el Coronel de Caballería. Barón de Ripperdá, Gobernador y Comandante General por S.M. de esta Provincia de los Texas, Nuevas Philipinas en el presente año de 1771, 1 January 1771, BA; Provincia de Texas: Estado General de la tropa de el Presidio de San Antonio de Béxar, Audiencia de Guadalajara, legajo 283, Archivo General de Indias, Seville, Spain; entry 20, SF Burials, book 11.

served at the Daughters of the Republic of Texas research library. It is addressed to "Don Antonio" and is one of the few pieces, if not the only piece, of personal correspondence involving Menchaca to have survived. Menchaca's oldest daughter, Joaquina, married Texas Revolution veteran John Glanton, though by at least one account Glanton gained the hand of his reportedly beautiful bride at gunpoint. Shortly after their marriage, Glanton headed west, leaving Joaquina and their infant daughter behind. A few years later, Yuma Indians in Sonora, Mexico, killed Glanton in retribution for atrocities he had committed as a "soldier of fortune, outlaw, and notorious bounty-hunter and murderer."[19]

WAR

The most often remembered—and one could add controversial—aspect of Menchaca's life is his military service during the Texas Revolution, particularly his exploits at the battle of San Jacinto. Historian Stephen L. Hardin avows that "Menchaca had no intention of enlisting in the rebel [Texas] army." He cites the recollections of Enrique Esparza, the son of Alamo defender Gregorio Esparza. At the time of the Alamo battle, on 6 March 1836, Enrique Esparza was eight years old and survived the battle inside the fortress walls with his mother and siblings. Some seven decades later the aging Esparza attested that Mexican general Antonio López de Santa Anna offered the Alamo defenders a period of amnesty before the battle and that "among the surnames of those I remember to have left during the time of this armistice were Menchaca, Flores, Rodriguez, Ramirez, Arocha, Silvero."[20] Although Esparza is the only known source who mentions the armistice and departure of these Tejanos, Hardin correctly notes that the most convincing evidence comes from the testimony of Menchaca himself; in his reminiscences he states that he left San Antonio just before the

19. Frederick C. Chabot, foreword to *Memoirs*, by Antonio Menchaca; Maximilian Neuendorff to Antonio Menchaca, folder 1, Neuendorff Family Papers, Daughters of the Republic of Texas Library, San Antonio; "Glanton, John Joel," *The Handbook of Texas Online*, http://www.tshaonline.org/handbook (hereafter *HOT*).

20. Stephen L. Hardin, "Efficient in the Cause," 66 (quotation), 67; Charles Merritt Barnes, "Alamo's Only Survivor," *San Antonio Express*, 12 May 1907, p. 14 (Esparza quotation). The Esparza account continued in the 19 May 1907 issue of the *Express*, p. 47; it is reprinted in its entirety in Timothy Matovina, *The Alamo Remembered: Tejano Accounts and Perspectives*, 77–89, quotation at 82.

Alamo battle and entered the Texan army afterward only when forced to do so. One key passage appears to be an apologetic about why he did not join his friend Jim Bowie and others in defending the Alamo; Menchaca states that Bowie and Tejano military leader Juan Seguín "made a motion to have Antonio Menchaca and his family sent away from here, knowing that they would receive no good treatment at Santa Anna's hands" (134).[21] But it is not clear why Menchaca and his family would have been in greater danger at Santa Anna's hands than anyone else who had chosen to join the Alamo defenders. After he headed east with his family, Menchaca explains, General Edward Burleson conscripted him into the Texas army.

Though long esteemed for his courage in the battle of San Jacinto on 21 April 1836, Menchaca mentions nothing about these exploits in his reminiscences, only that he fought in the battle and that the Texan commanders "made me take my men who were Mexicans and put large pieces of white paste board on their hats and breasts lest they should be mistaken for Santa Annas men and killed" (147). José María Rodríguez, a native San Antonian whose father, Ambrosio, was Menchaca's comrade in the battle, avers in his memoir that an unspecified "Mexican history of the battle" relates that "an officer of tremendous size, speaking Spanish, urged his men forward in a voice of thunder to give no quarter and that they slaughtered the Mexicans like sheep. . . . The man he referred to is supposed to have been Don Antonio." Hardin cites Henry Stuart Foote's 1841 account based on eyewitness interviews about the battle. Foote asserts that Texas soldier and statesman Thomas Jefferson Rusk claimed Menchaca refused to help a Mexican officer who begged him for mercy. Surrounded by Anglo-Americans apparently eager to hear how he would respond to the man's pleas, Menchaca reportedly retorted, "I'm no Mexican—I'm an American," and told his fellow Texan soldiers to shoot him. Hardin concludes that "such incidents indicate that Tejanos killed [Mexican] centralists with every bit as much relish as did vengeful Texians."[22]

Yet Hardin's conclusion and the single incident and primary source on which it is based are not corroborated in other primary documentation.

21. Page numbers for quotations from Menchaca's unedited reminiscences, given parenthetically in the text, refer to "The Memoirs of Captain Menchaca" and "The Unpublished Second Part of the Menchaca Manuscript," in this volume.

22. Rodríguez, *Rodríguez Memoirs of Early Texas*, 62; Hardin, "Efficient in the Cause," 60; Henry Stuart Foote, *Texas and the Texans; Or, Advance of the Anglo-Americans to the South-West* (1935), 2:310; Stephen L. Hardin, *Texian Iliad: A Military History of the Texas Revolution, 1835–1836*, 213.

Menchaca's alleged claim that he was no longer Mexican but American sounds more like the rhetoric of the aforementioned Newcomb or Hewitt than any known Tejano source; given that the battle of San Jacinto won Texas independence and was nine years before U.S. annexation, it seems particularly odd that a native Tejano like Menchaca would have identified himself as an "American." It is unlikely that, if such a dramatic incident occurred, Menchaca forgot it or thought it was too unimportant to record in his reminiscences, although he might have been too embarrassed or ashamed of such a brutal episode to recount it. But in the 1870s would Menchaca have been worried that associating himself with retribution on the Mexican army at San Jacinto could soil his reputation? Indeed, as we shall see, far from evidencing concern about a claim that he sought vengeance on the Mexican forces, Menchaca's recollections include a subsequent event that seems even more likely to have drawn his name into ill repute among his contemporaries: his offering the detested prisoner Santa Anna every form of assistance at his disposal. The strongest conclusion one can draw from extant sources is that Menchaca's reputation as a formidable adversary at San Jacinto is evident in Anglo-American, Tejano, and, according to Rodríguez, Mexican reports of the battle, even if not in Menchaca's own reminiscences.

Menchaca continued to serve in the Texas army until the Mexican forces withdrew from Texas after the battle of San Jacinto, at which point he went with several other Tejanos to escort their families back to San Antonio from Nacogdoches, where they had fled during the wartime hostilities. According to Juan Seguín, nearly everyone on this return expedition became ill, "and for several days, Captain Menchaca, who was the only person able to stand up, had to drive the whole train, as well as attend to the sick." After reestablishing his family at San Antonio, Menchaca engaged in further military service; the following March an order from Commander Seguín instructed Captain Thomas Pratt that "Capt. Manchaca accompanies you and is subject to your order although as he is acquainted with the Country and Language you may find it eligeable [sic] to consult with him on such points as may be necessary."[23]

Subsequently Menchaca provided intermittent service in military engagements with American Indians and in patrol duty to watch out for Mexican troops, although apparently he did not fulfill an 1842 mandate to raise a military company, as official correspondence ten months later in-

23. Seguín, *Revolution Remembered*, ed. De la Teja, 2nd ed., 113, 163. See also Seguín, *Personal Memoirs of John N. Seguín*, 18.

dicates that Texas Congress appropriations included funds only for troops under the command of renowned Texas Ranger Jack Hays. In September 1842 Menchaca was part of a group that sought to defend San Antonio from Mexican troops under the command of General Adrián Woll, whose last name the reminiscences mistakenly render as "Bull," but these Texan defenders quickly abandoned their effort when they discovered that the force aligned against them was a formidable contingent of the regular Mexican army. Menchaca's leg was reportedly injured in this skirmish when a cannonball dislodged a stone that then struck him. The Mexican army took him prisoner but quickly released him. An Anglo-American prisoner wrote in his diary that "Antonio Menchaca's release is likewise effected by the intercession of his family and that of his Mexican friends"; General Woll's official reports of his expedition state that he freed five prisoners "on account of being Mexicans whose families and themselves have offered to be hereafter faithful to the Supreme Government."[24]

Menchaca's recollection is consistent with Woll's official report, as he attests that Woll freed him "on one condition & that is that you will give me your word of honor never again to Take up arms against Mexico" (158). Menchaca goes on to state that he faithfully fulfilled his "parole of honor never more to take up arms against Mexico" (160). Though in 1844 Texas president Sam Houston appointed him to serve as an Indian escort, Menchaca's steadily advancing age and injured leg may have contributed to his decision about further military duty. Like many other Tejanos, he did not enlist for the war between the United States and Mexico that erupted in 1846; while at least 140 Tejanos applied for land grants as veterans of the Texas Revolution, in the War with Mexico only 20 soldiers with Spanish surnames were among the 6,000 Texas volunteers in the U.S. forces.[25] In

24. [M. B. Lamar] to Major Jones, 11 March 1839, in *The Papers of Mirabeau Buonaparte Lamar*, 6 vols., ed. Charles Adams Gulick Jr. and Katherine Elliott, 2:489–490; Sam Houston to the Texas Senate, 18 July 1842, in *The Writings of Sam Houston, 1813–1863*, 8 vols., ed. Amelia W. Williams and Eugene C. Barker, 3:105–106; Houston to certain citizens of San Antonio, 18 May 1843, ibid., 3:390–393; Joseph Milton Nance, *Attack and Counter-Attack: The Texas-Mexican Frontier, 1842*, 243, 273, 305, 318, 323–325; Frederick C. Chabot, *The Perote Prisoners: Being the Diary of James L. Truehart, Printed for the First Time Together with an Historical Introduction*, 100 (first quotation); Joseph Milton Nance, ed. and trans., "Brigadier General Adrián Woll's Report of His Expedition into Texas in 1842," 533 (second quotation). For other eyewitness accounts of General Woll's 1842 occupation of San Antonio that mention Menchaca, see Rodríguez, *Rodríguez Memoirs of Early Texas*, 17–18; E. W. Winkler, ed., "The Bexar and Dawson Prisoners," 295, 314.

25. Sam Houston, appointment of an Indian escort, 7 February 1844, in *Writings of*

any event, whether his motive was one or a combination of these factors, his participation in the 1842 defense of San Antonio during the Woll expedition was Menchaca's last military engagement mentioned in extant sources.

PEACE

Menchaca's military record earned him the acclaim of many contemporaries. Besides receiving public recognition at events such as Texas Independence Day celebrations, during the last years of his life he was a member of the Texas Veterans Association, a group of Texas Republic veterans founded in 1873. His renown also frequently drew him into the more elite Tejano circles of San Antonio. But his prominent status did not translate into economic luxury. Given the limited economic success of his parents and grandparents, it is not surprising that he was recorded as a *jornalero* (laborer) on 1830 census rolls, which listed two horses as his only noteworthy assets. By comparison, Juan Seguín, who was seven years his junior, was listed as a merchant head of a household that included two servants and as the owner of four cows, three bulls, six horses, a goat, and a mule. An 1838 joint resolution of the Texas Senate and House of Representatives granted Menchaca "one of the houses and lots in the city of San Antonio, which may be confiscated to the public use." The 1840 census of the Republic of Texas recorded him as holding one town lot in San Antonio, presumably the location of his private residence, and two horses. He was also the agent of record for his widowed mother, who owned one town lot. After U.S. annexation of Texas, his level of prosperity remained relatively constant. In 1850, on the first U.S. census conducted in San Antonio, he was listed as a "merchant" who owned real estate valued at $2,000; a newspaper report from seven years later mentions Menchaca as one owner of transport carts loaded with goods that left San Antonio for the coast under armed guard during the infamous Cart War.[26]

Sam Houston, ed. Williams and Barker, 4:251; Fane Downs, "The History of Mexicans in Texas, 1820–1845," 248; Henry W. Barton, *Texas Volunteers in the Mexican War*, 118.

26. *San Antonio Herald*, 7 April 1876, p. 3; Census, barrio del norte, 19 July 1829, and barrio del sur, 9 July 1830, BA; "A Joint Resolution for the Relief of Antonio Manchaca [*sic*]," 22 December 1838, in *Laws of the Republic of Texas Passed the First Session of Third Congress*, 21; Gifford White, ed., *The 1840 Census of the Republic of Texas*, 15; V. K. Carpenter, comp., *The State of Texas Federal Population Schedules Seventh Census of the United States, 1850*,

Still, in comparison to other San Antonio Tejanos, Menchaca's retention of his homestead and mercantile interests placed him ahead of many contemporaries. Although incomplete, the census of 1840 showed that Tejanos owned 85.1 percent of the town lots in San Antonio, along with 63.8 percent of all land acreage titled to local residents. According to the 1850 census, they owned only 9.1 percent of real estate values claimed. Similarly, in 1830, when Tejanos comprised nearly all the population of San Antonio, the census showed that most residents were farmers and only 14.8 percent were laborers. No employment listings were given in the 1840 census, but in 1850, 61.4 percent of the Tejano population was in labor positions. Menchaca was comparatively well off, but only in relation to a San Antonio Tejano population undergoing a significant downward trend in economic status from landowners to a working underclass.[27]

Menchaca did not complacently accept the woes of his fellow Tejanos. He was a frequent witness for Tejano parties in court cases, particularly for veterans seeking the compensation due them by law for military service in the Texas Revolution. Convinced that the just claims of many Tejano veterans had been denied or unduly delayed as compared to the more prompt approvals their Anglo-American counterparts received, Menchaca was one of nineteen Tejano signers in 1875 of a letter to the Texas comptroller of

---

entry no. 179, 1:121; *San Antonio Herald*, 25 September 1857, p. 2. For a brief overview of the Cart War, see John J. Linn, *Reminiscences of Fifty Years in Texas*, 352–354; J. Fred Rippy, "Border Troubles along the Rio Grande, 1848–1860," 103–104; Larry Knight, "The Cart War: Defining American in San Antonio in the 1850s," 319–336.

27. White, ed., *The 1840 Census of the Republic of Texas*, 12–18; Carpenter, comp., *State of Texas Seventh Census*, 1:111–189; White, *1830 Citizens of Texas*, 79–112. The downward trend in socioeconomic fortunes of Bexareños was not unique, either to Texas or to the Southwest generally. Arnoldo De León, in *The Tejano Community, 1836–1900*, was the first to explore this theme in a major work, not from the perspective of victimization, but from that of resistance and self-assertion. David Montejano, in confirming De León's findings, expanded the focus to include the legalistic dynamics of Tejano marginalization in the nineteenth century in *Anglos and Mexicans in the Making of Texas, 1836–1986*. Beyond Texas, Richard Griswold del Castillo, in *The Los Angeles Barrio, 1850–1890: A Social History*, and Albert Camarillo, in *Chicanos in a Changing Society: From Mexican Pueblos to American Barrios in Santa Barbara and Southern California, 1848–1930*, trace the very similar processes at work in southern California during the nineteenth century. Even in New Mexico, where they remained such a large percentage of the population, Laura E. Gómez demonstrates in *Manifest Destinies: The Making of the Mexican American Race* that Mexican Americans faced socioeconomic decline. In all these cases, the result was the formation and reinforcement of a distinctly Mexican-based identity.

public accounts that sought to "disabuse [Comptroller Stephen H. Darden's] mind of any prejudice" against Tejano veterans and that demanded for themselves and their comrades "simply justice and nothing more." His support of fellow Tejanos was so strong that apparently he did not even hold grudges against those who supported the Mexican side in the Texas Revolution. For example, he provided a deposition to support the legal claims of Francisco Esparza, a San Antonio native who, unlike his Alamo-defender brother Gregorio, had opted to fight in the Mexican army during the December 1835 Texan siege of San Antonio and was on reserve with the Mexican forces during Santa Anna's Texas campaign. James Newcomb summed up Menchaca's leading role as a legal advocate when he quipped that "in later years, when the titles to almost every foot of ground in the old city and county of Bexar were litigated in the courts, Captain Menchaca became a standing witness to prove up the genealogy of the old families."[28]

In his laudatory, and perhaps hyperbolic, recollections of his acquaintance with Menchaca several decades after Menchaca's death, Newcomb also recalled the Tejano's role as a leader in local social activities. Newcomb remembered "Captain Menchaca as the umpire at the Sunday cock fight. Amusements and entertainments in those days [the antebellum period] were limited to the Sunday cock fight—the fandango [dance]—the Saint's [sic] days." In sharp contrast to his claim that Menchaca had been received into the presumed-superior inner circle of Anglo-Americans, Newcomb went on to wistfully describe the era when Tejano festivities predominated as simpler and more serene than the bustling times of the early twentieth century in which he wrote. He also noted that Menchaca's umpire duties "required a man of stern character and unbending dignity to decide the fine points of these tournaments."[29]

Menchaca's political career and activism were another means through which he promoted Tejano interests. In the years after Texas independence he served several terms on the San Antonio City Council and as mayor

---

28. Antonio Menchaca, deposition, 1 January 1856, Antonio Fuentes file, and deposition, 28 July 1856, Carlos Espalier file, both in Memorials and Petitions, Texas State Library and Archives Commission, Austin; Juan N. Seguín, "Application for Pension," 2 October 1874, in Seguín, *Revolution Remembered*, ed. De la Teja, 2nd ed., 187–188; Tejano citizens to Stephen H. Darden, 12 January 1875, in James M. Day, ed., "Texas Letters and Documents," 84; Menchaca, deposition, 24 August 1860, Court of Claims voucher file no. 2557 (Francisco Esparza), Texas General Land Office, Austin; Newcomb, introduction to *Memoirs*, by Antonio Menchaca, ed. Chabot, 11.

29. Newcomb, introduction to *Memoirs*, ed. Chabot, 11.

pro tem from July 1838 to January 1839, completing the term of resigned mayor William Dangerfield. Like other Tejano elected officials, he sought with limited success to stem the tide of Anglo-American encroachment on local real estate, as in 1838, when as mayor pro tem he wrote the commissioner of the Texas General Land Office to alert him of Anglo-American attempts to take unlawful possession of land belonging to the City of San Antonio. He joined other San Antonio Tejano as well as Anglo-American leaders to press the national government of Texas for services such as local postal delivery and funding for military protection. A similar San Antonio coalition also offered financial and moral support for a federalist rebellion in the northern states of Mexico; this conflict potentially could have combined the population of that region with Texas to form a new nation in which the proportion of Mexican-descent to Anglo-American residents would have increased significantly.[30]

After a two-year disruption of local elections following the Woll expedition, Menchaca was once again elected to the city council in 1844, but subsequently his career as an elected official subsided along with those of his Tejano contemporaries. During the period of the Texas Republic (1836–1845), Tejanos elected to the city council accounted for 73.2 percent of the total, but they were just 24.2 percent of the total during the first fifteen years after U.S. annexation; in 1860 not a single Tejano served on the council. Menchaca was elected to the council one final time in 1849, but for unknown reasons he resigned a month before completing his term. The year after the anti-foreigner, anti-Catholic Know-Nothing Party swept the 1854 San Antonio municipal elections, he ran for the city council again but lost. Nonetheless, he remained active in political events and causes; in 1860 he helped organize a San Antonio visit by Governor Sam Houston to promote pro-Union views. Earlier that year Houston had warmly endorsed Menchaca for a federal-government appointment, but it apparently never materialized; Menchaca's only subsequent elected position was ditch commissioner, a position he filled just before the Civil War and once again during Reconstruction.[31]

30. Journal A: Minutes of the City Council of the City of San Antonio from 1837 to 1849 (typescript), Journals of the San Antonio City Council, Briscoe Center for American History, University of Texas at Austin; Seguín, *Revolution Remembered*, ed. De la Teja, 2nd ed., 43; Houston to certain citizens of San Antonio, 18 May 1843, in *Writings of Sam Houston*, ed. Williams and Barker, 3:390–393; Joseph Milton Nance, *After San Jacinto: The Texas-Mexican Frontier, 1836-1841*, 206.

31. Journal A: Minutes of the City Council of the City of San Antonio from 1837 to

In the years leading up to the Civil War, Tejanos in San Antonio split with their Democratic allies from the mid-1850s Know-Nothing political controversies because the Democratic Party supported secession and bitterly opposed Menchaca's friend and ally Governor Houston. But in the tumultuous decade following the war some Tejanos, particularly members of the older and more influential families like Menchaca's, realigned with the Democrats and resisted Reconstruction efforts that granted African Americans greater equality. Other Tejanos joined the Radicals, who advocated for African American voting and citizenship rights. Each group of activists formed its own political club and had its own Spanish-language newspaper. Menchaca's active involvement in the Democratic Party and platform was evident in his campaign efforts for Horace Greeley in his unsuccessful presidential bid against Ulysses S. Grant in 1872, as well as Menchaca's selection in 1875 as a delegate to the Democratic state convention. At a local celebration of Mexican Independence Day in 1871, Menchaca even publicly compared the heroic efforts of Father Miguel Hidalgo, who led the struggle for Mexican independence from Spain, to contemporary initiatives to elect Democratic candidates and overthrow Radical rule. Yet Tejanos from both political parties, including Menchaca, were able to unite in support of an 1876 municipal effort that attracted the first railroad lines to the city. Apparently, while the question of rights for African Americans in an Anglo-American-dominated society did not elicit a unilateral response among Menchaca and his fellow Tejanos, advocacy for their own rights and self-interests remained a powerful force for inciting their collective action.[32]

Menchaca died peacefully on 1 November 1879 after enduring a short illness. Earlier in the year he had been appointed a member of the local arrangements committee for the Texas Veterans Association, which was to meet in San Antonio in April 1880. Edward Miles, chair of the Bexar County chapter, reported Menchaca's death to Moses Austin Bryan, the association's secretary, on 2 November:

1849 (typescript); Journal B: Minutes of the City Council of the City of San Antonio from January 1849 to August 1856 (typescript); and Journal C: Minutes of the City Council of the City of San Antonio from 1 April 1856 to 21 February 1870 (typescript), all in Journals of the San Antonio City Council, Briscoe Center for American History, University of Texas at Austin; Sam Houston to Howell Cobb, in *Writings of Sam Houston*, ed. Williams and Barker, 7:451–452; *Alamo Express* (San Antonio), 1 October 1860, p. 3; *Mooney & Morrison's General Directory of the City of San Antonio, for 1877-1878*, 43.

32. De León, *The Tejano Community, 1836-1900*, 30–31; De León, *They Called Them Greasers: Anglo Attitudes toward Mexicans in Texas, 1821-1900*, 56–57.

Capt. Antonio Manchaca

FIGURE 2

Photograph of José Antonio Menchaca collected by Henry Arthur McArdle, an Irish-born artist who settled in Texas after the Civil War and painted two famous canvases of the battles of the Alamo and San Jacinto. In researching the paintings, McArdle collected a great deal of information on the participants, including this portrait of Menchaca. From The Battle of San Jacinto Notebook, The McArdle Notebooks, courtesy of the Archives and Information Services Division, Texas State Library and Archives Commission, Austin.

It again devolves upon me as a duty to perform to announce to you the death of Companion Capt. Antonio Menchaca who died yesterday (all Saints Day) at 6 O'clock P.M. and was buried this day (All Souls) at the hour of 5 P.M. in the 80th year of his age . . .

His funeral was largely attended and great numbers were already at the grave, not forgetting on this day long departed relatives & friends.

Our friend ever since the reunion at Galveston felt anxious to live long enough to meet his old companions in this "Historic City" on our next anniversary April 21, 1879 [sic].

The annual program did go on without him, and in attendance were his daughters Manuela and Antonia, "Mrs. J. B. Lacoste and Mrs. Antonio [sic] Neuendorf[f], daughters of Antonio Menchaca, soldier of San Jacinto." There to greet them on the left side of the stage in the meeting hall "was a large portrait of Antonio Menchaca."[33]

Besides lauding his Texas patriotism and military service, Menchaca's obituary in the San Antonio Express noted that one of his "most remarkable characteristics . . . was his retentiveness of memory. His stories of the war with Mexico, and of the thrilling scenes that marked the history of this city in her virginity, have ever won the listener." Employing a frequent mis-spelling of his name during his lifetime, the town of Manchaca in Travis County, south of Austin, is named for him; the genesis of this honor is that Menchaca had reportedly once camped at the nearby springs that also bear his name. After two previous post offices founded on the site had closed and two years after Menchaca's death, the arrival of the railroad in the area led to the establishment of the town on a more permanent footing and its formal naming as Manchaca.[34]

33. Minutes, Bexar County Texas Veterans Association meeting, 12 April 1879, box 2H122, folder "TVA Papers," Edward Miles to Moses Austin Bryan, box 2H120, folder "Miles, Edward" (first quotation), Texas Veterans Association Papers, Briscoe Center for American History, University of Texas at Austin; Proceedings, Constitution, By-Laws and Address of the Old Texas Veterans, Held at San Antonio, Thursday and Friday, April 22 and 23, 1880 (San Antonio: M. M. Mooney, Book and Job Printer, 1880), 5 (second quotation), 4 (third quotation). Menchaca's wife, Teresa Ramón, had preceded him in death by more than five years ("Genealogical notes: Neuendorff/Menchaca," folder 20, Neuendorff Family Papers, Daughters of the Republic of Texas Library, San Antonio).

34. San Antonio Express, 2 November 1879, p. 4; "Manchaca, Texas," HOT; "Historian tackles spelling of Manchaca," Austin American-Statesman, 10 June 2012, pp. B1, B6. Beginning in 2011, retired district judge Bob Perkins of Austin organized an effort to correct

MENCHACA REMEMBERS

Menchaca's long-standing activism on behalf of his fellow Tejanos continued into the last decade of his life, when he worked to resolve issues like pension discrimination against Tejano veterans and to provide a Tejano viewpoint on questions such as the advisability of expending municipal funds to attract railroads to the city. In this context, then, the mid-1870s reminiscences are part of a wider effort by the aging Menchaca to promote what he perceived to be Tejanos' interests as well as their legacy. The narrative opens with the observation "I was born in 1800, was baptized in the church of San Fernando de Austria on the 12th of January same year" (119). Menchaca proceeds to narrate his life and key events in San Antonio history during the first half of the nineteenth century. The manuscript is presented in eighteen chapters, though the original draft of the first nine chapters is lost and the full delineation for these chapters is not labeled on the published copies; in the extant versions, the first half has subtitles, but no chapter numbers or chapter titles. Menchaca's reminiscences of San Antonio can be roughly divided into four major sections, in the following order: the period of struggle for Mexican independence from Spain; the fight for Texas independence and its aftermath; local events during the period of the Texas Republic; and some final remarks on the history of San Antonio before 1800. Three of the four sections are roughly equal in length, with the exception being the section on the Texas Revolution, which is three times longer than the others and comprises nearly half the manuscript.

It is apparent from the text that Menchaca dictated his recollections and someone else wrote them down by hand, but it is unclear when that person employed his own editorial touches and when he merely took dictation. We cannot be sure when Menchaca began dictating his recollections, but from internal evidence in the reminiscences it appears to have been sometime in the mid-1870s.[35] It was during this time that Menchaca met newspaperman James Newcomb,[36] who showed an interest in the Te-

---

the misspelling of Menchaca's name on the south Austin street leading to the community of Manchaca known as Manchaca Road. The name was corrected on the community's elementary school after the new building was constructed in 1975.

35. Menchaca's comment about "Madam (signora) Antonio Cardenas a lady very nearly of my own age (a little over 76 years)" (163) indicates that he was working on what is here styled the second part of the reminiscences during 1876.

36. Newcomb, who was brought to San Antonio by his family in the 1840s, when he

jano's recollections. Arriving at a convenient stopping point, Menchaca handed Newcomb the first part of the manuscript, which covers his recollections through Santa Anna's capture after the battle of San Jacinto in April 1836. Menchaca then continued working with his collaborator, who Frederick C. Chabot tells us was Charles Merritt Barnes, backtracking some to flesh out the story of the aftermath of the battle of San Jacinto, including giving a much more detailed account of his encounter with Santa Anna. Unfortunately, the abrupt end of what Newcomb published in the *Passing Show* along with the mid-sentence beginning of the unpublished second half make impossible a definitive conclusion regarding the integrity of the whole of the reminiscences.

What we do know is what Newcomb tells us in his introduction to the portion of the reminiscences that he contributed to the *Passing Show* in 1907. Newcomb claims to have obtained the manuscript from Menchaca over a quarter century earlier; it would have had to be a few years before that, since Menchaca was dictating the last portion of his recollections around 1876. Newcomb never mentions who took down Menchaca's recollections or why he took so long to do anything with them. In his introduction, he explains:

> In accordance with his [Menchaca's] promise he handed me a plainly written history of events from the date of his birth to the battle of San Jacinto. I have never used the story and have had little opportunity to examine it critically. It is evident the amanuensis who took down the old Captain's story put it down without coloring, and one regrets that he did not enlarge more fully upon details that are so full of historic and romantic interest.[37]

For some reason, Menchaca apparently never attempted to recover the first part of the manuscript from Newcomb, who likewise apparently never attempted to follow up with Menchaca regarding any additional material. James Newcomb's son Pearson said in 1951 that either he or his father had passed their manuscript, that is, what was published in the

was a child, had entered the newspaper business and founded two newspapers in the city before having to flee to Mexico at the start of the Civil War because of his pro-Union views. When he returned to Texas in 1867, he again took up journalism and became part owner of the *San Antonio Express* and subsequently of other newspapers supporting the Republican Party. "Newcomb, James Pearson," HOT.

37. *Passing Show*, San Antonio, 22 June 1907, p. 1.

Passing Show, to the San Antonio Public Library, which has no record of the accession.[38]

Mention of Barnes[39] as Menchaca's collaborator first appears in Chabot's foreword to what he styled Menchaca's *Memoirs*, following James Newcomb, who had titled what he published in the *Passing Show* "The Memoirs of Captain Menchaca: Being an Unpublished Manuscript Detailing Events in San Antonio from 1807 to the Battle of San Jacinto." Chabot avers that "Antonio Menchaca dictated his narrative to Barnes, in whose handwriting they are preserved."[40] This assertion by Chabot is problematic in that Barnes, who became a reporter for the *San Antonio Express* and an increasingly prominent journalist in San Antonio, would certainly have known Newcomb, who at one time had owned the *Express*. Yet Newcomb's failure to name the "amanuensis" in 1907, while Barnes was still alive, argues against his being Menchaca's scribe, although it is possible that the aging Newcomb simply failed to mention this detail. Unfortunately no extant document containing Barnes's handwriting is available for comparison to determine whether it matches that of the second half of Menchaca's reminiscences, which is in handwritten draft form. However, there is evidence of some connection between Barnes and Menchaca. In his own published work on San Antonio, Barnes claims that "it was old Don Antonio Menchaca, the venerable seer of San Antonio, who in 1875, told me the legend depicting the origin of the San Antonio river,"[41] a legend recounted in the

38. Winnie Allen to "Mrs. Wm. Gordon Coogan, Jr." [Elizabeth Coogan], 24 February 1951, Antonio Menchaca Collection accession record, Briscoe Center for American History, University of Texas at Austin. There is no letter between Allen and Pearson Newcomb, so Allen may have acquired the information in a telephone call or personal visit with him. According to her, "Mr. Newcomb says that the first part of the manuscript, which was published in the *Passing Show*, was given to his father by Menchaca, and that he passed it on to the San Antonio Public Library." The ambiguity of the phrase "he passed it on" calls into question which Newcomb made the transfer. A search in the Newcomb Papers in the Texana Collection at the San Antonio Public Library turned up only a full set of clippings from the *Passing Show* from 22 June to 27 July 1907 containing the published portion of the reminiscences.

39. Charles Merritt Barnes, a native of Louisiana, came to Texas in the early 1870s and after practicing law for a few years became a reporter with the *San Antonio Express* in 1880. By the early 1900s he had become a feature writer focusing on prominent frontier figures. His *Combats and Conquests of Immortal Heroes*, published in 1910, derived from his interest in the nineteenth-century history of San Antonio and the surrounding area.

40. Chabot, foreword to *Memoirs*, by Antonio Menchaca.

41. Barnes, *Combats and Conquests of Immortal Heroes*, 76.

second part of Menchaca's reminiscences. Barnes does not, however, credit Menchaca with any of the other numerous stories that appear in his book.

Chabot further asserts that he is publishing the document that appeared in the *Passing Show* thirty years earlier: "The Yanaguana society is grateful to Mr. Newcomb for his kindness in permitting the publication of these memoirs, with the Introduction by James P. Newcomb (his father) published in the *Passing Show*, San Antonio, Texas, in weekly installments, from June 22 to July 27, 1907."[42] A comparison of the text as it appears in the *Passing Show* and in the 1937 Yanaguana Society edition indicates that Chabot made relatively significant changes to Newcomb's version but also that Newcomb and/or the *Passing Show* staff did a very poor job of proofreading the typesetting. The inclusion of two full paragraphs in the Yanaguana Society version that would have come at the point where the *Passing Show* version moves from 6 July to 12 July 1907 (as well as numerous other insertions) suggests that Chabot had access to the original manuscript and compared it to the printed version. Whether the differences represent Chabot's correction of what appeared in the *Passing Show* or his taking liberties with the text, we cannot know in the absence of the manuscript. Without the original manuscript we have decided to follow Newcomb's version as the one closer in date to the original and the one that is not otherwise readily available. It is the one presented here as "The Memoirs of Captain Menchaca" with some of Chabot's insertions incorporated where appropriate and clearly identified as such with brackets and underlining.[43]

If Barnes was responsible for taking down all of Menchaca's recollections, then he did it over the course of some period of time, thus allowing the first and second parts to become disconnected. However they became separated, it is clear from internal evidence that the published and unpublished portions are part of a whole, since in various passages from the unpublished second half of the recollections Menchaca makes reference to material already mentioned in the published first half.[44] What is here styled as "The Unpublished Second Part of the Menchaca Manuscript" remained in family hands until the middle of the twentieth century. In 1950 Elizabeth Coogan, Menchaca's great-granddaughter, not realizing that the manuscript in her possession was not complete, explained to University

42. Chabot, foreword to *Memoirs*, by Antonio Menchaca.

43. More information is presented in the Preface.

44. For example, on page 169 he refers to "Cordero" as the governor who had previously been referenced in the recollections, in part 1 (p. 119).

of Texas archivist Winnie Allen, "My father [Lucien LaCoste] kept these handwritten papers for many years, believing that this original account would be valuable for me to have, and hoping I would have an occasion to sell them to the right party. While my family and I have kept them safely these many years, I do believe that a library is the best place for these, and I should be glad to sell them to you."[45] When Allen asked her about the published part, Coogan was unable to explain to Allen how the two parts had become separated and recommended that Allen contact Amelie LaCoste, her aunt, who still lived in San Antonio. There is no record of Allen's having made contact with LaCoste and uncovering any other information on the provenance of Menchaca's reminiscences.[46] We are left, then, knowing that Chabot asserted that Barnes was the amanuensis of whom James Newcomb spoke and that after its transfer to the San Antonio Public Library, sometime in the first half of the twentieth century, the manuscript of the first, published, part of Menchaca's reminiscences became lost, while the second part remained in the hands of the LaCoste branch of the family.

Although considered a memoir by Newcomb and Chabot, the recollections as recorded might properly be deemed a *testimonio* in the way Rosaura Sánchez uses that term to connote a genre entailing a "mediated text" shaped by "uneven power relations between the oral producer of the testimonial and the transcribing interviewer." On the other hand, as Sánchez notes in her study of the sixty-two Californio *testimonios* produced under the directorship of book dealer and publisher Hubert Howe Bancroft during the 1870s, "The autobiographical element [of the *testimonios*] is evident in the narrators' interest in representing their own participation as public figures within the larger historical scheme." Sánchez also observes that the marked tendency of the Californio *testimonios* to focus on the public domain is correlative with a relatively scant treatment of their pri-

---

45. Coogan to Allen, 27 October 1950, Antonio Menchaca Collection, Briscoe Center for American History, University of Texas at Austin.

46. Corroboration that Elizabeth Coogan was Antonio Menchaca's great-granddaughter Elizabeth Merriam LaCoste comes from the California death record for a Helen Merriam LaCoste, daughter of (father) Merriam and (mother) Lovering, 4 May 1951 in Los Angeles, age eighty-four (California Death Records search, RootsWeb, accessed 31 October 2011, http://vitals.rootsweb.ancestry.com/ca/death/search.cgi/), which matches Coogan's comment that her mother passed away in early May in another letter to Allen, 21 May 1951 (Antonio Menchaca Collection, Briscoe Center for American History, University of Texas at Austin).

FIGURE 3
Relatively formal portrait of Antonio Menchaca that belonged to his daughter, María Antonia,
and her husband, Maximilian Neuendorff. From the Neuendorff Family Papers,
courtesy of the Daughters of the Republic of Texas Library, San Antonio.

vate lives. The texts produced thus reflect a strategic retelling of historical
events, but this does not necessarily mean their rendering of the past is
without veracity. Rather, they are an attempt of residents from the former
territories of northern Mexico to create historical narratives in which they
and other Mexican-descent residents play a prominent and meritorious
role. All these insights are consistent with nineteenth-century Tejano narratives of the past, including that of Menchaca. We have found it helpful

to bear in mind the similarities of Menchaca's recollections in genre and intent to other nineteenth-century Tejano and Californio self-narratives.[47]

Whoever Menchaca's scribe was, his influence in his role as transcriber is a primary issue for a critical study of the narrative. The manuscript is in English, but Menchaca's native language was Spanish. At one point in the reminiscences Menchaca states that he gave a public speech through an interpreter because "I did not like to Speak English for fear of making them laugh at my pronunciation" (161). The text of the manuscript is not polished and contains an occasional Spanish loan word. Does the mode of expression reflect the scribe's attempt to literally transcribe Menchaca's statements as he made them, his own shorthand rendering of them, or, most probably, some combination of the two? Moreover, did the scribe record Menchaca's words with little or no prompting, or are some of the major topics treated in the recollections a response to the scribe's queries and interests? There is no evidence that leads to indisputable answers to these questions. Suffice it to say the critical reader must bear in mind that not only is the manuscript the recollections of a septuagenarian Tejano looking back over a life in times of rapid political and social change, but it is also a record made through the pen of a scribe, possibly a young Anglo-American collaborator, Barnes, who in his subsequent journalism career displayed a marked interest in colorful stories about local events and characters. With this in mind, in what follows we will focus primarily on the broad themes of the reminiscences, especially two major concerns most likely to reflect Menchaca's own perspectives: his portrayals of the Tejano legacy and the Tejano character.

"A HISTORY OF THE SETTLEMENT AND INHABITANTS OF SAN ANTONIO"

While the bulk of the reminiscences consist of personal recollections from the first half century of Menchaca's life, the final section implicitly reveals a prideful conviction that Menchaca's ancestors and other Spanish-speaking residents founded and developed San Antonio. Entitled "A History of the Settlement and Inhabitants of San Antonio," this section begins with the observation that "Mexican & Canary [Islander] Settlers" (163) carried out

---

47. Rosaura Sánchez, *Telling Identities: The Californio Testimonios*, 9, 13–14. For an excellent overview on genre in self-narratives, see also Rudy V. Busto, *King Tiger: The Religious Vision of Reies López Tijerina*, 157–164.

the original development around San Antonio's Military and Main Plazas and, despite the obstacle of American Indians who "were very troublesome and continually harassed them" (163), built homes and established what came to be the city of San Antonio. Menchaca then presents a somewhat lengthy description of the various homes and buildings constructed on the town's central plazas and adjoining streets during the Spanish colonial era. In this narration, the aging Menchaca sets forth a mental map of how he remembers the city in his early days and how he perceives it in his memory, relating the names of Hispanic inhabitants of various properties that by the 1870s were owned by Anglo-Americans. For example, he recalls, "On Main Street where the Banking house of John Twohig Esq Stands — was the residence of Old Antonio Baccha [Baca] who died of a sunstroke while on the rode [*sic*] to Labahia [La Bahía] during the time of the difficulties & hostilities which were going on" during the struggle for Mexican independence (167).

As in other sections of the reminiscences, Menchaca here incorrectly presents some dates and details, such as his false claim that "my Great Grand Father Don Pedro Acon y Frillo and Old Captain Manchaca and his wife" (162) were among the original Canary Islander settlers. In light of the attempts to "Americanize" Tejano patriots like Menchaca in print and in public speech, his self-identification with the Canary Islander elite is no mere passing reference. Three other passages in the manuscript mention the Canary Islanders, all in a positive light. Other Tejanos, such as José María Rodríguez, went so far as to make the exaggerated claim that into the nineteenth century there were Canary Islanders, "people of pure Spanish descent," living in segregated isolation on the west side of the San Antonio River and that they "took great pride in preventing any intermarriage with mixed races and when one did mix he lost his caste with the rest."[48] In a racially conscious and stratified society like nineteenth-century Texas, Menchaca's claim of a European bloodline must be seen in part as a claim for legitimacy. At the same time, in connecting his family and community to the founders of San Antonio — note that Menchaca asserts that "*Mexican &* Canary [Islander] Settlers" (163, emphasis added) established the city around its two main plazas — Menchaca is showing his pride that San Antonio's origins are rooted not in Anglo-American or U.S. initiatives, but in the eighteenth-century efforts of Spanish-speaking pioneers.

Evidence of San Antonio's Mexican and Spanish origins was noteworthy in the "prominen [*sic*] historical land marks" (167) that Menchaca's reminis-

48. Rodríguez, *Rodríguez Memoirs of Early Texas*, 34, 38.

FIGURE 4

San Fernando Church, now cathedral, in which Menchaca was baptized, as he would have known it for most of his life. The cathedral's French Gothic nave dates from the 1870s, but its sanctuary and sacristy are part of the original building constructed in the 1730s–1750s. "San Fernando Church, Pre-reconstruction," 75–647, Photograph Collection, courtesy of the University of Texas at San Antonio Libraries Special Collections.

cences then proceed to highlight: the parish church of San Fernando; the Spanish missions, including the Alamo in its initial foundation as Mission San Antonio de Valero; and Alameda Street, which Spanish subjects had cleared through cottonwood trees as a promenade leading to a park area used for dances and other festivities. Expanding his treatment of the accomplishments in San Antonio during the Spanish colonial era enshrined in these historical sites, Menchaca adds a claim that a Canary Islander there sent as a gift to the king of Spain the first buffaloes ever transported to Europe. Though the name of the giver is not mentioned, Menchaca's recollection reveals his esteem for the exploits and the formative role of Hispanics in San Antonio.[49]

Menchaca's commentaries on early Hispanic settlers reveal his racial

49. For more on this story, including sources, see *Edited Reminiscences of José Antonio Menchaca, Part 2*, n. 110 (pp. 116–17), in this volume.

bias against their frequent adversaries, the American Indians who lived in the region before these newcomers arrived. Regarding the work of the Franciscan friars in the local missions, he states that "like in almost all other instances the Efforts to Christanize [sic] and civilize 'Lo the poor Indian' was a complete failure" (169). Yet he does admit that the missions were "all made in a mavelously [sic] solid and substantial manner when you consider the qualifications of the builders who were Indians" (168). His explanation for the noteworthy building campaign is that the Franciscans initially attracted some natives to the missions when they "succeeded in convert[ing] a very powerful chief," who "made them [the natives] very useful" to the friars (169).

Menchaca's reminiscences end rather abruptly with two legends that further accentuate the legacy of the early Spanish Franciscans in Texas. In the first a band of Franciscans is beset by a large and hostile group of American Indians, until the renowned missionary Antonio Margil de Jesús lifts up his eyes and "in the twinkling of a bed post the savages were transmogrified into deer" (170). The second recounts a traveling group of friars who, thirsty after passing several days without water, come upon a grapevine, pray over it, pull it out, and to their delight see water come bursting forth. According to Menchaca's recounting of the legend, this incident marks the origins of the San Marcos River, though other versions claim it was the San Antonio River.[50] These legends of miraculous assistance for Spanish friars, which Menchaca suggests were established tales among his Tejano contemporaries, further enhance his laudatory account of Spanish-speaking residents' efforts in San Antonio's early history with the implication that divine Providence accompanied them in their endeavors.

Consciously or not, Menchaca's eclectic rendering of San Antonio's early history contests Anglo-Americans' tendency to perceive their presence in Texas as initiating an era of progress for benighted Mexican-descent residents. Even Anglo-American defenders of Tejanos ascribed to a view of Tejanos as inferior. One San Antonio editorialist who objected to a fellow journalist's attack on the Tejano character in 1852 noted:

---

50. Charles Merritt Barnes, *Combats and Conquests of Immortal Heroes: Sung in Song and Told in Story*, 76–81; S. J. Wright, *San Antonio de Béxar: Historical, Traditional, Legendary*, 121–122, 127–128. Another account states that Margil de Jesús miraculously discovered a spring near Nacogdoches, although it cites the earlier works of Barnes and Wright, who gave the site as San Antonio. E. G. Littlejohn, "The Holy Spring of Father Margil at Nacogdoches," 204–205.

V. R. de el V. P. F. Antonio Margil de Jesus. Pred. Apost. Guard.
y Fundador de los tres Colegios de la SS. Cruz de Queretaro Guatem.
¡Zacatecas. Murio de 73 años ó 6 de Agosto. de 1726.

FIGURE 5

Portrait of Fray Antonio Margil de Jesús, founder of Mission San José and subject of a number
of early Texas legends, including one retold by Menchaca to his collaborator. For many Tejanos,
the missionaries, especially Fray Margil de Jesús, represented the civilizing power of Spanish
Catholicism in an increasingly Protestant world. Courtesy of the East Texas Research
Center, R. W. Steen Library, Stephen F. Austin State University, Nacogdoches, Texas.

It is lamentably true that our Mexican population, generally, do not occupy as high a position in the scale of morality and intelligence as is desirable; yet every one who knows their former condition, and will take into consideration their former mode of life, as well as the demoralizing effect of the Government under which they lived previous to the establishment of the Texas Republic, must admit that they are reforming as rapidly as could have been expected.[51]

Seen in this light, Menchaca's emphasis on the Tejano contribution to San Antonio and Texas history before Anglo-Americans ever arrived serves as a corrective to demeaning views of the Tejano past and integrity.

In this regard Menchaca's recollections parallel the extant memoirs of other nineteenth-century San Antonio Tejanos. José María Rodríguez dedicates nearly half of his recollections to reminiscences about his and other leading Spanish-surnamed families in San Antonio, and he points out, "I intend this [memoir] mostly for my children and their descendants as the recollections of one of their ancestors at the time when the government of this country was in a period of formation." Juan Seguín, who claimed that persecution by violent, anti-Mexican "adventurers" compelled him to leave Texas in 1842, returned to his hometown and published his memoirs in 1858 to vindicate his name. Seguín outlines Tejano contributions to the Republic of Texas and, in an often-quoted passage, opines that the growing Anglo-American population after Texas independence was not a pure boon of progress for Tejanos, but in fact made him (and others) "a foreigner in my native land." José Antonio Navarro explains in his historical writings that his first intention in writing them was "to correct some substantial errors" in an 1853 article on San Antonio history published in the *San Antonio Ledger*. His account goes on to describe Mexico's struggle for independence from Spain, particularly the valor of local Tejanos during battles between insurgent and royalist forces; his contention is that San Antonio had an honorable citizenry with aspirations for a free system of government long before Anglo-Americans arrived and that these "noble citizens of [San Antonio de] Béxar sacrificed their lives and property, performing heroic deeds of valor" in the cause of Mexican independence.[52]

---

51. *Western Texas* (San Antonio), 14 October 1852, p. 2.

52. Rodríguez, *Rodríguez Memoirs of Early Texas*, 6; Seguín, *Revolution Remembered*, ed. De la Teja, 2nd ed., 103, 113; Navarro, *Defending Mexican Valor in Texas*, 43, 58. See also Seguín, *Personal Memoirs of John N. Seguín*, iv, 19; Navarro, *Apuntes*, 13, 19.

FRIENDSHIPS, STRUGGLE, AND SURVIVAL

Menchaca's rendering of early San Antonio history—which in terms of its location in his reminiscences functions as an appendix to his own life recollections—is consistent with his accentuation of Tejano struggle and heroism beginning with Tejanos' initiatives to win Mexican independence from Spain when he was a young boy. Like the writings of his contemporary José Antonio Navarro, just mentioned, here Menchaca recounts the events of the insurgency and counterinsurgency in San Antonio from 1811 to 1813, the most turbulent years of the Mexican struggle for independence from Spain. In the latter year, Mexican insurgents wrested control of San Antonio, brutally killing Governor Manuel Salcedo and other crown officials, only to lose the town again and endure similarly harsh reprisals from the Spanish royalist forces under the command of General Joaquín de Arredondo. Menchaca's version of these events reflects the native San Antonian perspective of being caught in the violence and bloodshed, as he chronicles the names and the fates of various local families and individuals. Arredondo ordered that a number of women accused of insurgent loyalties be crowded into cramped quarters and coerced to prepare food for his troops. Many of their male counterparts suffocated to death in a crowded house used as a prison, were led before firing squads, or were forced into hard labor.[53]

Menchaca suggests that his sympathies and those of his fellow San Antonio residents were with the cause of independence, even making the exaggerated claim that local officials appointed to run the town after insurgents under José Bernardo Gutiérrez de Lara took it were "all gentlemen of the city of San Antonio, and descendants of the first families who migrated from the Canary Islands" (123).[54] He describes the period between

53. For an overview of these eventful years in San Antonio history, see Félix D. Almaráz Jr., *Tragic Cavalier: Governor Manuel Salcedo of Texas, 1808–1813*; Jesús F. de la Teja, "Rebellion on the Frontier," 15–30. Menchaca's account of Arredondo's harsh reprisals against San Antonio residents is consistent with his reminiscences that former Texas president Mirabeau Buonaparte Lamar recorded while conducting historical research in 1857. Notes taken from Menchaca and Barrera, 21 January 1857, in *Papers of Mirabeau Buonaparte Lamar*, ed. Gulick and Elliott, 6:339–340.

54. José Antonio Navarro attests that the secretary of this ruling group was Mariano Rodríguez, a leader not mentioned on Menchaca's list of appointed officials; José María Rodríguez notes that Mariano Rodríguez was his distant relative. Historian Carlos Castañeda cites primary documents to show Gutiérrez de Lara himself led the governing body after the insurgent victory and makes no mention of local officials, much less a Canary Islander–dominated ruling elite. Navarro, *Defending Mexican Valor in Texas*, 47;

the Spanish commander Arredondo's reconquest of the city and the winning of Mexican independence eight years later as a time of economic distress, weak leadership, and frequent American Indian depredations. Conversely, he maintains that San Antonio "underwent a great change for the better" in the years immediately following Mexican independence (129).

One of the most striking features of Menchaca's personal anecdotes is his narration of his honorable and charitable interactions with friend and foe alike, people of varied backgrounds and political persuasions. For example, he relates that, during the Arredondo occupation of San Antonio, a fellow San Antonian accused Menchaca's father of a minor infraction. When the Spanish authorities arrested Menchaca's parents and ordered that his father be publicly flogged and that his mother be placed in confinement and servitude of the royalist army, the thirteen-year-old Antonio reportedly rushed to plead their case with a Spanish officer he had befriended. He persisted until his parents were released.

Whether true in every detail or not, this self-narration as a person who could overcome difficulties with others, even befriend leaders of occupying armies, illumines Menchaca's self-perception of Tejanos like himself as people of honor, ingenuity, dedication to their families and communities, and resourceful ability to survive through a lifetime of turmoil and social change. These qualities are further evidenced in Menchaca's exposition of his relations during the struggle for Texas independence with key leaders such as James Bowie, Sam Houston, Antonio López de Santa Anna, and a Comanche chief whom Menchaca identifies as Casimiro.[55]

It must be recalled that Menchaca dictated his recollections in the 1870s, by which time Bowie's fame was legendary and still growing. Menchaca relates Bowie's arrival in San Antonio, marriage to Ursula María de Veramendi, and heartfelt loss at her death in a cholera epidemic. The first contact mentioned between Bowie and Menchaca is a confidential and urgent letter Bowie wrote him just before the December 1835 Texan siege and takeover of San Antonio from Mexican forces. After the Texan victory, Bowie and Menchaca reportedly were reunited for the first time since the death of Bowie's wife. Menchaca describes their encounter as a touching reunion:

When Bowie saw me he threw his arms around my neck and wept to think that he had not seen his wife die. He said, "My father, my brother,

Rodríguez, *Rodríguez Memoirs of Early Texas*, 52–54; Carlos E. Castañeda, *Our Catholic Heritage in Texas, 1519–1936*, 7 vols., 6:102–103. See also Navarro, *Apuntes*, 15.

55. For more on Casimiro, see *Edited Reminiscences, Part 2*, n. 48 (p. 94).

my companion, and all my protection has gone! Are you still my companion-in-arms?"

And I answered him:

"I shall be your companion, Jim Bowie, until I die."

"Then come this evening," Bowie said, "and I'll take you to meet Travis at the Alamo." (132)

Menchaca goes on to narrate his leading role in organizing a ball in honor of Davy Crockett, at which Menchaca states he was present when Bowie, Crockett, and William B. Travis first received the news that Mexican forces under General Santa Anna were marching toward San Antonio.

After he fled San Antonio with his family and was conscripted into the Texas army, Menchaca was among the forces under General Sam Houston that retreated eastward. He asserts that he personally confronted Houston when he learned that the Tejano troops under Juan Seguín's command had been ordered to guard horses rather than engage the Mexican army in the battle of San Jacinto. According to the reminiscences, Houston said that Menchaca impressed him because the Tejano "spoke like a man" (138). Consequently Houston allowed the Tejano soldiers to join in the fighting.

Once the battle of San Jacinto was won and General Santa Anna was taken prisoner in the Texas camp, Menchaca reportedly served as interpreter between him and General Houston. In contrast to his depiction of Santa Anna as an unsavory character when he provided some recollections for the historical research of former Texas president Mirabeau Buonaparte Lamar in 1857, in his own reminiscences Menchaca recounts no derogatory anecdotes about or descriptions of Santa Anna. Rather, Menchaca tells about how he secured a hot meal for the ravenously hungry Santa Anna, protested a Texan guard's refusal to let him see the Mexican general with this meal until Houston interceded, conversed with Santa Anna about the general's previous military service in San Antonio during the Mexican War of Independence, and even offered him financial support to assist with his needs while he was in captivity. Unlike the many Texas soldiers who wanted to execute Santa Anna in retribution for the killing of their comrades at the Alamo and Goliad, Menchaca states that he treated Santa Anna with the respect of a prisoner of war, a depiction of his actions that is consistent with the account in José María Rodríguez's memoirs.[56] Menchaca

56. Notes taken from Menchaca and Barrera, in *Papers of Mirabeau Buonaparte Lamar*, ed. Gulick and Elliott, 6:338; Rodríguez, *Rodríguez Memoirs of Early Texas*, 14.

FIGURE 6

William Henry Huddle's 1885 depiction of the surrender of Santa Anna omits the presence of any Tejano or Mexican participants on the Texan side in the battle of San Jacinto. Only Santa Anna and his aide, Juan Almonte, both of whom Menchaca claims to have interacted with, are depicted from the Mexican side. "Surrender of Santa Anna." Courtesy of the State Preservation Board; Accession ID: CHA 1989.046; Austin, TX; Original Artist: William H. Huddle, 1847–1892; Photographer: unknown; Pre-1991, PreConservation.
© State Preservation Board, Austin, Texas.

notes that Santa Anna was so moved by this kindness that "tears [came] to his eyes and he cried like a child" (148).

Menchaca further attests that he turned down a military promotion in order to be part of the lead forces that took the risk of closely monitoring the Mexican army's departure from Texas, which Santa Anna had ordered. Upon his return to San Antonio after completing this task, Menchaca found a nearly deserted city and a small band of Comanches under the leadership of one Chief Casimiro. According to the reminiscences, Menchaca and Casimiro were already acquainted, and the Tejano fed and supplied the natives at Casimiro's request. Apparently out of gratitude for this and similar kindnesses in the past, Casimiro reportedly forewarned Menchaca "that the Indians intended to come into San Antonio burn the town and kill all of the people" (155). He even offered to take Menchaca away and share with him all he had, shocking Menchaca when he stated that his offer included his four wives. Menchaca declined the offer, explaining that he preferred to remain in his own hometown and that in any event he had to go get his family members, who had been at Nacogdoches during the course of the war. He also requested that Casimiro not attack the inhabitants of San Antonio, telling him to "think of my kindness to you and do not harm them" (155).

Menchaca goes on to state that Comanches did descend on the town during his absence, but at Casimiro's order they desisted from their violence after killing a few residents. Though no other sources mention this specific episode, conflicts with the Comanches were frequent in and around San Antonio in the wake of the Texas Revolution. Menchaca's portrayal of tenuous but mutual respect between himself and this Comanche leader contrasts sharply with the conditions in other incidents, such as the Council House Fight, to which he subsequently alludes. In that conflict at San Antonio on 19 March 1840, representatives of the Comanches and Anglo-American leaders of the Texas government disagreed on an exchange of prisoners, and a violent confrontation erupted, leaving thirty-five Comanches, six Anglo-Americans, and one Tejano dead.[57]

Menchaca's diverse friendships and alliances reveal the Tejanos' dilemma of choosing sides as they were caught between opposing forces in the crucible of violence that was San Antonio. As he notes with regard to San Antonio during the Texas Revolution, "A great many families who sympathized with the Texas cause moved East and a great many Mexican families who either from choice or compulsion aspoused [sic] the Mexican cause went to Mexico" (154). His brief commentaries on Mexican and Texan expeditions into the other's territory, such as the March 1842 raid on San Antonio by Mexican forces under General Rafael Vásquez, as well as the eventual full-scale war between the United States and Mexico (1846–1848), reflect the ongoing tensions in which Tejanos at San Antonio and elsewhere lived after the political separation of Texas from Mexico.

Nowhere is the dilemma Tejanos faced more clearly expressed in the reminiscences than in Menchaca's narration of the September 1842 Mexican occupation of San Antonio under the forces of General Adrián Woll. Men-

---

57. Ray F. Broussard, "San Antonio during the Texas Republic: A City in Transition," 17–21. Contemporary accounts of the Council House Fight are in *Texas Sentinel* (Austin), 23, 25 March, 15 April 1840; *Telegraph and Texas Register* (Houston), 8 April 1840; Mary A. Maverick, *Memoirs of Mary A. Maverick*, ed. Rena Maverick Green, 31–37; Rodríguez, *Rodríguez Memoirs of Early Texas*, 24–26.

chaca relates that Woll had him arrested along with a number of Anglo-Americans who had pledged to defend the city and then accused the Tejano of being "the greatest traitor to your flag unhung and you deserve to be shot 25 times through the head but General Santa Anna who thanks you for the kindness you did him asked me if I captured you to spare your life" (158). General Woll reportedly did so with the condition that Menchaca promise never to take up arms against Mexico again. Menchaca agreed, but then immediately began to advocate for his Anglo-American friends, asking Woll that those to be taken away as prisoners to Mexico be allowed to travel via wagon or horseback rather than on foot. He also describes himself as a mediating force between Woll and Texas Ranger Jack Hays, the commander of the Texas troops that were amassing to retake San Antonio. Menchaca reportedly warned Woll that he had better leave town peaceably as Hays was about to attack, but to no avail. After the two forces fought, Woll prepared to withdraw. Menchaca reiterated his plea that the Mexican general show respect for his Anglo-American prisoners and not force them to walk all the way to Mexico, a request that went unheeded. Then he purportedly delivered a letter from those prisoners to Hays stating that Woll had treated them well and that no undue harshness should be shown Woll and his men if they were taken captive, though an account written at the time of this incident states instead that the prisoners' communiqué requested that Hays treat San Antonio Tejanos respectfully, not Woll, out of gratitude for *their* kindness to the prisoners in doing all that they could to alleviate their suffering.[58] As he does with other noteworthy leaders, Menchaca implies that he had a close relationship with Hays, describing how Hays "was much rejoiced to see me alive and well" (160).

Next, Menchaca maintains that after Woll's retreat he and some Anglo-American allies successfully subverted a proposal to burn San Antonio. Though Menchaca's recollection of this proposal is not corroborated in any other primary source, similar propositions had been proffered as early as 1836. After the battle of San Jacinto, General Felix Huston had commanded Juan Seguín to destroy the city, an order that Seguín convinced President Sam Houston to rescind.[59] Anglo-Americans who advocated the town's

---

58. Samuel Maverick, one of the prisoners, recorded this version of the communiqué in his journal, noting that "the Mexican population here" had supplied and assisted the Anglo-American prisoners "in the most liberal manner." Samuel Maverick, *Samuel Maverick, Texan: 1803-1870. A Collection of Letters, Journals, and Memoirs*, ed. Rena Maverick Green, 174.

59. Felix Huston to Sam Houston, 14 November 1836, Catholic Archives of Texas,

destruction after Woll retreated in 1842 argued that San Antonio's isolation had enabled the Mexican army to plant spies there and easily capture
it. Through an interpreter, Menchaca reportedly responded to such argu-
ments with a speech "bitterly opposing the sacrifice of San Antonio to the
flames" (161). He reminded his hearers that his aging mother and other residents "would be left destitute by the burning of the town" (161). Menchaca's recollection of defending his hometown against both Mexican attack
and Anglo-American destruction, all within the space of a few short weeks,
reflects Tejanos' commitment to their homeland. It also epitomizes Menchaca's self-narration of his Tejano capacity to survive by cultivating relations of respect, even friendship, among the leaders of the various groups
that came into the nexus of San Antonio life.[60]

NARRATING A TEJANO LIFE

What emerges from the pages of Menchaca's reminiscences is the story of
a man who prided himself on his heritage, his personal and family honor,
and his capacity as a survivor. Like other Tejanos, Menchaca had many
opportunities to succumb to bitterness and despair. His friends and neigh-
bors lost their lives in the insurgencies of the Mexican War of Independence and the Texas Revolution, regardless of which side they chose in the
conflicts, or even if they attempted to remain neutral. Living in the city
with more battles fought in or around it than any other in what is now the
United States, he witnessed many atrocities. In his early years, perennial
tensions with American Indians also led to attacks and counterattacks. As
successive national governments claimed sovereignty over San Antonio, he
was among the population caught in between, on one occasion having to
defend his hometown from both the Mexican and the Texan armies. Like
his Tejano contemporaries, his political career and activism had relatively

---

Austin; Houston to Juan Seguín, 16 January 1837, in Seguín, *Revolution Remembered*, ed.
De la Teja, 2nd ed., 152–153, 111–112; Linn, *Reminiscences of Fifty Years in Texas*, 294–296.
See also Seguín, *Personal Memoirs of John N. Seguín*, 15–16; *Telegraph and Texas Register*
(Columbia), 25 October 1836.

60. For the Tejano dilemma of being caught with opposing loyalties, see Jesús F. de la
Teja, "The Making of a Tejano," in Seguín, *Revolution Remembered*, ed. De la Teja, 2nd ed.,
1–70; Timothy Matovina, *Tejano Religion and Ethnicity: San Antonio, 1821-1860*, especially
Chap. 3, "Between Two Worlds: The Period of the Texas Republic, 1836-1845," 24–48.

limited influence on the new Anglo-American regime that gained ascendancy in his hometown.

Menchaca's life narration, however embellished or erroneous in detail, reveals a vision of the Tejano character and legacy that he undoubtedly held in common with many other nineteenth-century Tejanos who endured the tumult of that century in his homeland. Proudly accentuating his encounters with such diverse figures as James Bowie and Spanish military commanders, Comanche chiefs and Antonio López de Santa Anna, Sam Houston and Davy Crockett, General Adrián Woll and Texas Ranger Jack Hays, his fellow Tejanos and San Antonio's growing Anglo-American population, Menchaca displays a remarkable capacity to remember both friends and supposed enemies with similar respect. His narrative adds to historical studies of nineteenth-century Tejanos an insightful portfolio of the characteristics Tejanos valued and sought to deem their own: an unwillingness to forget that their ancestors were the original founders of places like San Antonio, an ability to maintain internal equilibrium amidst the many changes they faced throughout their lives, and the *aguante* (unyielding endurance) without which they would not have lived to tell their tale.

EDITED REMINISCENCES OF
JOSÉ ANTONIO MENCHACA

Part 1

I was born in the year 1800 and baptized in the church of San Fernando de Béxar[1] on 12 January of that year. Raised in San Antonio[2] up to the year 1807, I can remember when came the express order from the king of Spain to the governor, Lieutenant Colonel Antonio Cordero,[3] to select 250 men from the king's service to go and establish the Spanish line on the Sabine River. He did so and went to reconnoiter.[4] Having returned from the Sabine River, he left 100 men at Nacog-

1. The original reads "San Fernando de Austria." This misnaming was a common mistake, even among Bexareños, arising from the fact that the saint for whom the civilian settlement was named was St. Ferdinand, king of Castile and León in the thirteenth century, who was the namesake of Philip III's prominent war-hero third son, Cardinal-Infante Ferdinand. Following common practice, Spaniards named towns for combinations of religious figures and prominent Spanish nobles. Thus, the town of San Fernando de Austria (now Zaragoza, Coahuila) was named in honor of both St. Ferdinand and Cardinal-Infante Ferdinand, while the town of San Fernando de Béxar (now San Antonio, Texas) was named for the same saint, but for another Spanish military hero, Manuel de Zúñiga, Duke of Béjar, brother of the then viceroy, the Marqués de Valero.

2. For the sake of clarity, throughout the edited manuscript all references to "San Fernando" have been changed to "San Antonio" to reflect the modern designation of the city.

3. Manuel Antonio Cordero y Bustamante, who was born in Cádiz, Spain, was one of the most accomplished officers in Spain's frontier service. A veteran of the Apache wars on the northwestern frontier, he became governor of Coahuila in 1798 and served as interim governor of Texas from 1805 to 1808; he remained in the province until 1810 to complete settlement projects started under his direction.

4. In fact, the boundary between United States and Spanish territory had immediately come under dispute as a result of ambiguities in the French sale of Louisiana to the Jefferson administration in 1803. Spain continued to claim the Arroyo Hondo just east of the old Texas capital of Los Adaes as the true boundary. Menchaca's reference to the Sabine as the "Spanish line" is an ex post facto acceptance of the border established

doches for the safeguard of Spanish law, that it be respected and obeyed. When he had concluded his military business at Nacogdoches he returned to San Antonio.

Having arrived in San Antonio, Cordero took upon himself the task of improving the city. He straightened streets; Main Street,[5] so called now, was at that time a very crooked one, running straight from the plaza up to where the street from Lewis's Mill intersects it, thence to the mill. He cut the street straight, straightened Flores Street, built a bridge and the powder house. While he was governor he was very good and kind, doing many things for the welfare of the people.[6]

In 1811 Manuel Salcedo, lieutenant colonel in the Royal Spanish Army, succeeded Cordero.[7] While Salcedo was governor secret letters were received here from parties who desired to throw off the Spanish yoke in Mexico including Ignacio Allende, Miguel Hidalgo y Costilla, José Mariano Jiménez, and El Pachón,[8] inviting the citizens of San Antonio to join in

---

under the Adams-Onís Treaty of 1819. Governor Cordero's tour of East Texas was meant to reaffirm Spanish claims and reconnoiter American moves in the area after the signing of the Neutral Ground Agreement between Colonel Simón de Herrera and General James Wilkinson in 1806, which made the area between the Sabine and Arroyo Hondo off limits to the militaries of both countries.

5. This is now Commerce Street.

6. Cordero remained well respected, even during the Mexican War of Independence, during which time he was a royalist officer. In 1814 he married San Antonio native Gertrudis Pérez, daughter of Ignacio Pérez, one of the city's most prominent royalist residents. After independence, Cordero retained his rank and at the time of his death in 1823 was serving as commandant general of the Western Interior Provinces.

7. Manuel Salcedo actually arrived in Texas in 1808, having taken his oath of office before leaving Spain and traveling to Texas by way of the United States. He was the nephew of Nemecio Salcedo, commandant general of the Interior Provinces of New Spain, and son of a former Spanish governor of Louisiana.

8. Ignacio María Allende y Unzaga was a royalist military officer who had seen service in Texas at the beginning of the century. A sympathizer of the insurgency, he became its principal military leader when Miguel Hidalgo y Costilla stepped down following the defeat at Puente de Calderón. Hidalgo, parish priest of the town of Dolores in the state of Guanajuato, is considered the father of Mexican independence, having launched the revolt against Spanish rule on 16 September 1810, Mexico's independence day. José Mariano Jiménez was a trained mining engineer who joined the revolt in its early stages and rose to command artillery in Hidalgo's army. He was executed, along with Hidalgo's other top officers, after being captured in Coahuila on their way to Texas, following a trial conducted by Manuel Salcedo. *El Pachón* (the Bearded One) was

their enterprise. Many of these citizens answered them that they could rely upon help from here, that there were a great many here who would willingly enter into the plot. While considering the measures they were to adopt to secure their ends, the plotters were suspected and from fifteen to twenty of the leaders were arrested. Some were shot, others remained here in prison, and others were sent to prison in Chihuahua. Among those who were sent to Chihuahua was Captain José Menchaca,[9] who remained imprisoned till his death in 1820. The main leader, Juan Bautista Casas, was here in prison for a while, then taken to Monclova, where he was shot, his head severed from his body and placed in a box, and sent here and put in the middle of Military Plaza on a pole.[10] At the same time that Casas was killed, Ignacio Allende, Hidalgo, Jiménez, and El Pachón, who were on their way to San Antonio with $3,000,000,[11] were apprehended, killed, and all the property confiscated.[12]

---

the nickname of Encarnación Ortiz, another of Hidalgo's rebel leaders (Lucas Alamán, *Historia de México desde los primeros movimientos que prepararon su independencia hasta la época presente*, 5:224).

9. José Menchaca was the son of Luis Antonio Menchaca and Ignacia Núñez Morillo and no relation to Antonio Menchaca. He was also a royalist officer but had retired by the time the Mexican War of Independence erupted. He twice flirted with the insurgency, and the second time he tried to return to royalist loyalty, his pardon was disapproved by Commandant General Nemecio Salcedo. Tried for treason and convicted, he was sent to prison in Chihuahua, where he died after ten years.

10. Menchaca's recollections of events that took place when he was eleven years old are naturally muddled. The events he describes are known as the Casas Revolt, and they took place between January and March 1811. Casas was able to mount a successful coup against Governor Manuel Salcedo, who along with other Spaniards in San Antonio was sent under arrest to Coahuila. Bexareños quickly became suspicious of Casas, who was a native of Nuevo Santander and therefore not a part of the town's elite. Most of San Antonio's leading men soon thought better of their actions and under the leadership of Juan Manuel Zambrano staged a countercoup in the early morning hours of 17 March 1811.

11. The chief currency of Spanish colonial Mexico was the peso, or Spanish dollar. Until shortly before the American Civil War, it circulated in the United States as legal tender and was the model for the U.S. silver dollar.

12. Dissatisfied with Hidalgo's leadership, Ignacio Allende removed the priest as supreme commander and assumed control of the remaining rebel forces with the intention of retreating through Texas to the United States. The collapse of this first phase of Mexico's revolt took place in Coahuila, where counterinsurgents freed the deposed Texas governor, Manuel Salcedo; convinced local hacienda owner and retired military

On 11 March 1811 an order was received from Viceroy Félix María Calleja that San Fernando de Béxar and San Antonio de Valero should be incorporated under the name of San Antonio de Béxar.[13] In 1812 Juan Zambrano,[14] a citizen of this place, being a man who owned a great flock of 77,000 sheep, determined to put four droves of mules loaded with wool on the road to Nacogdoches. When he arrived at Nacogdoches some of his friends informed him of his projected death at the hands of José Bernardo Gutiérrez de Lara and Miguel Menchaca, who had 300 men.[15] Zambrano left Nacogdoches through the instructions of some of his friends, having lost all his wool, and returned to San Antonio, arriving here towards the latter part of August. He advised Governor Salcedo of what was going on at Nacogdoches, who immediately sent couriers to Mexico City and Chihuahua notifying his superiors of the expected insurgency.[16]

By November 1812 about 4,000 troops had arrived here from different

---

officer Ignacio Elizondo to assume command of loyalist forces; and ambushed Hidalgo, Allende, and other rebel leaders on 2 March 1811. Along with Casas, the other non-clerical rebel leaders were tried and executed at Chihuahua by a military court headed by Manuel Salcedo, while Hidalgo, because he was a priest, suffered the same fate only after being subjected to more exhaustive proceedings, including defrocking.

13. As a reward to the people of San Antonio for restoring royalist rule, the commandant general elevated the town's status from *villa* (town) to *ciudad* (city) pending royal approval. The incorporation of the suppressed Mission San Antonio de Valero (now the Alamo) actually took place in October 1809 by order of Governor Salcedo. Collection of *Bandos* by Governors, 16 January 1809, NAT; Castañeda, *Our Catholic Heritage in Texas*, 6:44.

14. Juan Zambrano was a member of one of the wealthiest families in San Antonio. Although an ordained priest, his main source of income was his family's livestock interests. He was also a capricious and querulous individual who ran afoul of Governor Salcedo; nevertheless, he was a devoted royalist. He led the counter-revolt against Casas and helped restore Salcedo to office.

15. José Bernardo Gutiérrez de Lara, a native of Revilla (now Nuevo Guerrero), Tamaulipas, was an early adherent to Hidalgo's cause and traveled to the United States in search of assistance. His political leadership of what is commonly referred to as the Gutiérrez-Magee Expedition resulted in the first Mexican Declaration of Independence on 18 April 1813. Conflicts with the Anglo-American members of the expedition led to his replacement by José de Toledo, and Gutiérrez de Lara returned to the United States. He continued to work for Mexican independence and in the early national period served as governor of Tamaulipas. Much less is known about Miguel Menchaca, who was a junior officer in the Nacogdoches garrison before deserting to join the insurgent cause.

16. Mexico City was the seat of viceregal government, and Chihuahua City was the headquarters of the commandant general of the Interior Provinces.

parts of Mexico.[17] At the same time that a republican army[18] advanced towards Goliad,[19] where they arrived on 26 November, the royalist troops[20] started from San Antonio to Goliad, where they took possession of Mission Rosario and Mission Espíritu Santo to consider their options.[21] They skirmished frequently with the republicans, but were always defeated. They put pickets out every night and kept the siege up during the months of December, January, and February 1813.

THE AFFAIR OF CORDERO, THE COMANCHE

On 11 February 1813 Captain Cordero, a Comanche chief,[22] arrived at San Antonio with 1,500 Comanches and presented himself to José Flores de Abrego, who was in command in the absence of the governor, asking him for a gift.[23] Flores de Abrego told him that he could give him nothing and

17. The reinforcement of Texas actually took place between 1801 and 1806, reaching a high of 1,368 in the latter year. There was no further reinforcement after the Casas Revolt as the royalists needed all available troops to fight the insurgency in the interior of Mexico.

18. Menchaca, or his collaborator(s), grouped all members of the Gutiérrez-Magee Expedition, known officially as the Republican Army of the North, under the label *American*, a common term at the time for any native of North America. To avoid confusion, all such references have been changed to *republican* unless the context specifically refers to Anglo-American members of the insurgent cause.

19. La Bahía, as the presidio-mission settlement on the lower San Antonio River was called during the Spanish colonial period, changed its name to Goliad, an anagram for *Hidalgo*, in 1829.

20. In the original, Menchaca refers to royal troops as *Mexican*, but since on occasion he also refers to insurgents as *Mexicans*, to avoid confusion the term *royalist* will be used throughout to refer to those loyal to the Spanish monarchy.

21. Mission Nuestra Señora del Rosario, established in 1754 upstream from La Bahía and Mission Espíritu Santo, was inactive at the time in question. Mission Nuestra Señora del Espíritu Santo de Zúñiga was the first of the three coastal missions. It fell into ruin in the course of the nineteenth century and was reconstructed in the 1930s as a Civilian Conservation Corps project. It is now part of Goliad State Historic Park.

22. Cordero was a Cuchanticas band chief who rose to prominence at the beginning of the nineteenth century. Menchaca's account cannot be corroborated from available records and is inconsistent with Gary Anderson's interpretation of Cordero as a peacemaker. See Gary Clayton Anderson, *The Indian Southwest, 1580–1830: Ethnogenesis and Reinvention*, 252–254.

23. Ignacio Pérez was left in command during Salcedo's campaign against the in-

that the governor was at Goliad in the war. Cordero then said that if he had nothing to give him that he wanted to speak with the governor and started for Goliad. When he arrived there with all his followers, he presented himself to Salcedo, insinuating that he wanted a gift. Salcedo told him that he did not have a gift to give, but that he could furnish him with powder and lead to assist him in fighting the Americans. However, the Indian chief answered him that he did not want to fight the Americans, that they were too brave and would kill too many of his men,[24] and that if Salcedo did not give him a gift he would come and destroy all the ranches and take all the horses. The Indians remained at camp three days, during which time, as soon as he found out their intentions, Salcedo sent an express to Flores directing him to have all the horses in the country brought into San Antonio and the town fortified, so that when the Indians returned they found all the ranches abandoned and the horses within San Antonio.[25] The horses, about 7,000 head, were herded by sixty men for fifteen days, at which time about 2,000 Indians came and took them all away.[26]

---

surgents at La Bahía. He met with Cordero in February 1812. In the 1780s Spanish officials and independent Indians in Texas and New Mexico reached a series of agreements by which a general peace was maintained based on the regular presentation of gifts to the Indians. This "peace by deceit" or "peace by purchase" policy was designed to make the Indians dependent on the Spanish and lasted into the period of the Mexican War of Independence, when financial circumstances led to the breakdown of the system.

24. This is an anachronistic statement, coming as it does before there was enough hostile interaction between Comanches and Americans to warrant Cordero's holding such an opinion.

25. While the comment on the prowess of Anglo-Americans as Indian fighters is anachronistic and based on contacts between Anglo-Americans and Comanches in the 1830s and 1840s, some of Menchaca's other observations here are consistent with contemporary sources. In 1813 few Anglo-Americans had had direct contact with Comanches and not in violent ways. For instance, in 1807 Cordero visited Natchitoches, Louisiana, seeking trade with Anglo-Americans. On the other hand, as a result of the War of Independence, Spanish authorities had been unable to continue the practice of gift giving, leading to a rise in Indian raiding. See Paul Carlson, *The Plains Indians*, 129–130; Pekka Hämäläinen, *The Comanche Empire*, 147–150; Anderson, *The Indian Southwest*, 252–255.

26. This statement is difficult to reconcile with available sources and the circumstances. Wild horses, which the number of animals given here suggests, were not the target of Indian raids. Raiders were interested in domesticated stock, and those numbers were vastly smaller according to available records—no more than a few hundred animals would have been in the area. See Jesús F. de la Teja, *San Antonio de Béxar: A Community on New Spain's Northern Frontier*, 112–113.

AMERICANS CAPTURE SAN ANTONIO

During all this time the royalists and republicans fought at Goliad, and continued doing so through part of March. On the tenth of that month the royalists, finding they could not whip the republicans, started for San Antonio. The republicans gave them time to arrive at San Antonio, then advanced and encamped on the Rosillo. The royalists went out from San Antonio and a fierce battle ensued in which the republicans were victorious, killing about 200 royalist soldiers and wounding a great many. The royalists retreated in a bad condition as the republicans remained on the field.[27] Three days later the republicans moved up and encamped at Mission Concepción. On Friday, Gutiérrez de Lara and Miguel Menchaca[28] sent a herald to Governor Salcedo stating that by ten o'clock the next day they wanted San Antonio's plaza evacuated. The answer was sent through Juan Martín Veramendi[29] that at any time they chose to come in, no resistance would be offered.

At the appointed hour on Saturday the republicans entered the city. At three o'clock the same day, the republicans imprisoned Miguel Delgado, Santiago Menchaca, Francisco Riojas, and twenty-one others of the republican side; and Manuel Salcedo, Simón de Herrera, Gerónimo Herrera, Francisco Povela, Miguel de Arcos, old Captain Gabriel de Arcos, son of Captain de Arcos, Miguel de Arcos Jr., Miguel Pando, Juan Francisco Caso, and four others of the royalist side, who were all taken to the Salado, and having arrived at the Rosillo that evening were beheaded. By eight o'clock Sunday morning the twenty-five republicans who had escorted the royal-

27. The battle of Rosillo was fought on 29 March 1813 at the confluence of the Rosillo and Salado Creeks, in the vicinity of Mission Espada.

28. Miguel Menchaca was most likely the son of Joaquín Menchaca and Juana Delgado and a cousin of José Menchaca, and therefore unrelated to Antonio Menchaca. He deserted from the garrison at Nacogdoches, helped distribute incendiary literature at San Antonio, participated in the Gutiérrez-Magee Expedition, and commanded the Mexican division of the Republican Army of the North at the battle of Alazán. General Joaquín Arredondo's report states that he was killed during the battle of Medina.

29. Juan Martín Veramendi was one of the town's leading citizens. He was a successful merchant, rancher, and farmer, and had served in the town government in the period immediately before the war. Although he participated in the junta that helped govern Texas during its brief interlude as a republic from April to August 1813, he eventually worked out a pardon for himself and was cleared of treason charges. He went on to become the lieutenant governor of Coahuila and Texas, and served as interim governor before dying in the cholera epidemic of 1833–1834.

RECOLLECTIONS OF A TEJANO LIFE

ists out of the city had returned and said that they had started the royalists for the coast to ship them to New Orleans, though they were infamously butchered as just stated.[30]

Then Bernardo Gutiérrez de Lara determined to establish good order in the City of San Antonio. He called a council, the president of which was Don Francisco Arocha, and was composed of Thomas Arocha, Ignacio Arocha, Clemente Delgado, Manuel Delgado, Miguel Delgado, and Antonio Delgado, all gentlemen of the City of San Antonio, descendants of the first families who emigrated from the Canary Islands in 1730, all adherents of the republican government.[31]

A MEXICAN ARMY MARCHES AGAINST SAN ANTONIO

The night of 11 June 1813 there appeared here 1,500 royalist soldiers under the command of Ignacio Elizondo,[32] a Spanish colonel, and Lieutenant

30. This is the most controversial event of the Gutiérrez-Magee episode. After San Antonio's capture, Governor Salcedo and at least sixteen other Spaniards and Creoles were taken prisoner, "tried" on various charges, and all found guilty. They were taken out of town and summarily executed. Some scholars believe that the Anglo-American participants in the expedition did not realize the sentence was death, while others maintain that the executions were tantamount to lynching, leading to the departure of a large number of disgusted Anglo-American volunteers. There is also disagreement on Gutiérrez de Lara's part in the incident. Menchaca's account sides with those who maintain that the killing of the Spaniards was in the nature of a massacre. For a succinct summary, see Félix D. Almaráz Jr., *Tragic Cavalier: Governor Manuel Salcedo of Texas, 1808-1813*, 170-172. See also Gerald Ashford, *Spanish Texas: Yesterday and Today*, 210-211; Donald A. Chipman, *Spanish Texas, 1519-1821*, 236; Harry McCorry Henderson, "The Magee-Gutiérrez Expedition," 52-53; De la Teja, "Rebellion on the Frontier," 23-24.

31. Menchaca's list coincides with popular opinion that it was Canary Islanders who headed the local rebels. Available documentation cannot confirm all the names on this list, although Francisco Arocha was one of four individuals explicitly excluded from the general amnesty that Arredondo issued in fall 1813. There is evidence, however, that others participated in the governing junta. Fernando Veramendi, Juan Martín's father, may have served as president and treasurer for a period of time, and two Americans may also have served.

32. Ignacio Elizondo was a Mexican militia officer sympathetic to the Hidalgo Revolt until convinced to switch sides by Governor Salcedo and Colonel Simón de Herrera, who were sent to Coahuila following the Casas Revolt. Subsequently, Elizondo carried out the capture of Hidalgo and his circle. General Joaquín Arredondo gave him a command during his campaign against Texas, during which he made an unsuccessful

Colonel Ignacio Pérez.[33] On the morning of 12 June they were within one and a half miles of the city at Alazán Hill. The republicans, seeing that they were there, took one of the city's old Spanish guns, a twelve-pounder, placed it upon the old powder house, which was built on the west side of San Pedro Creek, and saluted the royalists with five shots from the gun. Gutiérrez de Lara let them rest four days while he rested his troops. At 8 a.m. on the fifth day he took his troops out and attacked the royalists with such force and effect as to entirely rout them in about a half hour's fighting, killing forty or fifty, taking fifty or sixty prisoner, and putting the balance to flight. Gutiérrez de Lara brought the prisoners into the city and treated them very well.[34]

June passed and on 15 July the republican spies who had reconnoitered about Laredo returned and gave the intelligence to Gutiérrez de Lara that General Joaquín Arredondo[35] was raising a great many troops for the purpose of attacking San Antonio. On the same day that this news reached San Antonio, General José de Toledo[36] arrived from New Orleans and relieved

---

assault against the republicans in June 1813. Following the defeat of the republicans in August 1813, he pursued the fleeing rebels as far as Nacogdoches. During his return to San Antonio in September, he was attacked by one of his officers and died on the banks of the San Marcos River, where he was buried.

33. A native of San Antonio, Ignacio Pérez was a royalist officer throughout the Mexican War of Independence, serving as interim governor of Texas in 1816–1817 and leading military expeditions against Indians, filibusters, and interlopers until independence. He was also one of the province's leading cattlemen, and his daughter Gertrudis married former governor Antonio Cordero. At the time of his death in 1823 he was the owner of the house that came to be known as the Spanish Governor's Palace.

34. The engagement actually occurred on 20 June 1813. The exact location of the battle has not been determined, but descriptions of the distance from the town at the time, of the engagement occurring at a ridge, and of the area as a *charco* (pond) of Alazán Creek, point to an area on the west side of San Antonio above present-day Woodlawn Park, possibly in the Balcones Heights area.

35. Arredondo was a native of Barcelona, Spain, who had a distinguished career in the Spanish Royal Army, rising through the ranks until being appointed commandant general of the Eastern Interior Provinces, which included the province of Texas, in 1813. After defeating rebel forces in Texas he established his headquarters at Monterrey, Nuevo León. Seeing the writing on the wall, he granted permission to Moses Austin to pursue Anglo-American settlement in Texas and pledged his allegiance to the Plan of Iguala, General Agustín de Iturbide's project for the separation of Mexico from Spain. Soon after independence was achieved, he relinquished his command and retired to Cuba.

36. Sources disagree on his place of birth—Cuba or Santo Domingo—but Toledo did represent Santo Domingo at the Cortes of Cádiz before leaving for the United

General Gutiérrez de Lara from command of the troops. Upon being relieved, the latter left for Natchitoches.[37] Republican spies were incessantly on the lookout, that they should not be surprised. Watching Arredondo's movements, the spies came and told Toledo that the royalist army was on this side of the Atascosa River and advancing.

Toledo, who prepared to meet them, started from San Antonio in the direction in which Arredondo was coming and slept at Laguna de la Espada[38] on the first night. The next day he crossed the Medina River, and he thought a hill a short distance on the other side a convenient place to take the enemy at a disadvantage. Arredondo, also coming to a place he considered advantageous to his purpose, stopped at the water holes called "Charcos de las Gallinas" on the hill this side of the Atascosa and about five miles from the Medina River.[39]

On the day following Arredondo's occupation of the said water holes, he sent a detachment of cavalry about 400 strong under the command of Ignacio Elizondo and Ignacio Pérez, with two light pieces of artillery, to try and engage the republicans. They came up to the republican troops

---

States to work toward Spanish American independence. Having gained the ear of the Madison administration, Toledo conspired with William Shaler and other American agents on the Texas-Louisiana frontier to replace Gutiérrez de Lara, who had fallen out of favor with the Americans. It was Toledo who led the republican forces at the battle of Medina, from which disaster he managed to escape. He returned to the United States and subsequently made peace with Ferdinand VII, from whom he received diplomatic appointments and later a pension.

37. Established in 1714, this Louisiana border town was the headquarters for most intrigues concerning Texas throughout the eighteenth and early nineteenth centuries.

38. Mission Espada's lands were located mostly on the west bank of the San Antonio River in the direction of the Medina. The *laguna*, a lake or large pond, to which Menchaca refers has not been positively identified.

39. The most careful analysis of the movements of Arredondo's and Toledo's forces has been carried out by Ted Schwarz and Robert Thonhoff. Although the places mentioned by Menchaca cannot be conclusively identified, it appears that he confused Arredondo's campsite with Toledo's, since the location of Charcos de las Gallinas better fits the place described as where the insurgent leader set up his forward camp. However, since the battle site has not been conclusively identified, and given various possible locations, it could be that the reference to Arredondo's camping at Charcos de las Gallinas refers to a location on Gallinas Creek to the east of the Schwarz-Thonhoff location. In either case, the battle took place in the neighborhood of the Atascosa County–Bexar County line near present-day Rt. 281. See Ted Schwarz, *Forgotten Battlefield of the First Texas Revolution: The Battle of Medina, August 18, 1813*, ed. Robert Thonhoff, 72, 155.

and tried to engage them, upon which Miguel Menchaca, second in command on the republican side, came up to Toledo and asked him what his intentions were. Toledo remarked to him that the maneuvering was only intended as a decoy to ascertain the strength of his troops, that Menchaca might take some of his men and engage with the royalists but under no consideration follow them far if they retreated, and that Arredondo merely wished to get him out of his position in order to take him at a disadvantage.

THE BATTLE OF THE MEDINA

Menchaca went to attack them and did not return. He followed the detachment of royalists, killing all he could until he got up to the main body. He took two guns from the cavalry, but was attacked by the artillery and retreated for about a half-mile, from where he sent word to Toledo to advance with his troops, for he would not turn back. Toledo then sent word to him that it would be worse than madness for him to attempt to move forward and leave his position, for he would be sure to be defeated if he did. Upon receiving this reply, Menchaca, infuriated, himself came over to Toledo's position, where the balance of the force was, and told the troops that the fight had commenced; that under no consideration would he, having already commenced the fight, quit until he and the men under him had either died or conquered. He told them that if they were men, to act as men and follow him, whereupon all the forces became encouraged and moved in a body to follow Menchaca. Toledo unwillingly followed. They started out to meet Arredondo, but having no water and having to pull the guns along by hand, by the time they came to where Arredondo was and were placed in battle array, the troops were nearly dead from thirst.

The battle began with great fury. As soon as it commenced Menchaca, who commanded one wing of the cavalry, and Antonio Delgado,[40]

40. According to some sources, Antonio Delgado was responsible for the execution of Governor Manuel Salcedo and the other Spaniards who were taken prisoner when the Republican Army of the North took San Antonio on 1 April 1813. As the story goes, Delgado's father, Manuel, a devotee of Miguel Hidalgo, was beheaded by Salcedo in 1811 and Antonio's actions were in revenge for that execution. Other than the documents surrounding his involvement in the murder of the Spaniards, little is known of Delgado except that he was, apparently, a corporal in San Antonio's militia company and was executed following the battle of Medina when captured near the Trinity River. Available sacramental records do not contain his baptism, so whether or not he was the son of

who commanded the left wing, pushed their men up with such vigor as to compel the cavalry that opposed them to retreat to the center of the main body of Arredondo's infantry. The republicans were so thirsty that they even drank the water in which the rods for loading the cannon were soaked. The battle had almost been declared in favor of the republicans when by accident Colonel Menchaca was struck by a ball on the neck. He fell, and there being no one to cheer the troops on, they became discouraged and frightened, and disorder commenced. The royalists under Arredondo, seeing this, took courage and charged with fury, got into the republicans, and killed a great many of them. Though Menchaca was brought with them, he died on the way and was buried on the Seguin Road at the place called Menchaca Creek,[41] or "Cañada de Menchaca."

Arredondo, having come off victorious, came as far as the Laredo Road crossing of the Medina,[42] encamped to cure his wounded soldiers, have their clothes washed, and at the same time dispose of the prisoners he had taken, which he did by shooting them. The number he killed was about two hundred and fifty.[43]

After murdering his prisoners and resting his army, Arredondo marched into San Antonio. It was about 10 p.m. on 15 August that he arrived here.[44]

Manuel Delgado and Angela de Arocha is in question. Moreover, there is no record of the execution of Manuel Delgado by Governor Salcedo. In fact, José Antonio Navarro asserts that, contrary to the version of one prominent Anglo historian, Antonio Delgado's father was not executed by Salcedo, but "died of old age and sorrow at the Trinity River" (Navarro, *Defending Mexican Valor in Texas*, 62). See also De la Teja, "Rebellion on the Frontier," 24; Castañeda, *Our Catholic Heritage*, 6:99–100, 117–118.

41. Present-day Deadman Creek, southwest of the city of Seguin. The creek appears as "Manchaca Creek" in the 1854 General Land Office county survey map and as "Menchaca Creek" in updates through 1880. In the next map, prepared in 1919, the name is changed to "Deadman Creek." See maps 491, 3607, 3608, 3609, 3610, and 4692, County Map Collection, Texas General Land Office, Austin.

42. The Laredo Road crossed the Medina River east of present-day I-35 and west of I-37 in southeastern Bexar County. Neither the site of the battle nor the site of Arredondo's camp has been conclusively located.

43. In his battlefield report Arredondo put the number of enemy killed in battle at over 600 and prisoners executed after the battle at 112. He also claims to have captured an additional 215 on the way to San Antonio, of whom some were executed and others imprisoned. Other accounts, including one by American filibuster John Villars, put the number of men executed by Arredondo at approximately 300. Castañeda, *Our Catholic Heritage in Texas*, 6:115–116; Schwarz, *Forgotten Battlefield*, ed. Thonhoff, 107–109.

44. The battle of Medina was fought on 18 August 1813, and although an advance

The Catholic church was filled with poor men praying that their lives should be spared. All were taken out, some placed in the old Spanish guardhouse, and others crowded into the house of Francisco Arocha. Of those imprisoned in the latter place, it being so crowded, eight men suffocated to death by the next morning. On the following day they were all taken out in line to ascertain which of them deserved to be put to death, and which to be put to hard labor. Arredondo assigned Ignacio Pérez, a native of San Antonio, to name two persons of the natives that they might call out all such persons as were deserving of death, and to name also, all such as should be put to hard labor. Pérez nominated Luis Galán[45] and Manuel Salinas,[46] who, though natives of San Antonio, answered that they knew no one. Upon hearing this, Arredondo selected forty who should be put to death, and the balance, one hundred and sixty, were handcuffed in pairs and sent to work upon the streets. Of the forty who were selected to die, every third day they would shoot three on the north side of the Main Plaza, until the entire number was disposed of. The wives of these unfortunates were placed inside the "Quinta" to make "tortillas" for the soldiers.[47] They had to make 35,000 tortillas daily.

Six days after Arredondo's entry into the city, he ordered Elizondo and

---

royalist force entered San Antonio later that day, Arredondo did not occupy the city with the main army until the nineteenth.

45. Luis Galán was a longtime public servant in San Antonio, serving as administrator of the tobacco monopoly starting in 1799, and later as *alcalde* and administrator of the military hospital. During the Casas Revolt he had charge of the public treasury, and following the battle of Medina he was involved in managing property confiscated from the insurgents.

46. Manuel Salinas had served as *síndico de ranchos*, that is, as magistrate for one of the ranch precincts into which Governor Salcedo had divided the countryside around San Antonio.

47. José Antonio Navarro tells a similar tale, although with significant differences in detail, in his reminiscences, which were published in English in San Antonio between 1853 and 1858 and compiled and published in Spanish in 1869. While Menchaca claims that Arredondo chose forty men to be executed and their wives imprisoned and forced to make tortillas for the royalist army, Navarro claims the number of the executed was three hundred and the number of women imprisoned and forced to cook for the royalists was five hundred. Menchaca and Navarro agree that eight men suffocated during the first night of detention. They also agree that the women, whether Menchaca's forty or Navarro's five hundred, were held in a building known as *La Quinta* (the country house) and that the executions took place against the walls of the public buildings on the Main Plaza. For Navarro's version of events, see Navarro, *Defending Mexican Valor in Texas*, 54–55.

Pérez, with two hundred and fifty[48] men, to follow the fugitives who had started for Nacogdoches. After they left Arredondo displayed still further his cruel nature. He seemed furious to punish all those who had taken any part whatever in the revolutionary movement. As a result, anyone who wanted someone punished would merely complain to the officers and the chastisement would be inflicted by whipping them on the public square.

They very seldom excused anyone from punishment, although there was one instance. In the dead of night soldiers came to the house of my father, Mariano Menchaca,[49] who was accused of some trifling thing, and took him and my mother out of their bed. My mother was taken to the Quinta, and he was to be publicly whipped. I, who was then about fourteen years old and had become a favorite of Cristóbal Domínguez,[50] one of the ranking officers, seeing that they were going to whip my father, ran into the officer's bedroom, and begged him to intercede. Domínguez at first told me to go away, but I would not be put off. I begged him for all that was dear to save my father. The officer finally relented, and, stepping out, he spoke to the men who had charge of my father and made them turn him loose. I then asked him to please have my mother liberated. Domínguez gave me an order for her release, which I took to the officer in command of the Quinta and got her released too.

Elizondo and Pérez overtook the fugitives on the Trinity River, which had swollen from heavy rains. All the men of note had already crossed the river, and only the women and subordinate men remained on the south side. The royalists had along with them a priest named Esteban Camacho.[51]

48. Elizondo put his force at five hundred men.

49. Little is known of Antonio Menchaca's parents. See the section titled "Family" (pp. 4–10) in our Introduction for a discussion of the available evidence.

50. Menchaca would actually have been thirteen at the time of this incident. Captain Cristóbal Domínguez had served in Texas since 1810. He escaped to Natchitoches, Louisiana, during the Casas Revolt of 1811, and he escaped to the royalist camp during the Gutiérrez-Magee insurrection. At the battle of Medina he was with Arredondo, who later in August 1813 appointed him interim governor, in which capacity he served until the end of the year, when he was appointed second in command of the Eastern Interior Provinces. He remained in San Antonio until his death in October 1814. There is no independent evidence of the veracity of Menchaca's account of saving his father and mother from punishment at the hands of the royalists.

51. Probably José Manuel Camacho, a priest who had been active in San Antonio since 1809. José Antonio Navarro's more expansive description of the priest, to whom he refers as Pedro Camacho, has the clergyman breaking the confessional seal and contributing to the execution of captured insurgents (Navarro, *Defending Mexican Valor*, 56–57).

When the Spaniards arrived there, the men presented themselves to the royalist commanders. The commanders asked them why they had rebelled and told them that they would hurt nobody, as they would see. They told the fugitives that they would be treated kindly, and that the royalists' only object in following them was to bring them back to their homes.

Elizondo then asked if there was any man present who would cross the river and tell those on the other side that if they came over to this side a full pardon would be granted them. One of the men who had not crossed over agreed to go over and take the letter in which was guaranteed to the fugitives, in the most sacred terms, a full and complete pardon if they would but give themselves up. He went, the letter was presented, and after considerable debate, the terms being so moderate and couched in such plausible language, they consented to come over and give themselves up. When they did, the Spaniards took the precaution to tie their hands as they crossed over. All of them crossed that same evening, slept tied, and the next day were unmercifully slaughtered. The whole number so cruelly killed was 279.[52]

Having killed all the male fugitives, the next day they started on their way back to San Antonio with all the families afoot. On the second day thereafter, Don Manuel Serrano, captain under Elizondo, who felt deeply grieved at the barbarous manner in which the men had been killed, deliberately walked into Elizondo's tent, shot him dead and started towards Pérez's tent with the same view, shot at and missed him, and was apprehended and prevented from doing further mischief. They tied him and brought him to San Antonio, a raving maniac.[53]

They arrived here about 22 September, about 10 a.m., and formed all the female captives in a line on the main square. The line being formed, Arredondo, in full uniform, with his staff, came in front of the line of captives and asked who the Mexican Aunt was. When he said this, Da. Josefa Núñez

---

52. Menchaca's version of the capture and execution of fleeing insurgents at the Trinity is unique, and his number far greater than that reported by Elizondo to Arredondo. In fact, according to Elizondo, he began his return to San Antonio with over one hundred men, women, and children prisoners, having executed seventy-one.

53. The officer in question was Lieutenant Miguel Serrano, a veteran military officer who had seen service in Texas as early as 1805. According to Ignacio Elizondo's report of the incident before he died of his wounds, Serrano lost his mind, attacked and killed the commander's cousin, and then went to Elizondo's tent and attacked him with a sword. Severe wounds to Elizondo's wrist and right side led to his death and burial ten days later on the banks of the San Marcos River.

de Arocha,[54] wife of Francisco Arocha, answered, "Here I am, nephew." Arredondo then said, "So you have offered $500 for my paunch to make a drum with?" "Yes, I have and would have made it, had I got it," she answered. "You could not obtain my paunch," said he, "but now I can punish you as you deserve. You can go and rest at the Quinta, to make tortillas for my men and me." "I would rather you would give me fifteen shots, than that it should come to this," said she. Upon this Arredondo gave the order that the captives should be taken to the Quinta.

Arredondo remained in command in San Antonio until the month of November, when he was called to Mexico. On 8 December 1813 the Extremadura Regiment, numbering eight hundred and under the command of Colonel Benito de Armiñán,[55] entered San Antonio. They did not seem to be other than devils. They stole and committed many crimes. Armiñán remained in command here until November 1814, when he was ordered to Chapala, where his regiment, with the exception of about thirty-five, was killed. Ignacio Pérez remained in command here. In 1816 Manuel Pardo[56] relieved Pérez. In 1817 Pardo was relieved by Antonio Puertas. In 1818 Antonio Martínez relieved Puertas.[57] On 5 July 1819 San Antonio was inundated by a flood, in which twenty-eight persons were lost.[58] On the twenty-fifth of the same month, Antonio Menchaca, being a soldier of the king of Spain, took the message to Colonel Galica that Mexico was independent of Spain.[59]

---

54. Doña Josefa Núñez Morillo de Arocha was a descendant of one of the oldest San Antonio families. Her grandfather Miguel Núñez Morillo had come to Texas in the 1720s as a soldier, and her grandmother María Josefa Flores de Valdés was the daughter of San Antonio's second presidio commander, Captain Nicolás Flores de Valdés, who served from 1722 until 1730. No other source documents this exchange.

55. Armiñán also served as interim governor from late 1813 until July 1815.

56. Pardo served briefly as governor of Texas, from March until May 1817. A native of Santander, Spain, he remained in the Mexican military after independence.

57. There is no evidence that Puertas served as interim governor. Antonio María Martínez assumed the office directly from Pardo on 27 May 1817. Martínez, a native of Andújar, Spain, was a veteran of European wars before his transfer to the Americas. He was the last Spanish governor of Texas, continuing to serve after Mexican independence until replaced by Félix Trespalacios in August 1822.

58. The most severe storm in the city's history to that point, the flooding of the San Antonio River and San Pedro Creek swept away fifty-five dwellings and took nineteen lives.

59. Mexican independence did not take place until 1821. Word arrived in San Antonio of Arredondo's acceptance of General Agustín de Iturbide's Plan de Iguala in July 1821.

Because the city was surrounded by Indians, privations were such in 1814 that a sack of corn sold at $3.00, a pound of coffee cost $2.50, sugar cost $1.50, and tobacco sold for $1.00 per ounce. The people being under such pressure would risk their lives to go out in the country to kill deer, turkey, etc., and cook herbs for the support of their families. At planting time in 1815 there was not a single horse belonging to the military service in San Antonio. Detachments or squads of fifteen soldiers had to be sent afoot as far as the Leona to receive the mail from Mexico.[60] The persons who engaged at agriculture had to go in squads of fifteen to twenty or more to look for their oxen, and while working had to keep their weapons with them. There were so many Indians around the city that one day, while yet light, a lady sitting at her door was killed by a Tawakoni,[61] who walked up to her and shot her in the head. In the same month another lady was killed at the Alamo by a Tawakoni, and Domingo Bustillos, who was coming from the Alamo *labor*[62] in company with three others, was shot in the shoulder. It may be counted as a miracle that no more deaths occurred than there did, because the Indians would dress themselves with the clothes of their victim, and would promenade the streets at will. The people lived with this dread until 1820, when the Comanches and other tribes of Indians came to San Antonio to make peace, which was granted them; notwithstanding, they continued to kill and rob the settlers, who had to be on the alert continually. Very few of the people had milk cows, for the Indians had not

---

Governor Martínez led the town council and other officials and military officers in an oath to the new Mexican nation. The identities of the Antonio Menchaca and Colonel Galica to whom Menchaca refers are unclear.

60. This is probably at or near where I-35 crosses the Leona River in southern Frio County near Dilley, about seventy miles south of San Antonio. Until sometime in the nineteenth century, the stream was known as Arroyo de la Leona, or Lioness Creek. Menchaca is thus referring to the mail as coming up the Upper Presidio Road branch of the Camino Real between Río Grande and San Antonio.

61. The Tawakonis were one of the Wichita groups that had made their way into Texas during the eighteenth century. Like other north Texas tribes, the Tawakonis periodically raided as far as San Antonio either collectively or in single-warrior actions.

62. A *labor* is a collective farm made up of individually owned plots, or *suertes*, the owners of which would collectively operate and maintain the irrigation system. After the secularization of Mission San Antonio de Valero in 1793, its farmland was divided into three farms, the one south of the mission going to the remaining Indian residents, the one north of the mission being distributed among refugees from the closing of Los Adaes, and the outer farm set aside for worthy town residents. Subsequently, the term *labor* signified an area of arable land of 177.1 acres.

given them a chance to raise cattle. When the Indians came to seek peace, a good many of the settlers bought horses from them.

GOOD TIMES HERE UNDER A CAVALIER GOVERNMENT

In 1822, José Félix Trespalacios[63] relieved Martínez of command. During the command of Trespalacios, San Antonio underwent a great change for the better and money circulated more freely. Until 1825, when a provincial government was established, Texas was governed by six cavaliers,[64] until it was determined that a political chief should be named, the selection falling to Don José Antonio Saucedo.[65] He governed as political chief for two years, after which Ramón Múzquiz[66] was appointed.

63. A longtime insurgent and ally of James Long and Benjamin Milam, Trespalacios was appointed governor of Texas by Agustín de Iturbide and replaced Antonio Martínez in August 1822. During his eight-month tenure he helped organize the administration of the Austin Colony and established Texas's first bank of issue to ease the financial crunch caused by the failure of the central government to send regular military payrolls.

64. Menchaca is referring to the provincial deputation, a legislative body that had its origins in the collapse of Iturbide's empire in early 1823. Texas had been a member of the Provincial Deputation of the Eastern Interior Provinces, which had been organized at the end of the Spanish regime and included Coahuila, Tamaulipas, and Nuevo León. With the reorganization of government following Iturbide's overthrow, each province was allowed its own provincial deputation, and the one for Texas continued to function until September 1824, when it accepted the province's union with Coahuila. The Texas Provincial Deputation was overwhelmingly composed of leading Bexareños, hence the reference to "cavaliers."

65. José Antonio Saucedo was born in San Antonio in 1766. Although his father was in the military, he does not appear to have followed that career path, but instead went into the livestock business. By the end of the century he had accumulated some wealth and before the outbreak of the Mexican War of Independence had already begun public service. He remained a royalist throughout the rebellions, but that did not prevent him from keeping the trust of his fellow Bexareños. In 1823 he was appointed *jefe político* (political chief), a position he held until his retirement in 1827. During his tenure he was instrumental in helping Stephen F. Austin establish and organize his first colony, and after retirement he served as land commissioner for Green DeWitt. He died in San Antonio in 1832.

66. A native of Santa Rosa, Coahuila, Ramón Múzquiz spent his early years in Texas, where his father was stationed to military posts. The family returned to Coahuila during the decade of the Mexican War of Independence, but shortly after, Múzquiz made his way to San Antonio to pursue commercial interests. In 1825 he became secretary to the

In 1826, the regiment of Mateo Ahumada, a Mexican, arrived here.[67] He remained as military commander until 1828, when General Anastasio Bustamante[68] and General Manuel de Mier y Terán arrived. On the sixth day after their arrival, General Mier y Terán, at the head of Ahumada's regiment, started for Nacogdoches to suppress the Americans, where they were reported to be making preparations for fighting. Arriving in Nacogdoches and finding everything to all appearances quiet, Mier y Terán left Ahumada in charge and proceeded with a bodyguard to the Sabine River, and finding all quiet there returned to Nacogdoches. In 1830, leaving Ahumada in command at Nacogdoches, Mier y Terán came to San Antonio.[69]

In March 1830 James Bowie of Kentucky came to San Antonio in company with William Wharton.[70] From here, Bowie went to Saltillo. In the

---

jefe político and on 1 January 1828 assumed the office himself, holding it with interruptions until the summer of 1834. He briefly served as lieutenant governor of Coahuila and Texas in 1835 and remained in Texas until May 1836, when he moved his family to Monclova. He died there in 1867. Although a supporter of Anglo-American settlement, Múzquiz opposed the independence of Texas, requiring his departure from San Antonio.

67. Ahumada was appointed military commander for Texas in June 1825 and served until November 1827. He was succeeded by Antonio Elozua, who served in the post until September 1833.

68. Commandant general inspector of Coahuila and Texas and then commandant general of the Eastern Interior Provinces from 1826 to 1829, Bustamante made a visit to Texas in 1827, which may be the source of Menchaca's confusion regarding his presence during events that preceded his arrival.

69. Menchaca is confusing events from the Fredonian Rebellion and the Comisión de Límites. The short-lived Fredonian Rebellion at the end of 1826 was an effort by brothers Haden and Benjamin Edwards and a small group of collaborators to wrest East Texas from Mexico. The government quickly mobilized available military forces under Ahumada and militia units under Stephen F. Austin, who arrived in February 1827 to find that the conspirators had crossed into Louisiana. In 1827 President Guadalupe Victoria appointed Mier y Terán to head the Comisión de Límites, that is, the boundary commission required by the treaty with the United States to determine the border between the two nations. Mier y Terán was in Texas in 1828–1829 as head of the commission and visited the Galveston area in 1831 during his tenure as commandant general of the Eastern Interior Provinces.

70. In the *Passing Show* version of his reminiscences, Menchaca says that Bowie came to San Antonio with George Wharton. In the Yanaguana Society edition Menchaca says that Bowie came to San Antonio with Governor Wharton. Both versions are incorrect. In fact, Bowie accompanied William H. Wharton and others to San Antonio and then to Saltillo, where he became involved in land-speculation activities. Wharton was

same year Juan Martín Veramendi was elected lieutenant governor and proceeded to Mexico to take the oath of office.[71] There he met and became friendly with Bowie, and when he returned to San Antonio with his family, Bowie accompanied him. It was then that Ursula Veramendi, the lieutenant governor's daughter, and Bowie became engaged. Upon their arrival in San Antonio, Bowie, not having what he considered enough to justify his marrying, asked Veramendi to give him time to go to Kentucky and get funds, and he would then marry his daughter. Veramendi granted the request, and Bowie went and returned in the month of March 1831 and married.[72] He remained three months in San Antonio and then left for the interior of Texas to recruit forces for the war.[73] When he returned in

---

president of the Convention of 1833 and served in other government positions before his death in 1839. He was never governor of Texas.

71. In this section there are numerous anachronistic statements that are difficult to attribute. Since Texas was part of the Mexican nation, and part of the state of Coahuila and Texas, until 1836, Veramendi was merely traveling from one place in his state to another. Furthermore, as the elected lieutenant governor of Coahuila and Texas, it would have been more accurate for Menchaca to state that Veramendi was proceeding to Saltillo, which was then the state capital, to take the oath of office. As he was dictating his memoirs in the 1870s, Menchaca may have thought it easiest to present anything south of the current border as "Mexico." For purposes of clarity, all the references to general facts have been corrected, although not those regarding specific facts, such as Veramendi's travels, which Menchaca states as personal knowledge. Please consult the unedited version for the original language.

72. Juan Martín Veramendi was elected lieutenant governor by the legislature of Coahuila and Texas in January 1831. There is no record of his having traveled to Saltillo to take the oath of office, and it is clear from the documents that he met Bowie not in Saltillo, but in San Antonio, where the American also met Veramendi's daughter Ursula. Bowie and Veramendi attempted at least one business agreement, a venture to exploit beaver- and otter-pelt resources that Bowie had discovered on a trip into western Texas in search of silver mines, but neither project panned out. Bowie had to borrow money from Veramendi and Ursula's grandmother to take his wife on a honeymoon trip to New Orleans and Natchez following their wedding in April 1831. By the 1830s Bowie had no ties to Kentucky, and there is no evidence that he traveled to the United States to obtain funds with which to marry. A less-than-one-month round-trip for that (or almost any) purpose is highly unlikely.

73. Menchaca is here probably recollecting the initial confrontations between centralist government forces and settlers in eastern Texas. In June 1832 there was a clash between the local Mexican commander in southeast Texas, Juan Davis Bradburn, and Anglo settlers that led to the first of what is known as the Anahuac Disturbances. Upon receiving word of this clash, Bowie left San Antonio with fifteen mounted men to assist

1832 he went to look for the San Saba mines,[74] returned and remained four months, and again went to look for mines. (It was during the search for the mines that Bowie did some of his fiercest fighting with the Indians.)[75]

While Bowie was on this second trip, news reached San Antonio that José María Letona, the governor of Coahuila and Texas, had died. This made it necessary for Veramendi to go to Saltillo to take charge of the government.[76] While Bowie was on the Colorado, he received a command from Stephen F. Austin at San Felipe that he should repair immediately to San Felipe, that his services were greatly needed. Upon receiving this news Bowie wrote a letter to his wife telling her where he was going and on what business and that it was hard to tell when they would meet again.[77]

BOWIE'S UNEXPLAINED MISSION: WAS THIS A PLOT FOR THE INDEPENDENCE OF TEXAS?

Veramendi, having heard of Letona's death, made ready for his trip to Saltillo, where he arrived on 11 November 1832. As soon as he arrived, he received his commission as governor, which he exercised until 7 February

---

the settlers against the centralist military forces. He arrived in time to participate in the battle of Nacogdoches, which took place on 2–3 August 1832, and in which the Mexican commander for Nacogdoches, José de las Piedras, was captured and the Mexican military was driven out of East Texas.

74. By the beginning of the nineteenth century there was already a significant body of folklore regarding lost silver mines west of San Antonio. It all started with some mid-eighteenth-century expeditions in the direction of the San Saba River to a site called Los Almagres. Miners brought some ore back to San Antonio and then took it to Mexico City for assaying, but the results were not encouraging. From then on, the idea persisted that silver was to be found in the region, but commercial quantities were never discovered. The only commercial-quality silver deposits in Texas were in the Trans-Pecos, a region that did not become part of Texas until the 1840s.

75. This parenthetical note appears to be an editorial comment made by Mencha-ca's collaborator.

76. Letona died in September 1832, and the legislature sent for Veramendi to assume the state executive office, which he did at the beginning of January 1833 in Saltillo. He took his whole family with him, including Ursula.

77. There is no evidence for a call from Austin. Bowie was in the federalist camp and supported the transfer of the government from Saltillo to Monclova, which occurred in March 1833. He thereafter traveled to Natchez on business, and was unaware of the death of his wife and father-in-law in the cholera epidemic then sweeping northern Mexico.

1833,[78] when Bowie with seven other Americans arrived there also. On the following day he had an interview with Veramendi, and was introduced to the members of congress. As soon as his acquaintance with the leading members became such as to warrant it, he told them what his object was. He received the assurances of Marcial Borrego and José María Uranga that they would aid him in his enterprise. He tried and succeeded in making them change the congress from Saltillo to Monclova. Congress having been established at Monclova, he returned to Texas.[79]

In July of the same year Veramendi sent $10,000 to Múzquiz to be sent to New Orleans.[80] In September Veramendi's family as well as Bowie's wife, with $25,000 worth of goods, were taken to Monclova, where they arrived on 27 September. On that day cholera broke out there. Madam Veramendi was the first victim of the disease, and, after her, Governor Veramendi and then Madam Bowie died. The rest of the family stayed in Monclova until the first of November, when I brought them back to San Antonio.[81]

78. The writing here is unclear, implying that with Bowie's arrival Veramendi ceased serving as governor. In fact, Veramendi served until his death from cholera on 7 September 1833, and there is no evidence that Bowie traveled to Monclova at this time.

79. Menchaca's claims regarding the role played by Bowie in the transfer of the legislature from Saltillo to Monclova are both unsubstantiated and highly improbable. The dispute between Saltillo politicians and representatives of the rest of the state had been developing for some time. Until independence, the capital of Coahuila had been Monclova, although Saltillo was the state's largest city and for a time seat of the provincial deputation that included Texas, Coahuila, Nuevo Santander, and Nuevo León. San Antonio had been the capital of Texas. With the union of Coahuila and Texas and the establishment of the capital at Saltillo, much of the state, both north and south of the Rio Grande, was farther away from the seat of government than it had been under Spain, Saltillo being located at the southeastern corner of the new state. There was, therefore, considerable support among Texans, both Anglo and Tejano, and also among representatives of parts of Coahuila and Texas for the removal of the capital to Monclova. Marcial Borrego and José María Uranga were both legislators during that period and both staunch supporters of the Monclova federalist camp, Borrego serving as interim governor in 1835. The truth of the statement that Bowie met with Veramendi, Borrego, Uranga, and others regarding the move, which was legislated only a day after Menchaca claims Bowie arrived in Saltillo, is highly questionable. There is no documentary evidence of Bowie's whereabouts during this period other than Menchaca's statements, on which all historians have relied.

80. The nature of this statement is very obscure. It may have been part of a private financial transaction, since both Veramendi and Múzquiz were involved in commerce between Louisiana, Texas, and the Mexican interior.

81. While he may have brought back to San Antonio the remaining members of

The year 1834 passed and in July 1835 Colonel Nicholas Condelle with 500 infantry and 100 cavalry arrived here, for it was reported that the Americans were gathered at San Felipe. With these last troops there were 1,100 Mexican soldiers, 1,000 infantry, and 100 cavalry in Texas.[82] On 20 October I received a letter from Bowie in which was enclosed a note addressed to Marcial Borrego and J. M. Uranga. The letter told me to deliver the note in person, to trust it to no one, and to be as quick about it as possible. I went while the report in San Antonio was that the Americans were at Gonzales[83] and delivered the note, and on my return got as far as San Fernando de Rosas,[84] where I was detained and was not allowed to pass, though my liberty was given me upon my giving bond. Six days after the capitulation of San Antonio[85] a friend of mine, Pedro Rodríguez,[86] furnished me with two men and horses to bring me to San Antonio. I crossed at night at Eagle Crossing,[87] and arrived here on 20 December. The companies that had assisted in the siege were still in San Antonio. As soon as I arrived here I sought Bowie, who as soon as he saw me put his arms around my neck and wept to think that he had not seen his wife die. He said, "My father, my brother, my companion, and all my protection has gone! Are you still my companion-in-arms?" I answered, "I shall be your companion, Jim

----

the Veramendi household following the deaths of Juan Martín, his wife, his daughter Ursula, and possibly one or two grandchildren, Menchaca's description of the events is confused. Cholera had appeared in Monclova in August, and the Veramendis succumbed at the beginning of September. It is highly unlikely that the family would have traveled to join Juan Martín during the cholera outbreak, and there is no evidence of a shipment of goods at this time. There is documentation for Veramendi's business transactions in the interior of Mexico during previous years.

82. Why Menchaca would neglect to mention that General Martín Perfecto de Cos arrived in San Antonio on 9 October 1835 with 500 men is a mystery.

83. Menchaca would have to be referring to sometime in mid-October, since volunteers did not start gathering at Gonzales until after 2 October, and by 24 October Austin had moved them to San Antonio, where they lay siege to the Mexican garrison.

84. San Fernando de Rosas is present-day Zaragoza, Coahuila.

85. This is a reference to the final assault by the Texans against the Mexican defenders of San Antonio on 9 December 1835 during the Siege of Bexar.

86. Rodríguez was a longtime military man with service going back at least to 1816. He was stationed at San Fernando de Rosas in early 1835.

87. Eagle Crossing is present-day Eagle Pass, at the mouth of the Escondido River into the Rio Grande downstream from Zaragoza, Coahuila. The choice of route was logical as Eagle Pass is on an old smugglers' trail that allowed travelers to avoid Presidio del Río Grande.

Bowie, until I die." "Then come this evening," Bowie said, "and I'll take you to meet Travis at the Alamo." That evening he introduced me to Travis and to Colonel James Neill.[88]

On 26 December 1835 Don Diego Grant left San Antonio for Matamoros with about 500 men, Americans and Tejanos, of those who had assisted in the siege, while here we kept up guards and night patrols.[89] The 250 men who went to keep a lookout on General Martín Perfecto de Cos (who had gone to Mexico) returned to San Antonio on 5 January 1836. On 13 January 1836 David Crockett presented himself at the old Mexican graveyard, on the west side of the San Pedro Creek.[90] He had in company with him fourteen young men who had accompanied him from Tennessee. As soon as he got there he sent word to Bowie to come and receive him, and conduct him into the city. Bowie and I went, and he was brought and lodged at Erasmo Seguín's house. Crockett, Bowie, Travis, Neill, and all the officers joined together to establish guards for the safety of the city, fearing the Mexicans' return.[91]

88. Bowie was not in San Antonio at this time. He had left for Goliad at the end of November and missed out on the final assault on the Mexican garrison. Under orders from Sam Houston, he returned to San Antonio in mid-January to assess the situation and make preparations for the abandonment of the city. In addition, Reason Bowie, James's father, had died in about 1821 and Rezin, James's brother, was in poor health and living in Louisiana at the time of the revolution. Of the other individuals mentioned, only Neill, who had been placed in command of the Texan garrison, was in San Antonio at the end of December. Travis did not arrive in San Antonio until 3 February.

89. James (Diego) Grant was a British land speculator with federalist leanings who had had to abandon his properties in Coahuila during the centralist takeover in 1835. He fled to Nacogdoches, where he became involved in the Texan cause, participated in the Siege of Bexar, and with Francis Johnson developed a scheme for attacking the centralists at Matamoros. The number of volunteers he took from San Antonio at the end of 1835 was approximately 200. He died on 2 March 1836 near San Patricio with a party of his men that had gone to capture mustangs for their expedition, when they were ambushed by a Mexican force.

90. Crockett and his small party actually arrived on 8 February 1836. The cemetery, old in the 1870s, was established at the beginning of the nineteenth century at what is now the site of Santa Rosa Hospital.

91. Crockett declined a commission and served as a "high private."

ARRIVAL OF THE COURIER

On 10 February 1836 I was invited by the officers to a ball given in honor of Crockett, and was asked to invite all the principal ladies in the city. On the same day invitations were extended and the ball given that night. While the dance was still going on, at about 1 a.m. on the eleventh, a courier sent by Plácido Benavides arrived from Camargo with the intelligence that Santa Anna was starting from Presidio del Río Grande with 13,000 troops—10,000 infantry and 3,000 cavalry—with the view of taking San Antonio. The courier arrived at the ballroom door, inquired for Colonel Juan Seguín, and was told that Colonel Seguín was not there. Asked if Menchaca was there, he was told that I was. He told me he had a letter of great importance, which he had brought from Benavides from Camargo. I seated my partner and came to see the letter, opened it and read the following: "At this moment I have received the very certain notice that the commander-in-chief, Antonio López de Santa Anna, marches for the city of San Antonio to take possession thereof, with 13,000 men."[92] As I was reading the letter Bowie came up to me to see it, and while reading it Travis came up and Bowie called him to read the letter. Travis declined, stating that at that moment he could not stop to read the letter for he was dancing with the most beautiful lady in San Antonio. Bowie replied that the letter was one of grave importance and for him to leave his partner. Because of the reply, Travis came and brought Crockett with him. Travis and Bowie understood Spanish, Crockett did not. Travis said, lightly, "It will take 13,000 men, from the Presidio del Río Grande thirteen or fourteen days to march to this place. This is the fourth day. Let us dance tonight and tomorrow we will make arrangements for our defense." The ball continued until 7 a.m.[93]

92. This is the first of a number of instances in the memoirs where Menchaca downplays Juan Seguín's role and places himself at the center of events. Although Seguín in his memoirs does not address how news arrived in San Antonio of Santa Anna's advance, other sources normally credit members of Seguín's company acting as spies with bringing word of the Mexican army's approach in February 1836. Carolina Castillo Crimm, in *De León: A Tejano Family History*, 156, does maintain that Plácido Benavides, who was involved during February 1836 in a spying mission, but to Matamoros, not Camargo, in an attempt to rescue his captured brothers-in-law from the centralists, reported back to Victoria with news of General José de Urrea's and Santa Anna's campaign preparations.

93. Menchaca here contradicts Travis's communications with the Texas government,

TRAVIS CALLS COUNCIL OF WAR:
MENCHACA RETREATS TOWARDS HOUSTON'S ARMY

After the ball, Travis invited the officers to hold a meeting to consult as to the defense of the place. The council gathered and many resolutions were offered and adopted, after which Bowie and Seguín made a motion to have me and my family sent away from San Antonio, knowing that should Santa Anna come, I and my family would receive no good treatment at his hands.[94] I left San Antonio and went to Seguín's ranch, where I remained six days preparing for a trip. From there I went as far as Marchelino, then to an old pond three miles farther on the east side of the Cibolo. At sunup the next morning Nat Lewis passed on foot from San Antonio with a wallet on his back.[95] I asked him why he went afoot and he answered that he could not find a horse; that Santa Anna had entered San Antonio the previous day. I asked what the Texans had done and he said they were in the fortifications inside the Alamo. I asked why he did not remain there and he answered that he was not a fighting man, that he was a businessman.

I continued my journey to Gonzales and arrived at the house of Green DeWitt,[96] where I met up with General Edward Burleson,[97] who had just arrived with seventy-three men. I slept there and on the next day attempted

---

which indicate that the Texan officers did not expect the Mexican army to arrive before mid-March.

94. This is a perplexing statement because it makes one wonder what made Menchaca's family more vulnerable than others. In fact, while documentation exists that a number of Tejanos left the service on the eve of Santa Anna's arrival in San Antonio on 23 February, there is no evidence of Menchaca's whereabouts except for his own comments.

95. In the nineteenth century, along with the modern meaning, the word *wallet* could still refer to a sack or pouch for carrying provisions. It was not meant to be carried on one's person, hence Lewis's explanation regarding the unavailability of a horse. Nathaniel C. Lewis was a recently established San Antonio merchant who has, controversially, been considered one of the Alamo couriers. Menchaca's is not the only account taking him away from San Antonio at the time the siege began, rather than later.

96. DeWitt was, along with Stephen F. Austin, the earliest Anglo *empresario* operating in Texas. His colonization contract extended over the present-day counties of DeWitt, Gonzales, Caldwell, Lavaca, and Guadalupe.

97. An Austin colonist, Indian fighter, and War of Independence hero, Burleson was one of the leading officers at both the final assault on Bexar in December 1835 and the battle of San Jacinto in April 1836. He arrived in Gonzales in early March with a company of men and was elected colonel of the First Infantry regiment.

to pass to the other side of the river with my family but was prevented by Burleson, who told me that my family might cross but not me, that the men were needed in the army.

ARRIVAL OF SEGUÍN WITH MESSAGE FROM TRAVIS: ORGANIZATION OF COMPANY OF MEXICANS

At Gonzales I also met up with fourteen Tejanos from San Antonio, and we united and remained there until a company could be formed. The Texans were gradually being strengthened by the addition of from three to fifteen daily. Six days after being there Captain Seguín, who was sent as a courier by Travis, arrived there and presented himself to General Burleson, who upon receipt of the message forwarded it to the Convention assembled at Washington, Texas.[98] On the following day, the Mexican company was organized with twenty-two men, having for captain Seguín, for first lieutenant Manuel Flores, and me for second lieutenant.[99]

On 4 March news reached us that Texas had declared her independence. The few who were there, 350 men, swore allegiance to it, and two days later General Sam Houston arrived and took command of the forces.[100]

When Santa Anna took the Alamo and burned the men he had killed, he sent Madam Dickinson,[101] a lady whose husband had been killed in the Alamo (accompanied by William Travis's servant and Juan N. Almonte's servant), with propositions to those desiring to make Texas their home.[102]

98. What later came to be referred to as Washington-on-the-Brazos was a settlement in Austin's colony where the interim government had gathered. It was there that the Texas Declaration of Independence was signed on 2 March 1836 and the Constitution of the Republic was drafted over succeeding days.

99. The muster roll book for the battle of San Jacinto lists Flores as first sergeant and Menchaca as second sergeant. Seguín, *Revolution Remembered*, ed. De la Teja, 2nd ed., 136.

100. The news of the Alamo's fall did not reach Washington-on-the-Brazos until 15 March, by which time Houston had left for Gonzales, which he reached on 11 March.

101. Susanna Dickinson was the wife of Almaron Dickinson, one of the defenders. All the defenders' bodies were cremated following the battle save for that of Gregorio Esparza, whose brother Francisco secured permission to bury him from General Santa Anna. Dickinson and her daughter Angelina were freed along with all the other women and children and other noncombatants.

102. *Ben* was the name of the black servant (slavery had officially been abolished in Mexico) of Juan Almonte, one of Santa Anna's most trusted advisors. Dickinson and Ben were tasked by Santa Anna to take news of the Mexican army's victory over

The propositions were in these terms: Any American Texan who desired to live in Texas would present himself to General Santa Anna and upon surrendering his weapons would be treated as a gentleman.[103] When the Americans heard what Santa Anna proposed, they in a voice cried, "General Santa Anna, you may be a good man, but the Americans will never surrender; go to h—1 . . . and hurrah for General Sam Houston."

On the following day, Texan spies arrived with the intelligence that the Mexicans were on their way to Gonzales and encamped on the Cibolo. On the same day the Texans started for the Colorado River, and slept at Rock Creek.[104] On the following day, at Lavaca,[105] Colonel George W. Hockley[106] with 160 men reported to General Houston for orders. On the next day the army encamped on the San Antonio,[107] and there General Alexander Somervell[108] presented himself with 250 men.

---

the Texans at San Antonio and to warn the settlers not to continue in their rebellion. Shortly after leaving San Antonio, Dickinson and Ben met Joe, William Travis's slave, who had also been released by Santa Anna. The small group of Alamo survivors delivered Santa Anna's message to Sam Houston at Gonzales on 12 March.

103. Santa Anna's proclamation following the battle of the Alamo was a bit more complicated than what Menchaca remembered. Santa Anna drew a distinction between "a parcel of audacious adventurers," who "must also necessarily suffer the just punishment that the laws and the public vengeance demand," and "the inhabitants of this country, let their origin be whatever it may, who should not appear to have been implicated in such iniquitous rebellion." The latter would, upon presenting themselves to the local Mexican commander within eight days of returning to their homes, be given a safe conduct. The full text of Santa Anna's proclamation was published in the *Telegraph and Texas Register* on 11 October 1836.

104. This "Rock Creek" is now Rocky Creek, flowing from northeastern Gonzales County southeastward into Lavaca County past Shiner. The road between Gonzales and Columbus passed along Rock Creek between the Bartholomew McClure and George Blair grants after crossing Peach Creek in northeastern Gonzales County.

105. The Gonzales–Columbus Road intersected the La Bahía Road just north of the Lavaca River, at present-day Moulton in Lavaca County.

106. George W. Hockley had been Houston's aide and had been with him the whole time. Houston's army was reinforced with the arrival of various groups of volunteers, so Menchaca's observation that the Army of Texas, as the regular army of the upstart republic was called, continued to grow during the retreat to the Colorado is generally correct.

107. It is difficult to be certain what Menchaca meant here, possibly the San Antonio Road. Certainly it could not have been San Antonio itself, or the river, both of which were in the opposite direction of travel.

108. Somervell was a volunteer who joined the army on 12 March 1836 and was with

From thence they started and arrived at Mr. Burnam's on the Colorado, and there remained ten days.[109] On the sixth day after they got there, General Joaquín Ramírez y Sesma, of the Mexican side, approached with 400 men.[110] There were 900 Texans in camp. As soon as the Texans saw that the Mexicans were trying to draw them into an attack, the Texans prepared to attack; but Houston told them that not a single man should move out, that that move was only made to draw him out and ascertain his strength, something that he did not intend to let them know. The Texans murmured, whereupon Houston told them that such was his determination and that nothing would tempt him to depart from it; but that if they were determined to do otherwise, all they had to do was to choose some other commander, for he would not take the consequences upon himself. He, then, would fight as a private but never as a commander. The soldiers upon hearing Houston's position saw that it was useless to argue and gave in. They then started for the Brazos River with the intention of crossing at "La Malena,"[111] the Nacogdoches road crossing about eight leagues above San Felipe de Austin,[112] and arrived there two days after and took a position in the river bottom on the west side.

From there Houston sent Moseley Baker[113] in command of 250 men to

---

Houston by the time the Army of Texas reached the Lavaca. Available documents do not indicate how many volunteers came into camp with him or what rank he held at the time. On 8 April he was elected lieutenant colonel of volunteers.

109. Houston's army arrived at Burnam's Ferry, a Colorado River crossing near present-day La Grange, on 17 March and crossed to the east bank. The army then marched eastward along the river until on 19 March it reached Beason's Ferry, where it remained until 26 March. It was at Beason's that Houston temporarily checked General Ramírez y Sesma's advance.

110. Ramírez y Sesma led one of two advance columns that Santa Anna sent in pursuit of the retreating Texan forces following the battle of the Alamo. He arrived with his column of about 800 men at Beason's Ferry on 21 March but was prevented from crossing both by the presence of the Texan army on the east bank of the Colorado and by the swollenness of the river due to spring-rain flooding. Although he had intended to fight the Mexican army at the Colorado, when news arrived of James Walker Fannin's defeat at Goliad, Houston decided to withdraw to the east. The march began on 26 March.

111. The Texans camped at Mill Creek.

112. Seat of Stephen F. Austin's colonial enterprise, San Felipe too was burned by the Mexican army during its pursuit of the retreating Texan forces.

113. An early advocate of Texas independence from Mexico, Baker fought in the early battles and was elected captain of Company D, First Regiment of Texas volunteers, on 1 March 1836.

San Felipe to take all they could in stores and burn the balance. Baker went to San Felipe with his men, crossed the river, encamped in the bottom, and then commenced to haul all they could away from San Felipe and to hide it in the bottoms until Baker told them that he could wait for them no longer, when he burned the stores. While the stores were being burnt, a great many barrels of liquor that had been crossed over were ordered to be broken, which was done. Texan spies came on the other bank and told Baker that Houston wanted him to come back, that the Mexicans were on the march, and were then at San Bernardo. Baker immediately set out to join Houston and arrived at Leonard Groce's house on the following day, where he received word to await further orders.[114] On that same day the steamboat *Yellow Stone*, captained by John E. Ross, came up the Brazos, and Houston stopped it and told the captain that on his return he should stop there and await his orders, which he did, and remained there twelve days.[115]

The Mexicans, the greatest part of them, turned to Fort Bend, only 500 going to the San Felipe crossing. On the eighteenth day that Houston was in camp, Santa Anna, with 700 men, crossed at Fort Bend towards Galveston. He was seen by an American, who took the news to Houston. The American arrived at Groce's at about 5 p.m., his horse very much fatigued and having ridden two other horses to death. He gave Houston the news, and on the following day Houston began to cross his troops on the steamboat.

After crossing, the Texans went as far as Isaac Donoho's house.[116] On the

114. The Texan army arrived at the Brazos above San Felipe on 28 March, but moved westward the following day. Because Baker refused to retreat further, Houston made the best of a bad situation and "ordered" him to stay. Baker was to defend the San Felipe crossing. According to Juan Seguín, his company was detached to support Baker's defense of the crossing, which may be why Menchaca emphasizes this set of events in his recollections (*Revolution Remembered*, ed. De la Teja, 2nd ed., 81). By the time Santa Anna arrived at the Brazos across from San Felipe on 7 April, the town had been burned. Because Baker's force prevented the Mexicans from crossing, Santa Anna continued downstream and was able to cross between San Felipe and Fort Bend, forcing Baker to withdraw.

115. The steamboat was at Groce's Landing taking on cotton when Sam Houston and his army arrived on 31 March. On the twelfth and thirteenth of April, Houston used the ship to get his army across the river before allowing it to proceed.

116. Isaac Donoho originally obtained a grant as a single man under the Austin and Williams contract in February 1836. Because the interim government had ordered the land offices closed the previous November, Donoho had to reapply for the quarter-league grant located northeast of present-day Hempstead, Waller County.

following morning at about eight o'clock, Colonel Bell, Colonel Allen, and Mirabeau B. Lamar, with 54 Americans, presented themselves to Houston for duty.[117] From this point they marched to the edge of the pine woods and camped.[118] On the following morning an old man in company with a young one arrived at camp with word from Santa Anna asking, where were the Americans? That he had heard every oak produced six Americans. Houston replied that though he did not have many men, with what he did have, he would surely call upon Santa Anna.[119]

The army next halted at the headwaters of Buffalo Bayou,[120] where camp was pitched on the west bank. As soon as camp was established, General Houston sent 25 horsemen to reconnoiter and ascertain what was going on. The horsemen found that Santa Anna had crossed towards Harrisburg.[121] They captured two couriers, one from Ramón Múzquiz of San Antonio and the other from Mexico, who were taken to General Houston.[122] Gen-

117. This Colonel Bell was possibly Peter Hansbrough Bell, who served as a private in the San Jacinto campaign, but went on to become assistant adjutant general in 1837, inspector general in 1839, a captain in the Somervell expedition in 1842, and a lieutenant colonel in the Texas Rangers during the War with Mexico. Menchaca's identification of him as a colonel may stem from his later service. The Colonel Allen to whom Menchaca refers is possibly John M. Allen, who was appointed captain of infantry after joining the army in December 1835. Lamar served as a private during the San Jacinto campaign until the eve of the battle of San Jacinto, so none of the men who came when he joined the army at Groce's would have been under his command.

118. A reference to the Big Thicket or Piney Woods region, the southwesternmost extent of which in the 1830s would have been in the Waller-Grimes-Montgomery-Harris Counties area. Houston's army briefly entered the Piney Woods on its eastward march.

119. No other source relates the incident of an old man and a young man entering the Texan camp.

120. Buffalo Bayou rises in northwestern Fort Bend County before flowing southeastward through Harris County.

121. Santa Anna arrived in Harrisburg on 14 April and burned the settlement on the eighteenth. According to J. H. Kuykendall, the army camped on the seventeenth at the headwaters of Buffalo Bayou and on the eighteenth less than a mile from Harrisburg. It is here that the capture of the Mexican couriers took place. Kuykendall's version matches Seguín's in placing the capture of the couriers while the Texans were camped near Harrisburg. Kuykendall, "Reminiscences of Early Texans: A Collection from the Austin Papers," 140; Seguín, *Revolution Remembered*, ed. De la Teja, 2nd ed., 81.

122. As in the case of the siege of the Alamo, there are conflicting reports on the number of couriers captured by the Texans during the last days of the San Jacinto cam-

eral Thomas Jefferson Rusk called the Tejano officers to read the messages. It happened that I opened the official dispatch from General Filisola to Santa Anna in which the former said that he sent Santa Anna 800 choice men, for he had heard from a reliable American that the Texans were 6,000 strong, and that he awaited instruction from Santa Anna in order to know what to do.[123]

As soon as General Houston heard the contents of the dispatch he said that he did not care a cent for the Mexican disposition, that all he wanted to know was where Santa Anna was; that as Santa Anna was separated from the main body of the army, Houston felt confident he could defeat Santa Anna. Houston then gave orders that 200 men should be placed under the command of Captain P. R. Splane to guard the horses and equipage, which was to be left there by the Americans who were to march the next day to meet Santa Anna. General Sidney Sherman[124] then said that his orders would be obeyed, and immediately started to select the company that was to remain.[125]

---

paign. According to Seguín, because of intelligence gathered by his men, three Mexicans were captured by Captain Henry Wax Karnes and "Deaf" Smith near Buffalo Bayou, including an army captain, a civilian, and a courier from Mexico (*Revolution Remembered*, ed. De la Teja, 2nd ed., 81). Like Menchaca, other sources indicate the capture of two couriers. Menchaca is incorrect, however, in claiming that one of the couriers carried an express, or official communication, from Ramón Múzquiz. Múzquiz did not hold a public office at this time.

123. The first military express taken from the courier, who was a Mexican army officer, was from General Vicente Filisola, Santa Anna's second in command, and, according to Houston, he was assured from its contents that "Santa Anna was in command of the advance of the army." The other express was mail from Mexico City congratulating Santa Anna on the success of the campaign. Lester C. Edwards, *The Life of Sam Houston: The Hunter, Patriot, and Statesman of Texas*, 111.

124. A resident of Kentucky in 1835, Sherman sold his business interests, recruited a company of volunteers, and set out for Texas, arriving early in 1836. Houston appointed him colonel of the Second Regiment of Texas volunteers, under whose command Juan Seguín's company, including Menchaca, fought at San Jacinto.

125. The baggage train, ammunition, and sick and wounded were left in the charge of Major Robert McNutt protected by two companies, one of 45 men under the command of Kuykendall and another of 20 men under Captain P. R. Splane.

MENCHACA PROTESTS TO HOUSTON

Houston told Sherman to have the Tejano company left at camp, that they knew but little about fighting, but were good at herding. General Sherman then went to the Tejano company and asked for Captain Seguín, and he was told he was not there. Then Sherman instructed me that as soon as he came, to tell him that his company was ordered to remain and guard the equipage and horses. I asked General Sherman why our company was ordered to do this duty and the general explained that those were his orders. When Seguín came, I told him what Sherman had said, and Seguín asked me what I thought about it. I replied that I wanted to see General Houston, and we both went. When we got to General Houston and saluted him, he asked what we wanted. I answered that Sherman had given me orders to remain in camp and I wished to know why it was. Houston replied that as a general he had given that order. I then told him that he could not deprive me of my commission; that when I joined the Americans I had done so with a view of aiding them in their fight and that I wanted to do so even if I died facing the enemy. That I did not enlist to guard horses and would do no such duty; that if that was the alternative I would go and attend to my family, which was on its way to Nacogdoches without escort or servants. Houston answered that I spoke like a man. I answered that I considered myself one; that I could handle any and all kinds of arms from a gun to an arrow, and that having a willing heart I did not see why I should not be allowed to fight. Houston then told me that he would gladly let me and my company go to fight.[126]

On the following day after breakfast (19 April 1836) the army was marshaled and addressed by General Houston and General Rusk. Houston spoke very eloquently. He dwelt long and emotionally of the suffering of those who had fallen at the Alamo and of those who fell at Goliad under Fannin. Houston having concluded, Rusk addressed the troops with such force and effect as to make every man, without a single exception, shed

126. No independent corroboration of this event is possible. It is improbable, however, that in his capacity as a sergeant under Seguín's command, Menchaca would have made the case for the Tejanos. In his memoir, Seguín gives no indication that there was any hesitation on the part of Houston to employ the Tejanos in the upcoming battle. Again, here Menchaca assumes the leading role among Tejano participants so far as to refer to the Tejano company as his. Stephen Hardin in *Texian Iliad* (209) relies on Menchaca's memoirs, but records that Houston's comment that he "spoke like a man" was about Seguín, although Menchaca is clear that the comment was directed at him.

tears. When General Rusk concluded speaking, provision was made for crossing the bayou, which was done by making rafts on which the guns, two four-pounders, were crossed, and also the horsemen.

SKIRMISHES BEFORE THE BATTLE

It took until 5 p.m. of 19 April to get over. The march was continued until 10 a.m. of the twentieth. The men slept on their weapons and proceeded very early the same morning to the bridge at Harrisburg,[127] and at 7 a.m. crossed it. We halted on a hill to await reports from spies. The spies came and reported that Santa Anna was within one and a half miles from there. Upon hearing this, General Houston ordered that the troops should discharge their arms and clean and reload, for, he said, the time was close at hand when they would be needed.

After this order was complied with, the Texans moved forward to a bend in the bayou, where they were halted in line. They were ordered to lie down and cautioned not to shoot until ordered to do so. Shortly after the Texans were on the ground, three Mexican companies came in sight, shooting scattering shots to draw the Texans on, for they could not see the Texans. When the Mexicans saw that no one answered their shots they halted and an officer came and ordered them back.

They remained about half an hour without shooting, and General Houston ordered General Sherman to advance with cavalry and ascertain what the Mexicans were doing. Sherman did so, and as soon as he reached the spot indicated the Mexicans attacked and wounded two of his horses badly. Sherman ordered that those men whose horses were wounded should be taken up behind two others, and he retreated in good order.

The Mexicans, about forty, followed the Texans, and when they came in good range a gun was fired at them, which killed some eight or ten, and they retreated. When they reached the mott[128] they commenced to shoot at the Texans with Jaegers.[129]

127. This would be the famous Vince's Bridge, which the army crossed in the early morning hours of 20 April (having crossed to the south side of Buffalo Bayou below Harrisburg) and which was destroyed the day of the battle by Deaf Smith at Houston's order.

128. *Mott* is from the Spanish word *mata*, a southwestern regionalism for a small grove of trees, particularly live oaks.

129. According to Hardin, where Menchaca says "yangers," he means "Jaegers," as

Houston gave orders that those men who lived upon the Navidad and Lavaca and killed deer at a hundred paces offhand should come forward and take a shot at the Mexicans. Immediately about fifty men were formed in line and went to a good distance from where the Mexicans were, fired one volley and hushed them. General Houston, seeing that the Mexicans fired no more, after some time elapsed sent some men over to find out if the Mexicans still occupied the mott and they found no one there. As soon as this report was brought to the general, he sent a detachment of one hundred men to occupy the place and to let a man climb a tree and see what the Mexicans were doing. The sentinel in the tree reported that they were cutting timber and fortifying from point to point the space upon which no timber grew.

The hundred men were relieved by another hundred men until three o'clock that day, at which time Houston ordered the line to be formed where the troops had first lain down. He then gave Sherman command of three companies of infantry and Lamar[130] the command of the cavalry, with orders to advance and ascertain what the Mexicans were doing.

When Sherman got to the edge of the prairie he ordered his companies to fall flat, the cavalry going out. The Mexicans, upon seeing the Texan horse coming out, engaged with their cavalry. When the Mexicans observed that the Texans would not retreat, they sent some infantry to support their cavalry. Then Sherman ordered his men to the relief of the horse, upon which the Mexicans retreated. In this skirmish three Americans were wounded: Colonel Neill and two others.[131] The Americans under Sherman and Lamar then came over to where Houston was. Fifty men were placed on guard on the Texan side that night.

On the twenty-first, early in the morning, about ten or twelve Mexican

---

it appears in this edited version. *Jaeger* is "hunter" in German. The Jaeger was a short, stocky, usually large-caliber flintlock rifle designed for hunting in the fields and forests of Europe. Using the old-world Jaeger as a starting point, German gunsmiths in Pennsylvania developed the American long rifle. During the Napoleonic Wars, "Jaegers" were light-infantry skirmishers in Prussian service. This tradition extended to the Spanish and Mexican armies in which such troops styled themselves as *cazadores* (Spanish for "hunters"). The weapons Menchaca encountered were likely the British Baker rifles used by the Mexican *cazadores*.

130. Although he had entered the service as a private, Mirabeau Lamar received a colonel's field commission to command the cavalry on the eve of San Jacinto.

131. Neill was actually wounded during an artillery exchange that preceded Sherman's probe of the Mexican lines.

mules were in sight of the Texan camp and were driven in by the Americans. At about ten o'clock the spies came in with their horses very tired and told General Houston that General Cos had crossed with eight hundred men and had burned the bridges;[132] that if he wanted to trouble them he could do so, as they were then close by; but Houston said no, that they were his anyhow, to let them rest.

THE BATTLE OF SAN JACINTO

About 2 p.m. that day, Houston ordered the troops to fall in line in three divisions, the right wing under Rusk, left under Sherman, and the center under himself. When they were so arranged, he called the officers together to give them his instructions, and after having done so ordered that the whole front should move at the same pace that he did. He then ordered Sherman to advance with his division to Santa Anna's right, and that Lamar should march with him. The attack was made and the battle began. The Mexicans were taken by surprise, so much so that eleven rows of stacked arms were not touched. The fight lasted two hours and a quarter, when those who were not killed, taken prisoner, or wounded, fled in great disorder.[133]

On the following day Santa Anna was brought in by two Americans, a lieutenant and Louis Robinson of Nacogdoches. He was found in the woods, under the care of two mulatto girls.[134] He was taken to General

132. Cos brought about 450 reinforcements into the Mexican camp, but it was the Texans who burned Vince's Bridge later in the day, on Houston's order.

133. Menchaca was part of Seguín's company, part of Sherman's division, which occupied the Texan left flank and advanced along the swamp that made up the eastern boundary of the battlefield. Considering that he gave such a detailed account of the preliminaries, Menchaca's description of the battle itself is curiously brief. And he is in error on the length of the engagement, which is generally recognized as having lasted only eighteen minutes, although the slaughter of Mexican soldiers went on for some time. He is correct that the Texans caught the Mexican camp by surprise. In his 1841 two-volume *Texas and the Texans*, Henry Stuart Foote, quoting Thomas Jefferson Rusk, documents Menchaca's presence in the battle and his refusal to save the life of a Mexican officer who recognized him (2:310). However, in his 1859 *Texas Almanac* recollection of the campaign, N. D. Labadie maintains that it was "one Sanchez, a Mexican, in Capt. Seguin's Company, composed of some thirty Mexicans fighting on our side," who identified the Mexican officer, a man named Bertrand. Labadie, "San Jacinto Campaign," 54.

134. This would be a group that included Sion Bostick, Joel W. Robison (or

Houston and many were in favor of putting him to death. But as he was a Freemason and most of the officers were Masons, he was protected.[135] The next day a steamboat from Galveston arrived with three hundred men, four guns, and provisions. Houston ordered that the provisions be divided into two equal parts, one for his troops and the other for prisoners and the wounded, which was done. On the next day Don Lorenzo Zavala arrived and spoke to Santa Anna, abusing him severely.[136]

Orders were given that Sherman and Burleson with two hundred and fifty men should march down to Fort Bend to see what Filisola, who was with the main body of the Mexican troops, determined upon. When they reached Fort Bend they found that Filisola had left for Matamoros. They then crossed the river and arrived at a lake, remaining there the balance of the day.[137]

Robinson), and James A. Sylvester. Menchaca misidentifies Robison as Louis Robinson here. The three men's stories do not include mention of two "mulatto" girls. "Reminiscences of Sion R. Bostick," 92–95; Kuykendall, "Reminiscences of Early Texans," 244; Edwards, *Life of Sam Houston*, 144–145.

135. None of the major sources point to the possibility that Santa Anna's Masonic connection had anything to do with his survival. In fact, many of the officers on both sides were Masons, and that did not stop them from fighting and killing each other. The consensus interpretation of why Houston fought to save Santa Anna's life rests in the presence of thousands of Mexican troops under the command of General Filisola and General Urrea, whom the Texans were ill prepared to fight. In return for sparing his life, Santa Anna agreed to order Filisola to withdraw the Mexican army south of the Rio Grande.

136. Colonel James Morgan and thirty volunteers (not three hundred) along with Lorenzo de Zavala arrived aboard the steamboat *Cayuga* on 23 or 24 April. The only other record of the meeting between Zavala and Santa Anna can be found in José Enrique de la Peña's diary, in which he claims to have spoken with Alexander Alsbury, a witness to the event, who supports Menchaca's description of the encounter. The two men had become political enemies as a result of Santa Anna's abandonment of federalism. Labadie, "San Jacinto Campaign," 60; Margaret Swett Henson, *Lorenzo de Zavala: The Pragmatic Idealist*, 72–73, 110; José Enrique de la Peña, *With Santa Anna in Texas: A Personal Narrative of the Revolution*, 10.

137. This statement is another curious discrepancy with the available record. As Seguín notes in his memoirs and as his correspondence with the Mexican army confirms, it was his and Captain Henry Wax Karnes's companies that were sent to observe the movements of the Mexican army, not those of Sherman and Burleson. Burleson, who was at Fort Bend holding that crossing, met up with Karnes and Seguín a few days later. It is possible that Menchaca considered Seguín's and Karnes's units as part of Burleson's command and so his recollection combined them all into a single force.

At about 3 p.m. General Pedro Ampudia came into the Texan camp and asked permission to take all the wounded and sick away. He was told that he could do so and would not be molested. Two men with two horses loaded with roasted meat and gourds of water for the wounded and sick were sent with Filisola. He took them with him and overtook the main body at the Colorado River.[138]

Seguín, *Revolution Remembered*, ed. De la Teja, 2nd ed., 28, 84; Gregg J. Dimmick, *Sea of Mud: The Retreat of the Mexican Army after San Jacinto, An Archeological Investigation*, 259–260.

138. Menchaca is wrong in this regard. Before crossing the Colorado, the Mexican rearguard abandoned a group of wagons that had bogged down and contained the most seriously ill soldiers.

EDITED REMINISCENCES OF
JOSÉ ANTONIO MENCHACA

Part 2

The Mexican prisoners on the banks of the San Jacinto and Buffalo Bayou were drawn up into a line. Among them were General Almonte and Colonel Juan Bringas, who surrendered to me.[1] I found among them a great many badly wounded men, and I made those who were not wounded make slings with their hands and carry to our camp the wounded, many of whom did not live to reach it. It was now growing dusk and Rusk, Allen, and Edwin Morehouse[2] asked me to take the prisoners who were well and make them cut wood and build fires as it was cold. I made them make three fires in a line about fifty yards long, and we laid down the wounded beside them. We had about fifty physicians and surgeons[3] more or less skillful in their profession and Houston sent for them and told them to dress the wounds of our men and the Mexican prisoners. These surgeons got us to light about four hundred candles for them

1. According to Seguín, Juan Almonte, Juan Bringas, and a number of other officers surrendered after one of them gave himself up. Seguín does not specifically take credit for the capture, allowing for the possibility that Menchaca had an active part in the surrender of one or more officers. See *Edited Reminiscences of José Antonio Menchaca, Part 1*, n. 133 (p. 76).

2. Morehouse, who had been in Texas since 1826, was commissioned a major in the Texas army and went to the United States to recruit. His unit was marching to join Houston but arrived too late to participate in the battle of San Jacinto.

3. Houston's official report lists only six surgeons and no physicians in the medical staff of the Army of Texas. On the Mexican side, according to General Filisola, Santa Anna had entered Texas without doctors or surgeons. Consequently, all the San Jacinto wounded on both sides had to be attended to by the six Texan surgeons and their assistants. J. W. Winters, *True Veterans of Texas: An Authentic Account of the Battle of San Jacinto*, 4; Filisola, *Memorias para la historia de la Guerra de Tejas*, 2:302, 311.

to see how to dress the wounds. We had lost in the battle only seven men and about thirty wounded.[4]

On the next day we went to the battlefield and found it covered with dead Mexican soldiers. We dug trenches and buried them with our own seven dead[5] and returned to our camp, where I found General Houston surrounded by his staff, and they were all in high glee over the brilliant victory of the day previous and all the army were in fine spirits.

The battle of San Jacinto was the most brilliant feat of arms I have ever witnessed and has immortalized Houston, his brave staff, and the army that participated in it and makes a beautiful page not only in the history of the then Republic of Texas but also in the history of the United States.

SANTA ANNA IS CAPTURED!

On the second day after the action at San Jacinto, 23 April 1836, two young gentlemen volunteers in the Texas service named Lewis Robinson of Nacogdoches and the other Pitt from New Orleans[6] rode out two miles from our camp to scout. As they were looking out for prisoners, one of them spied a fine-looking man with a commanding personal appearance dressed, however, in a very filthy ragged suit with a blue cap having a leather front piece. He was sitting down on the ground at a little distance from two likely looking young mulatto women, who were parching corn to feed him and who evidently were mistresses of his.[7] The young men rode up to the party and asked the mulattoes who that man was and they answered confusedly that they did not know and told them to ask him who he was. They did so, and he said he did not understand them. They then repeated the question, and he said, "I am Carlo, General Santa Anna's private secretary."[8] They told him he was a liar, that Carlo was a prisoner at

4. Houston's report lists two killed and twenty-three wounded, six mortally. Winters, *True Veterans of Texas*, 3.

5. Menchaca is at variance with other accounts, which note a dispute between the Texans and the Mexicans over burial duties and, consequently, that the Mexican dead remained on the field. A year later, their bones still littered the field.

6. This was actually Joel W. Robison, and there is no Pitt mentioned in other accounts of Santa Anna's capture. See *Edited Reminiscences, Part 1*, n. 134 (pp. 76–77).

7. No other account of Santa Anna's capture mentions any women, "mulatto," young, or otherwise. See *Edited Reminiscences, Part 1*, n. 134 (pp. 76–77).

8. Santa Anna's secretary was Ramón Martínez Caro.

that moment in General Sam Houston's camp. They then told him to get up and follow them; they did not care who he was and intended to take him into the camp to their general. They were on horseback, he was on foot, and after he had walked about fifty yards they saw that he was very much fatigued and young Robinson got down off his horse and ordered him to get up into the saddle. The man pretended not to understand him, but Robinson said, "I'll make you understand," and he caught hold of him by the slack of his trousers and made him mount and then got up behind him and the three rode into camp. As they rode in, one of the Mexicans who knew the prisoner said, "There is General Santa Anna!" And when the news, which seemed to spread over the army by electricity, was known, the whole army cheered the two young men and their distinguished prize.

They rode up near General Houston's tent and dismounted, and Santa Anna took a seat on a trunk and crossed his legs and kept his sharp bright eyes occupied in watching the army, which crowded up close all around him in a circle. And those in the rear got up on the shoulders of the men in front of them to get a look at Santa Anna, who sat like a lion at bay. He sat thus silently for some time and his eyes seemed every now and then to single out the officers, whom he distinguished not by the difference in dress from their subordinates but by their authoritative appearance.

Finally he said, "I am very thirsty. Will not someone bring me some water?" One of the Texans went down to the bayou and returned with a large tin cup filled with it, and Santa Anna took the cup and as he was about to drink it, he made the Masonic sign of distress. As he did so, all the officers and men of that fraternity—General Houston among the rest—drew their weapons and closed around him to protect him.[9]

Just at this juncture General Somervell, who was not a Mason and who was just beyond the circle of men around Santa Anna, came up cursing and swearing that he was going to kill Santa Anna. He had a bowie knife in one hand and a pistol in the other. Houston said to him, "Somervell, your blood is too warm, go down to the bayou and take a bath and that will cool it off." Somervell answered, "I don't care what you say, I intend to kill him," and became still more excited. Houston then told General Rusk, who stood beside him, to go and take Somervell away and make him promise not to harm their prisoner and if he did not, to kill him on the spot. Rusk went with Morehouse, Sherman, and Lamar up to Somervell, and they each had a pistol in one hand and a bowie knife in the other, just as Somervell had. They told him to follow them and come away from there or it would not

9. On the improbability of this event, see *Edited Reminiscences, Part 1*, n. 135 (p. 77).

be well for him. Somervell referred Rusk to the Devil and said he was still hungry and wanted to chaw up Santa Anna. Rusk then went close up to Somervell and said, "General Houston has given me orders to take you off and make you promise not to kill or hurt his prisoner, and if you do not instantly comply with those orders I shall kill you here." Somervell did not weaken until Rusk took his bowie knife and stuck it into his flesh a matter of an inch deep just over his heart, and then he said, "I will accede to my commander's orders." Rusk said, "Will you give your sacred word of honor to not molest Santa Anna in any way?" Somervell said, "Yes," and he then put up his pistol and bowie knife and marched away with them to his quarters.[10]

SANTA ANNA SPEAKS

Santa Anna then drew a long sigh of relief as Somervell was led off and said after a short pause, "Is there not someone who speaks Castilian and English?" He asked this question in Spanish, and Houston's own interpreter answered him in the same tongue and said, "I do, sir." Santa Anna replied, "You can tell your commander in chief that I am Don López de Santa Anna, President of the Republic of Mexico." Hallet[11] complied, and Houston, who was lying down near him suffering from a painful wound in his foot,[12] politely arose and shook his hand and at the same time bade Hallet to ask Santa Anna to tell him why he had not told that to the young men who had taken him prisoner. Santa Anna answered with much confusion that he feared if he did so, the two soldiers would have killed him.

Houston then said, "Tell Santa Anna that I have no soldiers; all of my brave men are honorable gentlemen who are above such brutality and, if not, they fear me too much to do a thing that I would not countenance on account of its barbarity."

10. No such confrontation is recorded in any other source. If something like it did take place, it is quite reasonable to assume that Menchaca gave it a Masonic interpretation without understanding that Houston's desire to save Santa Anna's life rested in his concern about the remainder of the Mexican army still in the field under General Filisola and General Urrea. See *Edited Reminiscences, Part 1*, n. 135 (p. 77).

11. N. D. Labadie claims to have served as interpreter initially until the arrival of Lorenzo de Zavala Jr. and Juan Almonte. Labadie, "San Jacinto Campaign," 57–58. No Hallet is mentioned in other available sources.

12. The wound was to Houston's right leg, above the ankle.

Santa Anna said, "Give me another interpreter." Dr. Ald[. . .] but neither he or [. . .][13] who came up to interpret pleased Santa Anna, who had spied General Almonte and asked that he be permitted to act as his mouthpiece. Almonte was called and came up. He, Houston, and Santa Anna then had a general and political conversation that lasted some time. Houston then said, "I see, General Santa Anna, that you are extremely fatigued, and I will have you a tent erected close to my own and have a bed prepared for you to rest upon," and he gave orders to that effect that were promptly executed.[14]

Santa Anna then asked Houston through Almonte if he did not have some Mexican gentleman among his command. I, who had been standing close during the whole conversation that had occurred since Santa Anna first asked for water, stepped forward, bowed, uncovered my head, and put my left hand over my bosom and then addressed Santa Anna thus: "You see before you General Santa Anna a Mexican; your humble servant and ready to do your bidding."[15]

He said, "You are a very fine-looking fellow, and your face seems familiar to me. What is your name?"

I answered, "My name, General Santa Anna, is Antonio Menchaca."

He said, "You are from San Antonio, are you not Menchaca?"

I said, "I am, sir."

He then replied, "Menchaca, I know you very well."

I said, "I know you also very well General Santa Anna, and I remember you when you came to San Antonio with General Arredondo and you were then a young cadet fresh from school."[16]

He then told me that when he was in San Antonio last he had heard me very highly spoken of.

13. The manuscript is worn and faded at the bottoms of a number of pages here, making some of the text illegible.

14. In fact, Houston ordered that Santa Anna's own tent and other belongings be brought in from the battlefield.

15. This entire conversation is problematic. Up to this point, Menchaca has been careful to distance himself from Mexicans. The familiar and obsequious tone he assumes here both contradicts his expressed attitudes and is inconsistent with the earlier part of his narrative. Even more problematic is the possibility of Santa Anna's singling Menchaca out for conversation among the Tejanos. Seguín never makes any such claim for himself, and he was the ranking Tejano at the scene.

16. This fanciful conversation would have us believe that the thirteen-year-old Menchaca was (a) well acquainted with the royalist officers occupying San Antonio, and (b) already prominent enough in the community to be pointed out to royalist officials.

I said to him [. . .] prisoner I s[. . .][17] by treating you kindly that my good repute in San Antonio may not be undeserved. Please tell how I can be of any service to you."

He replied to me, "Major Menchaca I have not tasted any food for three days but parched corn and I have not had more than enough of that than barely to keep me alive and I am very hungry indeed. Will you get me something to eat?"

I said, "General Santa Anna, the provisions in the American army are very low and we fare but little better than you have done, but I will get what I can for you."

He said, "Please get me some meat and roast it with your own hand as some of the rest of the men might try to poison me."

Then Santa Anna and Almonte were conducted to the tent prepared to receive them and Rusk with a picked detachment of twenty-five men, most of [. . .] and all reliable [. . .][18] and not cannibals like Somervell who might feel hungry and wish to feast on Santa Anna's bones.

Santa Anna was strongly hated by the Texas volunteers on account of his brutality in murdering the men who were in the Alamo when it was carried by storm. During the battle of San Jacinto the battle cry of the Texans was "remember the Alamo," and they made me take my men, who were Mexicans, and put large pieces of white paste board on our hats and breasts lest we should be mistaken for Santa Anna's men and killed.[19]

As I stated before, I started off in quest of some food for Santa Anna. As I got to my camp, four companies of men from Galveston sent to reinforce General Houston arrived (they were "just *behind* the battle Mother"[20] and the fighting was all done when they came in), and they marched in front of my camp. As they were passing I went out to meet them, and when they halted close by I went to one of the men and asked him if he had any green coffee[21] to sell, and he said that he had. I asked him what he charged me

17. Worn and faded; illegible.

18. Torn; illegible.

19. Menchaca's reference to this occurrence is unique among the battle accounts.

20. This statement is a jab at the late arrivals referencing the popular Civil War song "Just before the Battle, Mother," by George Frederick Root. In fact, volunteers continued to arrive in the days immediately following the battle of San Jacinto, among them Edwin Morehouse.

21. "Green coffee" refers to unroasted, or raw, beans, which would have been cheaper, not having undergone the roasting process. For a humorous description of green coffee in the military, see *Punch* 27 (1854): 59.

for it and he said $5 a cupful. I bought a cup of it and also two cups of sugar for $5 more, and also fourteen cups of flour for the same price and paid him in bills of a bank in New Orleans of which I had $7,000 in my belt; and they were at par with gold or silver with us, and even at a premium with the latter, as they were so much easier to carry in large quantities without danger of losing them.

These provisions I conveyed to my camp and asked one of my men named Flores, who was an excellent cook, to parch the coffee and drip some of it, make some bread with the flour, boil some of our mess beans, roast some meat *a la mexicana*, and fry some in the same mode, which he set himself to do. And when Flores had finished cooking it, I saw to having it dished up in some tin pans.

In the meantime, while Flores was cooking this supper, a court-martial was being held at headquarters in front of General Sam Houston's tent, and I went to ascertain what they intended to do. Santa Anna was looking on at the court from where he was standing at the front opening of his tent, which was about ten or fifteen paces distant from the place where the tribunal was in session. The court was discussing what they would do with Santa Anna and whether they would execute him or not. The court finally concluded not to kill him but to send him as a prisoner of war to the national capital of the United States, Washington City, and present him before the president of that government to answer for the wrong he had done some of its citizens who were murdered in the Alamo.[22]

After this decision had been reached, I thought I would go and see about Santa Anna's supper, which I found ready. I made four of my men take the pans and coffee pot and follow me over to Santa Anna's tent. When I reached it the guard halted me and would not let me pass. I told him prisoners were human beings with appetites like other men and it was a shame not to permit me to feed them. Houston heard me remonstrating with the

---

22. This is another episode well off from the record. No such court-martial was held. The decision to send Santa Anna to Washington was made months after the battle. In any case, the whole notion that he should be sent to Washington, D.C., to answer for war crimes at the Alamo is anachronistic. The United States did not have jurisdiction in Texas, nor had it yet recognized Texas as an independent nation at the time that this supposed court-martial took place. Therefore, Santa Anna could not have been tried in the United States for his actions in Texas. Santa Anna did return to Mexico by way of the United States, but that did not happen until November 1836, essentially because of the continued state of war that existed between Texas and Mexico, which the captive Mexican president was supposed to help bring to an end.

guard and immediately gave me a written pass to go at any hour day or night into the quarters of Santa Anna and the Mexican prisoners. I was then admitted and I got my four men to go and cut branches and boughs and spread them as even as possible to make a table in the tent. When this had been done and a cover was spread on them, I took three cups of coffee and made places for the two generals, Santa Anna and Almonte, and Colonel Bringas, and when Santa Anna sat down to eat, I took out my knife and scraped all of the mud that I could get off his trousers and the breeches of the other two officers. Santa Anna was so ravenously hungry and thirsty he drank two cups of coffee one right after the other without intermission and called for a third cup to wash his supper down with. He ate like a wolf and did not look around until he had finished his supper.

After his supper had been eaten he commenced to talk to me and ask me why the Americans hated him so; why they wanted to kill him; and if the court-martial had ordered his execution yet. I told him the cause of the hatred the Texans bore for him, but told him he was not to be killed but sent to the president of the United States as a prisoner of war, and his fate would be determined there. He told me he thought that I was deceiving him, that this information was almost too good to be true.[23]

I told him that I gave him my word as gentleman of honor that it was as I told him. He then put his hand in his belt and pulled out a splendid watch, which he had concealed there, and offered it to me. It was a watch that cost $3,700 and had been presented to Santa Anna by the government of Mexico as a token of appreciation for his services as its president. As he extended his hand to give it to me, I motioned to him to put it back in his belt and asked him why he had offered it to me; he said, "To pay you for the splendid supper you have given and the good news you have told me." I said to him, "General Santa Anna, would you insult me by saying this and offering me that watch? You are my prisoner; were you free you should fight for this." I then saw tears come to his eyes, and he cried like a child. I then said, "General Santa Anna, I do not need your watch, which is the only thing of any value that you have about your person. But you, who are a prisoner, do need some assistance. I have in my belt nearly $7,000 in the bills of a New Orleans bank. Take it. It may be of some service to you to pay for your servants and living when you are taken to Washington."[24]

23. As in the case of the first encounter between Menchaca and Santa Anna, this is likely a completely fabricated conversation.

24. The following statement is interlined in the text at this point: "It showed the goodness of heart of Manchaca to be sorry for hurting Santa Anna's feelings and offering

Santa Anna said I was mistaken in believing he needed any pecuniary assistance. He informed me that he had the incredibly large sum of $33,000,000 in gold in Mexico and his check for that amount at any time he saw to draw it would be paid. I then left him to retire as it was late, and I saw the men who had been left to guard baggage during the battle come in with it as our camp was not at the same place where we had it when the battle was fought. My wallet and other baggage that had been among it turned up missing, and I lost all of my changes of clothing and linen.

Sunday morning just exactly a week after the battle[25] I took one of the members of my company down to the bayou to wash out the shirt that I had on. As I sat on the bank waiting for it to dry, I saw a skiff coming up Buffalo Bayou in the direction from Galveston and as it came close to me and the person spoke to me, his face resembled the countenance of young Zavala so closely that I knew it must be his father. I said to him, "How do you do, Don Lorenzo Zavala," and he replied, "I am very well."[26]

It was Zavala Sr. who had been the vice president of the Mexican Republic, but he had been banished by Santa Anna from Mexico and had to work on the streets of London and Paris when he reached those cities, he was sent off in such destitute circumstances.[27] Zavala, though, was a statesman and a scholar and was warmly welcomed by the Texans because he espoused their cause. Sam Houston fired a grand salute with his cannon when Zavala landed and went down with his officers, followed by Santa Anna, to the side of the water to meet him. Zavala and Santa Anna were of course bitter enemies, but the latter thought it just as well to be polite as their fortunes were now reversed, and so he went to the bayou with the rest who went to welcome Zavala.

After Houston and his officers and also Santa Anna had held a long con-

---

to rob himself of his last cent to give to Santa Anna." The statement constitutes a gloss by the individual who assisted Menchaca in preparing the original manuscript.

25. The battle took place on a Thursday.

26. Zavala arrived in camp on the steamboat *Cayuga*. See *Edited Reminiscences, Part 1*, n. 136 (p. 77).

27. A marginal notation (in a different hand) with the following text constitutes the only corrective gloss in the entire text: "This is not quite correct as Zavala was in Paris at the time Santa Anna usurped the supreme power and Zavala wrote and denounced him and refused to serve under him longer. That letter is still in existence. He was Minister to the Court of St Cloude at the time." The gloss is itself in error. In 1835, France was in the early phase of the "July Monarchy," a period of constitutional monarchy under Louis-Philippe. The annotator thus anachronistically refers to the Palace of St. Cloud, which had been Napoleon's official residence, but which no longer served that function.

versation with Zavala, the latter asked to see the documents which contained a record of the proceedings of the Congress of the Republic of Texas. Rusk told him that I had them and asked him to accompany him over to my quarters.[28] When they reached there I had not returned and they asked where I was and sent after me. My shirt had not yet dried sufficiently for me to put it on, so I went back without it. When I came into the presence of the august ex-vice president of the Republic of Mexico, I had no shirt on, and both he and Rusk looked a little surprised and smiled visibly. Rusk asked me to explain why I came on dress parade before one of the generals of the army with such a pretty brown shirt that fit me so tightly. I told him all of my other shirts but one had been stolen by one of his own men who were guarding some of the baggage and that one was drying on the bank of the bayou. He then said he would make me a present of a shirt and sent to his tent by one of my men to bring me one.

After I got inside of it he asked me to show the vice president those papers already alluded to. As he was looking over them his son, young Zavala, came into my tent with a large official paper in his hand that he handed to me. I could not at first imagine what it could be, but I found on reading it that it was a commission as quartermaster general of the Army of the Republic of Texas, to which position the court-martial had just appointed me.[29]

While I was looking at it Seguín, my old captain, passed and saluted me, saying, "You have just been made a high officer without any more fighting to do and I will have to leave you now, Major." I said, "Seguín, have you got orders to leave here?" and he said, yes. He was to go with Burleson's division, which Houston had then ordered to march to the Atascosito Crossing.[30] I handed the commission back to young Zavala and told him to go for me to the court-martial and say for me that I was deeply grateful for the high honor they desired to confer on me, but that it was my intention to stay with my command as long as there was a bit of fighting to be done, and that I would be compelled to decline the high position of quartermaster

28. Zavala had been with the rest of the government on Galveston Island at the time of the battle. There would not have been a need for Zavala to ask Menchaca to see the government's records, and Menchaca would not have had the government's records to begin with.

29. There is no record of such an appointment. Colonel Almazon Huston served as quartermaster general from 14 November 1835 to 18 March 1837.

30. On the specifics of Seguín's detachment to observe the withdrawal of the Mexican army, see *Edited Reminiscences, Part 1*, n. 137 (p. 77).

general. I then ordered my boy to go and saddle my horse, and I rode off without telling either Santa Anna, Almonte, Zavala, Houston, or anyone else good-bye. And I never saw Santa Anna afterwards.

I had some money then, and had I accepted the position of quartermaster general and stayed with Santa Anna I might have been very wealthy today in my old age. I do not regret going off and losing those opportunities when I reflect that I was doing my duty to my country in its strictest and best sense, and this is a great consolation to me now though I am a very poor man with but a meager subsistence.[31]

After I had gone some distance, I waited for Burleson and his command to come up. Sherman was with him, and they both took the direction of Fort Bend and marched at easy stages until they got within about five miles of that place when they discerned a troop of six horsemen with five small red flags, which they knew to be Mexican standards. The party, we soon ascertained to be General Adrián Woll, one of Santa Anna's generals.[32] He rode up very close to us and must at first have mistaken us for Santa Anna's men, as I with my Mexicans marched at the head of the column.

When he rode close to us, we halted him, and Burleson asked Sherman to accost him, which he did, asking who he was and where he was going. He said, "I am General Adrián Woll of Santa Anna's Mexican Army and in search of my chief. Can you tell me where to find him?" Sherman told him of Santa Anna's capture and whereabouts and then asked him why he rode up to us with such sangfroid,[33] and if he was not afraid that we would kill him. He said, "No, I am a Frenchman and I do not fear death. Neither am I afraid that the Americans would kill me." Sherman asked him how he knew this, and he said because they were not in the habit of shooting prisoners.

He then gave his parole of honor that if Burleson would give him a pass-

31. Menchaca's economic circumstances in the 1870s and his effort to elicit sympathy may well have been the reason for his references to considerable wealth and opportunity.

32. The French-born Woll, who had served in the Napoleonic armies, immigrated to Mexico following the restoration of Bourbon rule in France. There he participated in the Mina Expedition and then as an officer under Santa Anna. Following independence, he rose through the ranks and was quartermaster of the army during the Texas campaign. He remained a centralist, and later a monarchist during the brief reign of Emperor Maximilian. Sent to France to report to Napoleon III on the situation in Mexico, he never returned to Mexico.

33. A number of internal clues indicate that Menchaca received considerable assistance from his collaborator, including here the use of the term *sangfroid*, or coolness under stress, a term with which Menchaca is likely to have been unfamiliar.

port to Houston, and guards and pickets to protect him, that he would ride on to meet Santa Anna, whom he particularly desired to find. Burleson wrote him the safe conduct for himself and his bodyguard and parted company, Burleson with his command going on into Fort Bend and Woll going to Houston's camp on the San Jacinto. When Woll reached there, I am told that Houston was very indignant with Burleson and Sherman for giving him this safe conduct and for not taking him westward with them and sending him on his parole back to Mexico.[34]

SMUGGLERS SINK

Our command marched into Fort Bend, and after a short rest we marched onward and at the end of the afternoon of the second day we stopped at some holes of water in a lane called Smugglers Sink.[35] Here we overtook a party of Mexicans with their General Pedro de Ampudia.[36] We halted and made our camp here and Ampudia struck up a conversation with Sherman. And as he was a quartermaster general in Santa Anna's army, they (Burleson and Sherman) might have known that he had a camp with supplies around somewhere in the neighborhood. That night Ampudia stole off and made good his escape.[37]

It was ascertained next morning that he had a camp within two miles of us and had there 150 mules and horses, a large number of wagons loaded with all sorts of military supplies, and two wagons loaded with cannonballs and other artillery charges. One of our men, Felipe Jaimes,[38] who

34. Filisola sent Woll to the Texan camp to obtain intelligence and was detained by Rusk, who had taken command of the army when Houston left for New Orleans to have his leg wound attended.

35. In his memoirs Juan Seguín refers to this place as Contraband Marsh. *Revolution Remembered*, ed. De la Teja, 2nd ed., 84.

36. Lieutenant Colonel Pedro de Ampudia, an artillery officer, was in charge of the rearguard, which included the artillery and wagons carrying the sick and wounded.

37. There is no evidence of Ampudia's having come into contact with either Sherman or Burleson. There is no evidence that Sherman was with Burleson. Both Filisola's and Ampudia's communications and subsequent accounts refer to Seguín and Henry Wax Karnes as the Texan commanders with whom they dealt. Dimmick, *Sea of Mud*, 251–261.

38. Felipe Jaimes does not appear in any service records from the War of Independence. He does appear on the roster of a company of men led by Juan Seguín in 1839 in a campaign against Comanches. Seguín, *Revolution Remembered*, ed. De la Teja, 2nd ed., 185–186.

was captured as a courier for Santa Anna and who had taken allegiance to the Texas government and was acting as one of our scouts at the time, stumbled on a lot of sick and wounded, twenty-one in number, with the two wagons loaded with ordnance. They communicated the fact of Ampudia having escaped from the Texans and then coming over to his own camp and gathering up all of the supplies and provisions, leaving only the two heaviest wagons with the cannonballs and ammunition in them. They said he had left them not a morsel of food and that they were very hungry, and likewise implored him to go and bring them food from his camp. He went and told his superior officers, Burleson and Sherman, this, and they both felt sheepish at letting themselves be caught napping, but they ordered Jaimes to take them food, which he did.

He was sent back on the following morning with more food for the wounded and to do all he could for them, as the officers of the Texas army did not like to leave their wounded enemies to starve like their own officers had done. But, lo and behold, when Jaimes went to the place where the wounded had been, he found the two wagons that had contained ordnance, as well as all of the wounded, gone and nothing left but the cannonballs, shells, etc. thrown promiscuously out on the ground. When he went back with this news to Burleson and Sherman, they again opened their eyes very wide and looked very suspiciously and then laughed at the smartness of the Mexicans. The supposition is that the first food sent by Jaimes strengthened some of them so as to enable them to get out and capture some mules and horses on the prairie that night, and they came back with them, pitched out the loads of artillery ammunition, and hauled off their wounded companions in the two wagons that had contained it.[39]

Burleson and Sherman now sent forward scouts to the Colorado to reconnoiter and report if they came up with the Mexican army, there on either side, as they rightly conjectured that they were then getting tolerably close upon it. Some of the scouts returned very soon afterwards and

---

39. Menchaca's account is at considerable odds with documents written at the time of the narrated incidents. Ampudia, in fact, requested that Seguín, with whom he was in communication, attend to the sick and wounded. In his communication of 4 May 1836 to Seguín, Ampudia states that "with Lt. Col. Don Ignacio Barragán, the bearer of the present dispatch, I forward to the sick the necessary supplies, until His Excellency, Don Vicente Filisola, can take measures for their removal; and inasmuch as those sick men are on the ground occupied by your camp, I hope you will in future attend to them, as I have been informed you will" (in Seguín, *Revolution Remembered*, ed. De la Teja, 2nd ed., 137–140).

informed us that Ampudia with his train and the wounded men had both crossed the Colorado and formed a junction just on the west bank of the river with General Filisola, who with his division was camped within a hundred yards of the river's bank. We were within eight miles of the Colorado then, and we reached it at night. That night people were crossing the river in both directions unmolested by either army.

"Boots and Saddles!!"

Next morning at daybreak we heard Filisola's buglers play "Boots and Saddles"[40] on their bugles, and Sherman ordered his own buglers to play the same strain. When we crossed the river and came upon his camp, which was just as the sun rose, it was deserted and nothing but the ashes of his campfires was left. They could not have been very far ahead of us, but we were marching a little more leisurely behind them, that they were in front of us. Houston's orders to Burleson and Sherman had been to avoid bloody battles as long as their enemy retreated in the direction of his own country. And to follow him without pressing him too close.

At ten o'clock Sherman ordered a detachment of ten scouts to ride ahead and see how far off the enemy was. They rode about two or three miles and found 1,000 head of beef cattle lying almost exhausted in the road from hard driving, and they concluded correctly that they had been left behind by Filisola in his hurry to get beyond the reach of Texas powder and lead.

The next day's march brought us to the San Antonito Creek[41] twelve miles west of the Colorado River, where we halted a week. From here we took up our march to Victoria and below the town about a mile and a half.

We remained at Victoria eighteen days, and during our encampment there we were joined by General Rusk, who came up from San Jacinto with 800 men.[42] A short time after his arrival, Rusk asked me if I would like to

40. This bugle tune is used to call a cavalry unit to prepare to mount and dates to at least the beginning of the nineteenth century. It would have been a familiar sound in Menchaca's San Antonio of the 1870s. Whether it was the same call as used by the Mexican army in 1836 is uncertain.

41. San Antonito Creek is possibly present-day Skull Creek, southwest of the Atascosito Crossing of the Colorado River on the Atascosito Road, which was the road connecting Goliad and East Texas.

42. The headquarters of the Mexican army evacuated Victoria on 16 May, and Rusk, with the main body of the Army of Texas, arrived by the end of the month. Rusk had

go with my men and Seguín's to San Antonio and I told him I would. He said, "There is some risk attendant upon the venture as General Juan José Andrade, with 2,500 men and 30 pieces of artillery, is marching in the direction from San Antonio on his way to Matamoros." I told him I did not feel a bit afraid. He said, "If you fall in with him and get captured, let me know as soon as possible by a courier and I will come to your assistance. I have orders not to fight unless it is necessary, but I would like very much indeed to pitch once more into the Mexicans."[43]

On the road to New Goliad[44] we met Colonel Domingo Ugartechea[45] with an escort of five men on his way to get supplies for Andrade's army. He asked Seguín and me which way we were going with our men, and we said to San Antonio. He said, "I wish to see General Rusk, who is at Victoria, and if you will give me a passport through to him and an interpreter, I will give you one through Andrade's lines to San Antonio." Seguín wrote him a passport and called one of my men, Pedro Flores,[46] and sent him with Ugartechea, and he left us his corporal and a written passport to Andrade and we separated, going in different directions. Our companies halted to prepare their dinner at a little house by the roadside about nine miles from Goliad. And very shortly after we had stopped, the corporal left by Ugartechea came to Seguín and me and informed us that Andrade's command

---

taken command of the army on 4 May because Houston departed for New Orleans to be treated for his wound.

43. Rusk ordered Seguín to occupy San Antonio, where he arrived at the head of his small company on 4 June. By the time he arrived, only a small detachment under Lieutenant Francisco Castañeda remained. It surrendered the city and withdrew on 6 June. General Juan José Andrade had been left in command at San Antonio when the Mexican army moved on after the fall of the Alamo. He was withdrawing on orders of General Filisola.

44. This is a reference to the settlement on the north side of the San Antonio River, present-day Goliad, which began after the war, when the old town site surrounding the presidio was largely abandoned, although at the end of May 1836 it was still occupied by the Mexican army.

45. One-time commander of Mexican forces in Coahuila and Texas, Ugartechea had been left in command of recruits at Goliad during the Mexican army's advance into the interior of Texas. Seguín does not mention this encounter between his detachment and Ugartechea in his memoirs.

46. Possibly Pedro Flores Morales, a member of Seguín's 1839 Comanche campaign, who does not appear on the roster from the battle of San Jacinto or that from the Siege of Bexar.

was marching toward us. As Andrade's advance guard came up, some of the officers in front accosted the corporal and asked what he was doing among those Texans, and he explained to them. In the meantime, Andrade and his staff rode up, and Andrade asked who commanded those troops. Seguín answered, "I do, sir." Andrade then said, "My corporal informs me that you have a passport from Colonel Ugartechea, let me see it." Seguín handed it to him and he read it and said, "You and your command can march on ahead to San Antonio undisturbed."[47] Andrade's army marched then by us in silence, and our men kept perfectly silent, too, as they passed on in a regular, slow, and orderly manner. They came to a halt at a creek about a mile beyond us, and about an hour afterwards we took up our march.

BACK TO SAN ANTONIO

After three days more marching, we got into San Antonio and made Múzquiz's house headquarters of our division. We found the city almost deserted. A great many families who sympathized with the Texas cause moved east, and a great many Mexican families, who either from choice or compulsion espoused the Mexican cause, went to Mexico.

We had returned and remained in town about a week when six Comanche Indians with their chief Casimiro[48] rode into the town. They were all horribly filthy and as lean and gaunt as wolves. They asked some of the Mexicans who was in command here, and they were told Seguín and Menchaca. Casimiro said he did not know Seguín but he did know Menchaca, and he came to me and asked me how I came on and I told him very well. He then informed me he was very hungry (all Indians always are) and wanted something to eat. He also asked me if I did not have something to give him. I told him I would give him aplenty, and I took the key to one of Santa Anna's storehouses, which was full of provisions, and told him to follow me there. I unlocked the door and told him to pitch in and help himself. He ate like a

47. This is one of the few instances in which Menchaca's and Seguín's memoirs coincide. Seguín reports encountering Andrade at Cabeza Creek on the La Bahía Road about six miles west of Goliad. Seguín, *Revolution Remembered*, ed. De la Teja, 2nd ed., 85.

48. In some passages of Menchaca's reminiscences the name is spelled "Cassimiro." The only other reference we have found to this Comanche leader is in the work of Joseph Milton Nance, who spells his name "Casemiro" but does not reference any incidents with him at San Antonio akin to those that Menchaca recounts. Nance, *Attack and Counter-Attack*, 111, 189.

hungry hound with his men and, after they had satisfied the immediate ravings of their appetites, Casimiro began to look around the storehouse. He spied a large sack of bread cooked with lard seasoned with salt and he asked to be permitted to take it with a sack of beans and three strings of peppers, which I agreed to. He then turned to go, but before he left, he looked at me in a very strange, pitying manner and said to me, "Menchaca, I feel a great deal of compassion for you and am truly sorry for you." I asked him why this sudden outburst of pity and compassion and if there was any danger overhanging me. He told me that the Indians intended to come into San Antonio, burn the town, and kill all of the people. I said, "Casimiro, this is the worst piece of barbarous ingratitude that I ever heard of. The people of San Antonio have never yet harmed the Comanche and have always fed them when they came and asked for something to eat."[49]

He said, "Menchaca, I have twenty horses, two Mexican prisoners to wait on me, and four wives. If you will come and live with me and my band, I will divide equally with you each of these articles."

I told him I was not quite as well fixed with wives as he was, but still I was satisfied to remain where I was. He said, "Do you intend to stay in San Antonio?"

I said, "I live here, Casimiro, and I am going to get my family, which left during the war, and bring them back."[50]

He said, "How many moons will you be gone?" (Indians reckon time by the number of new moons.) I told him it might take me five or six moons to go and return.

He grunted, "Umph! Good!" and asked me if I had any mescal, and I told him a little and that I would give him six bottles. He then wanted *piloncillo*[51] (sugar), and I gave him fifty of them. And then I said, "Casimiro, recollect what I have told you about killing people in San Antonio and think of my kindness to you and do not harm them." He and his men then went away.

On 10 June 1836, I left San Antonio to go to get my family, who were

49. It is difficult to know who the intended audience might be for this comment. Although there were periods of peace between Comanches and Tejanos, there is abundant evidence of conflict between them going back to the arrival of the Comanches in Texas in the mid-eighteenth century.

50. Presumably, Menchaca's family was with Seguín's in East Texas. Seguín credits Menchaca with bringing his whole family back safely as they all fell ill during the return trip to San Antonio. Seguín, *Revolution Remembered*, ed. De la Teja, 2nd ed., 85, 88–89.

51. *Piloncillo* typically is brown sugar in the form of small cones. It can be consumed both as a sweetener and as candy.

then at Nacogdoches, and arrived there on 20 July. I remained there with them until 15 August and started with them back to San Antonio.

While we were on the road I heard that 1,500 Comanches on 15 August had been into San Antonio and killed a Mexican woman and two girls and then gone down to the San José Mission and there killed two very good men and a lady. On the sixteenth they came back to San Antonio and dismounted in the Cíbolo Square[52] and said they wanted to kill all of the people. Casimiro was their chief and after a while ordered them to ride out of town. He was the last to go, and before he left he told a Mexican to tell me that he had been in town and stayed all day with his band, which wanted to kill everybody in town, and that he had ordered them off without letting them carry out their threats. He asked the Mexican if I was in town, and he told him I had gone to Nacogdoches. One of Casimiro's men said it was so because he had seen me when I got to Nacogdoches. Casimiro then left town.

I did not reach home from Nacogdoches until November 1836. Soon after my arrival General Rusk, who had 4,000 men near Lavaca, sent 300 of them to Seguín and me to protect San Antonio from the Indians, squads of whom we sent out on scouts to fight them. Seguín and I were the commanders of this point as officers of the Texas Republic from November 1836 to 1838.[53]

Early in the latter year a Colonel Henry Wax Karnes[54] was sent by the

---

52. We have been unable to locate any mention of a Cíbolo Square or Plaza. *Cíbolo* was the common Mexican Spanish word for the American buffalo; thus Cibolo Creek, which flows from northwest to southeast around San Antonio, was named for the presence of bison there in the early eighteenth century.

53. Seguín received a lieutenant colonel's commission and orders to raise a battalion with which to garrison San Antonio in September 1836. He was able to raise 80 men, with whom he arrived in San Antonio in November. Rusk did not have 4,000 men, nor did he provide Seguín with the men for his unit. Menchaca served as first lieutenant in Seguín's unit from October 1836 to March 1837 and as captain thereafter until Seguín's command was disbanded in October 1837. Menchaca appears to have subsequently provided additional military service, specifically as a captain of cavalry in February, March, and April 1838 under General Albert Sidney Johnston. Menchaca, Antonio, Republic Claims, PE reel 229 frame 429, AU4219 reel 69 frame 668, and AU 9590 reel 69 frame 679, State Library and Archives Commission, Austin, Texas; Seguín, *Revolution Remembered*, ed. De la Teja, 2nd ed., 29–31.

54. Karnes was a highly respected soldier, having served throughout the War of Independence. It was he along with Seguín who commanded the units that shadowed the Mexican army during its withdrawal following the battle of San Jacinto. As Joseph

president of the Republic to relieve us. He commanded until 1839. Karnes always kept a guard to watch the horses at the San José Mission, but in March 1839 a band of Indians from Presidio del Río Grande captured all of the horses and the two guards who were watching them and took them away.

In September 1839 Colonel Karnes was superseded by Colonel William S. Fisher,[55] who moved his quarters to the San José Mission. A short time after Fisher was placed in command, a band of seven Comanche Indians and their chief wanted to make an overture for peace. Fisher told them they would first have to go and bring him all the Mexican or American prisoners they had. And they told him they would go and return with the prisoners in the course of twenty days. He told his interpreter to tell the chief that if he caught him telling a lie, he would kill him and all of the men he caught with him. The Indians left and returned at the end of twenty days and camped at the spot where the market near Main Plaza now stands. There were about twenty of them, including five women and some children, but they did not bring any of the prisoners with them.[56]

Fisher was very indignant when he learned that they had returned without keeping their word to bring the prisoners, and so he determined to teach them a lesson. He took his command and surrounded them and killed every man but one among them, who escaped badly wounded by running down the river, swimming across and following down the timber. He did not kill the women and children but kept them as prisoners.

At the end of three months, a Comanche chief came in unattended by his band. His name was Potsanaquahip,[57] and he offered to exchange five

---

Milton Nance points out in *After San Jacinto* (55, 71–74), Karnes must have assumed command in San Antonio late in 1837, as Menchaca's own pension record indicates. Menchaca, Antonio, Pension Claims, PE, NA reel 229 frames 423–450, State Library and Archives Commission, Austin, Texas.

55. Fisher, a settler in DeWitt's colony and veteran of the battle of San Jacinto, did assume command at San Antonio about this time.

56. The events described here constitute the 19 March 1840 "Council House Fight," during which thirty-five Comanches were killed while in San Antonio for negotiations over captives. Fisher and the other Texans were dissatisfied that the Comanches had brought in only one white hostage, Matilda Lockhart. Fisher's men opened fire when the Comanches refused to become hostages until all white hostages in Comanche hands were released.

57. Known to Texans as "Buffalo Hump," this was the Comanche chief who led the Linnville Raid of August 1840. He was the only remaining Penateka Comanche chief, having escaped the Council House Fight.

Mexican prisoners for the five Comanche women and the children in the custody of Fisher, to which the latter agreed. Potsanaquahip brought in his prisoners, delivered them up, effected the exchange, and retired with his women and children.

In 1840,[58] while General Lamar was president of the young republic, he had an expedition fitted out that March under General Hugh McLeod, assisted by the young José Antonio Navarro, whose father has already been mentioned as one of the former governors of San Antonio under the Spanish regime.[59] The expedition numbered 400 men and was sent to attend to some troubles that were going on out on the Texas border near Paso del Norte.[60]

They went out there and crossed the Rio Grande and marched into Chihuahua but were attacked and captured after a short engagement by Mexican General Manuel Armijo with 3,000 men and taken prisoners to Veracruz.[61] In September of the same year, Karnes was sent back to San Antonio to organize another expedition to fight the Indians, who were

58. Actually taking place in 1841, the Texan Santa Fe Expedition was President Mirabeau Buonaparte Lamar's scheme to enforce Texas's claims to all the territory north and east of the Rio Grande, which included the important New Mexican trading centers of Santa Fe and Albuquerque. The expedition proved a complete disaster, with its members taken prisoner after becoming lost on the southern Plains.

59. One of numerous Americans who arrived too late to participate in the Mexican War of Independence, McLeod joined the army in June 1836 and quickly rose through the ranks. He served as adjutant general and did considerable Indian fighting before participating in the Santa Fe Expedition. He went on to serve in the Texas Congress and during the Civil War returned to military service as an officer in the state militia. Navarro, born in February 1795, was one of two Texas-born signers of the Texas Declaration of Independence. He reluctantly assumed the role of one of four civilian commissioners to the people of New Mexico on behalf of the Texas government, which claimed the lands east of the Rio Grande as its territory. At age forty-six when the expedition took place in 1841, he was hardly "young." His father, Angel, was a native of Corsica who migrated in the 1770s to San Antonio, where he became a leading merchant and served on the city council and as *alcalde* on various occasions. He was never governor of Texas.

60. Paso del Norte is now Ciudad Juárez and is located on the south bank of the Rio Grande; it had nothing to do with the expedition.

61. Armijo was governor of New Mexico, which was a separate territory from the State of Chihuahua, which the Texans never entered. Armijo never had even 1,000 men, and the expedition surrendered without a shot being fired. The prisoners were marched to Mexico City and subsequently held at Perote prison in Veracruz until most were released in April 1842.

then very troublesome. The expedition went to San Saba and had a fight with the Indians in which they killed twenty of the Indians and took from them over 100 horses without losing a single man. The Army of Texas then in this place was disbanded and the discharged soldiers permitted to go to their homes as the government was considered to have been established on a firm basis.[62]

But while there were only sixty able-bodied American and Texas men, mostly lawyers and professional men and a great many treacherous Mexicans, in San Antonio, we learned that Mexicans under a General Rafael Vásquez[63] were coming into San Antonio from Mexico. The sixty Americans who organized and were commanded by two lawyers, Barnes and John D. Morris,[64] prepared to defend the town. Vásquez came to the edge of town with 1,500 men in March 1842 and sent word to Barnes and Morris that if they would surrender the town without fighting, the people who chose to leave might be permitted to depart unmolested, but if they did

62. Menchaca is conflating a number of campaigns and fights with the Comanches, in some of which Karnes had a role. In August 1838 Karnes was at the head of a troop of rangers that reportedly fought off 200 Comanches at Arroyo Seco near the Medina River. In February 1839 a troop of rangers under the command of John H. Moore clashed with Comanches at the mouth of the San Saba River. In summer 1839 Karnes commanded two companies of volunteers that responded to reports of Comanches in the vicinity of San Antonio.

63. Vásquez, a centralist, had been operating in northern Mexico since at least 1839 and had conducted minor raids into Texas prior to leading a force of approximately 700 men into San Antonio at the beginning of March 1842. Seguín had warned the government regarding Vásquez's movements, but the Houston administration did not send help. Many Tejanos, including Seguín, decided to leave the city before the arrival of the Mexican army, which may account for Menchaca's comment regarding treacherous Mexicans in San Antonio. The Anglo residents attempted to organize a defense, but they too withdrew, and Vásquez occupied the city from 5 to 7 March.

64. Menchaca is incorrect in identifying these men as the leaders of the Anglo-American defenders. A committee of public safety composed of William B. Jacques, John Madley, William Elliot, and Samuel A. Maverick had elected John Coffee Hays to command the defenders. Hays is one of the most colorful figures in Republic history, having acquired a reputation as an Indian fighter and ranger captain. John D. Morris, a lawyer who settled in San Antonio in 1837, had been elected to represent the area in the Sixth Congress and participated in the defense efforts. Hays sent him, Cornelius Van Ness, and Mike Chevallie to negotiate with Vásquez. After the Mexican withdrawal Morris participated in Hays's pursuit of Vásquez's column. No one by the name of Barnes appears as a leader among the defenders.

not surrender without firing a shot, he would kill every soul among them. Barnes and Morris held a consultation with the people, and finally all agreed to accept the terms offered. Vásquez marched into town, and the Texans and other American people all marched out via the Seguin Road.[65]

Vásquez remained twelve days[66] and then retreated on hearing that 1,500 Texans were after him, who passed through the following day after his departure in hot pursuit after him. They, however, did not overtake him and gave up the chase very soon because Vásquez distanced them so badly. He was in a terrible hurry to get back across the Rio Grande and never stopped longer than necessary before reaching its opposite bank. And the Texans returned through San Antonio to the places from whence they came.

ANOTHER "*BULLY*" BOY WHO CALLS HIMSELF GENERAL ADRIÁN WOLL COMES TO TOWN AND IS TAKEN BY THE HORNS

San Antonio was a very quiet place from the time that Vásquez left until the following September. On the eleventh of that month the same General Adrián Woll[67] who was met by the roadside by Burleson and Sherman near Fort Bend marched into San Antonio at the head of a force of 1,500 men. He took fifty-four Americans and me prisoners and put us in the Calaboose. I stayed locked up three days when on the third day Woll sent an interpreter named Martínez to bring me to his presence. He said, "You are Antonio Menchaca, the greatest traitor to your flag unhung, and you deserve to be shot twenty-five times through the head. But General Santa Anna, who thanks you for the kindness you did him, asked me if I captured you to spare your life, which I will do on one condition and that is that you will give me

65. Seguin had been founded as Walnut Springs in summer 1838, but the name was changed to honor the Tejano war hero early in 1839. Most of the first residents were rangers, and it proved a popular place for rangers and volunteers to rendezvous.

66. Vásquez withdrew after two days.

67. Either Menchaca's memory failed him or his collaborator misunderstood Menchaca in reference to Adrián Woll's name. In the manuscript he is referred to throughout as "Adrián Bull," hence the pun "bully" boy and the joke about taking him by the horns. This play on words does not work in Spanish, which is the language they would have been speaking, and constitutes further evidence of the collaborator's interference in the creation of the narrative. It would have been easy enough for Menchaca to confuse *Woll* and *bull* in English, but there is no way to confuse the Spanish *toro* with *Woll*.

your word of honor never again to take up arms against Mexico." I agreed to comply with his condition, and he then told me I was free.[68]

He then said he contemplated sending the other fifty-four prisoners to Mexico and asked me if I thought they would be able to walk there. I said they were most of them dear friends of mine and all of them good people, and it would hurt me very much to see them have to walk all of the way to Mexico. I told him he did not have to walk from Fort Bend to San Jacinto, and I thought if the prisoners had to go to Mexico they had better be sent on horseback or in wagons and not be made to foot it.

At the end of a week he sent Martínez again to my house saying that he wanted to see me. When I came to his quarters he offered me a seat, which I took, and then he asked me if I still remembered his sparing my life. I told him I did. He said, "Now tell me candidly, if you think I am running any risk by staying in San Antonio?" I told him that he had now been in San Antonio ten days and in three or four days more he would have to fight if he stayed. He asked me how I knew this and why I thought so. I said, "General Vásquez came here and was in quiet possession of the town for twelve days, but at the end of the twelfth he had to fly as fast as his legs could carry him back to Mexico. And I expect it would be very prudent for you to begin to think about following his illustrious example."[69] He asked me if I could not be mistaken in my opinions. I told him perhaps I could be mistaken, but my belief was very firm that it would not be very long before the brave "Bull" would run from the cowboys who would be trying to pen him. Woll said, "Can I rely on your word, Menchaca?" I told him that other people relied on it, and it might be very wise in him to do so in time. He then said, "I will give you a passport through my lines, pickets, and guards or into my quarters to pass you any hour, day or night, and if

---

68. According to Nance, Menchaca was one of several individuals released, in his case as a result of having been "lamed by a stone detached by a cannon ball and he, too was released on the 14th, being unable to travel" (*Attack and Counter-Attack*, 323n84). Aside from any exaggeration, there is no doubt of Menchaca's participation in the brief defense of the city. Anderson Hutchinson, justice of the fourth judicial district, who was holding court in San Antonio, wrote a diary of the events, reporting that when the skirmish began between the defenders and the Mexican army, "at this moment Manshaca [*sic*], who was the only Mexican in our company, cried out that our d——d Mexican friends had retreated" (E. W. Winkler, ed., "The Bexar and Dawson Prisoners," 292). Menchaca was referring to a company of Tejanos that received special consideration from Woll after the Texans' surrender.

69. As noted above, Vásquez remained in San Antonio only two days, not twelve.

you learn anything of importance, please come and inform me." I assented, took the passport, and left his presence.

On the fifteenth day after Woll's arrival in San Antonio, a Mexican named Brunovisso[70] came into town from the San José Mission and came to my house and inquired for me. He told me that on his way to town he was stopped by Colonel John Coffee Hays and two of his men, who caught his bridle rein just as he was on the point of fording the river and led his horse into the timber thicket at the side of the ford. They asked him if I was alive and in town. Brunovisso said he believed so, as I was seen the week before. Hays then told Brunovisso he would let him go on provided he promised as soon as he got into town to tell me to go out to him as he wanted me to see him tell General Woll good morning with his rifles next morning.

I went and communicated all this to Woll and told him that if he was going to leave town he had the best opportunity he ever would have of leaving. He said, "Can I rely on this information as being true?" (He was a very suspicious Frenchman.)

And I said, "If you wait until tomorrow morning you will find out whether Colonel Hays will greet you or not." I then left Woll and went back to my house.

Sure enough, next morning early ten or fifteen rangers, with red shirts, rode into town by the Alamo Street.[71] Then a corps of 250 dragoons quartered in the Alamo who saw them blew their bugle to get ready to attack them. At the same time Woll, who was with his infantry in the plazas, gave orders for them to form, and he marched them with his dragoons towards the Salado.

There "Woll's Ball" began, and a hot fight ensued. Woll sent sixty men to the front to commence the attack and they were every last one killed by Hays's men. About this time fifty Americans under a Texan captain, Nicholas Mosby Dawson, came up to join the main body of Hays's command, but they with their leader were all cut off and killed by the dragoons, who surrounded them, outflanked them, and cut them to pieces.[72] Woll

70. This is not a typical Spanish name and is most likely the collaborator's effort to phonetically spell what he heard from Menchaca.

71. Except for his role in it, Menchaca's account of events is generally accurate. Hays did capture a "Mexican" and he did send spies into town. The Texan commander in the area, Matthew "Paint" Caldwell, did ask Hays to enter San Antonio with his company in order to draw out the Mexican army. On the morning of the eighteenth, Hays and six of his men did ride as far as the Alamo to taunt the Mexicans.

72. This is the episode commonly referred to as the "Dawson Massacre," although

stubbornly fought all day long, losing his men like sheep and gaining no advantage over Hays. At four o'clock he began to send his wounded, who were very numerous, into San Antonio, and at dark he commenced to retreat with the survivors of his army to San Antonio.

Next day he made preparations about evacuating. He sent for me and had further conversation in relation to the American prisoners. He said he had heard that the thirteen lawyers and private citizens were gentlemen but that the remainder were vagabonds and thieves. I told him I believed them all to be gentlemen. He then said they should all in that case be permitted to ride when taken to Mexico. The prisoners gave me a letter to take to Colonel Hays, which said they were treated well by Woll and if he fell in with any of his men asking that they be treated well. I got a horse from a merchant of this place, a Mr. William B. Jacques,[73] and I took the letter to Hays, who was then on the Salado with his men. He was much rejoiced to see me alive and well, and Hays then read his letter.[74] He next moved his men to the San Pedro Springs and waited there for Woll to evacuate, which he did at three o'clock in the morning.

For several days Hays permitted no one but me and one of his young men named Clay Davis[75] to go into town. Recruits now began to pour into Hays's army, and at the end of three days after they first camped at the San

---

the available record indicates that it was a conventional action in which approximately the same number of Mexicans and Texans were killed and in which fifteen Texans were taken prisoner. Nance refers to it as the "Dawson Fight" (*Attack and Counter-Attack,* 364–374).

73. Originally from New Jersey, William B. Jacques had lived in Mexico City before coming to Texas in 1837. He settled in San Antonio, where he represented the firm of Jacques and Browning.

74. The prisoners had been led out of San Antonio on the fourteenth and had begun their march toward the Rio Grande the following day, five days before Woll withdrew from San Antonio. It is true that the prisoners drafted a letter immediately after their capture describing the events and the fair treatment they had received, but Menchaca could not have delivered it to Hays as he was still a prisoner. On the fourteenth Woll had the prisoners sign a statement exonerating the local Tejano population of any blame, but this document does not match Menchaca's description of the document delivered to Hays.

75. Henry Clay Davis had been at the Council House Fight and later participated in the Mier Expedition, which he abandoned after it reached the Rio Grande. He is credited by some with founding Rio Grande City. There is no evidence that anyone was kept out of town once the Mexican army withdrew.

Pedro Springs he had 2,500 in his ranks. A court-martial was now called by Hays and his officers.[76]

GENERAL ANTONIO MENCHACA, COMMANDER IN CHIEF OF THE ARMY OF THE REPUBLIC OF TEXAS

While this court-martial was in session, five members of a committee sent by the court rode up to my door, and the chairman handed me a commission that gave me the rank and title of Chief Commander of the Texas forces.[77] I was full of gratitude, and it hurt me this time to be forced to decline the honors that had been given to me unsought for. I, however, bade the chairman take back the commission to the court, give it my heartfelt thanks and deep regrets, and tell the members of the tribunal that my only reason for declining was that I had given my parole of honor never more to take up arms against Mexico; that this parole was given to General Woll on the condition that he would spare my life, and I could not violate it.

The Texas army was for some time without a chief commander, and before they had elected one they followed Woll, who had retreated slowly, and attacked him. But their attack was ineffectual inasmuch as there was but little discipline or harmony of action in the engagement and the Texans had to fall back after killing a few of Woll's men and losing some of their own. They came here on a retreat, leaving the enemy himself retreating in the opposite direction.[78]

After the return of the Texans to San Antonio, General Burleson came

76. As noted above, Matthew Caldwell was in overall command of Texan forces, not Hays. Nance states that the number of volunteers who gathered in San Antonio after the Texans gave up their pursuit of the Mexicans was in the hundreds. There is no evidence of a court-martial or council prior to a meeting held on 25 September under the auspices of Vice President Burleson, who had arrived in San Antonio on the previous day.

77. It is interesting that it was at this otherwise undocumented "court-martial," which was held prior to the council of the twenty-fifth, that Menchaca was supposedly elected commander of Texan forces. On 3 October 1842 President Houston appointed Alexander Somervell to command the western forces and organize an expedition against Woll.

78. The Texans were not without a commander during the initial pursuit of Woll. As stated above, Matthew Caldwell was in command of Texas forces until his return to San Antonio after breaking off pursuit of Woll. Vice President Burleson, who was a general and had been on an Indian campaign when he got news of Woll's invasion, appears to have assumed temporary command.

in and they then called a court-martial, which was composed of some of the officers besides General Burleson and some civilians, among them me and Messrs. Barnes (already mentioned) and Terrell[79] and two attorneys. We were members of the court by invitation from General Burleson, who courteously requested us to participate in the deliberations of the court.

"SHALL WE BURN SAN ANTONIO?"

The main question that was under discussion was what should we do with San Antonio? It was so far from other cities of the Republic of Texas that it was then a perfect hotbed of Mexican spies and always the point first attacked and easiest captured by the Mexicans. These serious drawbacks were all exhausted by Colonel George W. Terrell,[80] the attorney of Eastern Texas, who strongly advocated burning the town, and he was the first to address the court. He said that the families who lived here could be permitted to go to other cities of Texas or to Mexico, those who preferred the latter government.

General Burleson, after Terrell finished, introduced me to the court as a man in whose opinion he had as much confidence as in the opinion of any general in his army and requested me to present my views to the court. I said I did not like to speak English for fear of making them laugh at my pronunciation, and I asked Barnes to interpret for me while I spoke in Castilian. I made them a short speech bitterly opposing the sacrifice of San Antonio to the flames. I said I had an aged mother here who would be among the people who would be left destitute by the burning of the town and I said that for myself I did not care so much. I moreover asked, if San Antonio was burned, who would give the money to support the people who would be left penniless paupers, until they could go somewhere else and earn a livelihood? There were too a great many old people here who could not well be moved.

Barnes then slipped a little note in my hand asking me to give way

79. As noted above, there is no mention of a Barnes in the available records, but the attorney named Barnes that Menchaca mentions in this passage is not the Charles Merritt Barnes to whom, according to Chabot, he dictated the reminiscences, who was not yet born when these events occurred. With regard to Terrell, see the following note.

80. Possibly George Whitfield Terrell, who was attorney general at the time. There is no record of his having held a military rank, however. Menchaca's is the only mention in the records of Terrell in connection with the Woll episode.

to him and let him make a speech in behalf of saving San Antonio, and I gratified his request. Barnes was a beautiful speaker and a much more eloquent man than I, and at the conclusion of his warm and impetuous speech there was not a dry eye except his own on the whole court. When General Burleson took the vote on the question, San Antonio was saved!

THE MEXICAN WAR WITH THE
UNITED STATES COMMENCES

It was sometime in April 1845 when Colonel William Selby Harney left San Antonio with 400 cavalry to meet the U.S. general Zachary Taylor (old Zach) at Corpus Christi, where he was with 1,500 regular U.S. troops that he had brought from New Orleans by sea. Taylor, however, intending to push on into Mexico, ordered Harney not to come to Corpus Christi but to march his cavalry via Presidio del Río Grande and join him somewhere close to Monterrey.[81]

Taylor won a victorious battle at a lane near Matamoros called Point Isabel, in which he entirely destroyed the command of the Mexican Rómulo Díaz de la Vega and captured him.[82]

Taylor passed on to Monterrey and here was joined by Harney, who came with his cavalry from San Antonio. Soon after, the Mexican campaign opened in earnest and all of the battles, described already in the his-

81. U.S. troops entered Texas with the permission of the Republic and under orders from President James K. Polk before annexation in summer 1845. General Zachary Taylor made camp at Corpus Christi while Harney's old unit, the Second Dragoons, was stationed at San Antonio. Because he had been relieved of command at a court-martial, Harney did not rejoin his unit until the beginning of 1846. Harney never tried to go to Corpus Christi, and without orders from Taylor he struck out for Presidio del Río Grande with 600 troops composed of his dragoons, militia, and Indian scouts in July 1846. He changed his mind and returned in August to San Antonio, where General John E. Wool was already organizing his ultimately unsuccessful expedition into Chihuahua. In late September 1846 Harney headed Wool's vanguard as he retraced his July route to the Rio Grande.

82. There were two battles fought on 8–9 May 1846 just north of the Rio Grande opposite Matamoros, the battles of Palo Alto and Resaca de la Palma. Overall Mexican command at both was in the hands of General Mariano Arista. Díaz de la Vega, a brevet brigadier general, was in command of an artillery battery at the time he was captured during the Resaca de la Palma action.

tory which is written of the Mexican War, were fought; among the most bloody of all was Buena Vista.[83]

In 1816 some laboring men were plowing in a field that is now the site of the Vance Hotel, kept by Captain William G. Tobin and owned by the Vance brothers,[84] and these laborers were fired on by the Indians and six were killed. I believe there were sixteen Indians who made the attack. From that time to the present the city has grown in size, wealth, and prosperity. The lot of about 300 yards long by 100 wide, which is on the Main Street, and which formerly sold in 1808 in the time of Governor Cordero for $60, could not today be bought for $60,000.[85]

A HISTORY OF THE SETTLEMENT
AND INHABITANTS OF SAN ANTONIO

The first settlers who came here were sixteen families of Spanish descendants from the Canary Isles who reached here in 1735. Among them was

83. After Wool found it impossible to penetrate the mountains dividing Coahuila from Chihuahua, Harney received permission to join Taylor's forces, thus bringing Harney to Monterrey. However, soon after General Winfield Scott's arrival at Brazos Santiago, at the mouth of the Rio Grande, Harney's regiment was reassigned to his command and Harney was not at the battle of Buena Vista. Known in Mexico as Angostura, *Buena Vista* was the name of a nearby hacienda, but the battle took place at a narrow pass through the mountains, hence *Angostura*.

84. William Vance and brothers John and James came to Texas with Zachary Taylor at the outbreak of the War with Mexico. After the war, they settled permanently in San Antonio, where they built and operated a mercantile store and the first army barracks and headquarters for the U.S. Army. In 1872 the Vances with William G. Tobin converted the headquarters building into a hotel called Vance House at the site now occupied by the Sheraton Gunther Hotel on North St. Mary's Street. Tobin, who had come to San Antonio before the Civil War, served as city marshal and army volunteer in the late 1850s and then as a captain in the Confederate Army. He should be considered an early promoter of Tex-Mex food, having contracted with the U.S. Army to supply it and the navy with canned chili con carne just before his death in 1881.

85. This orphan paragraph may represent a random thought of Menchaca's that served to lead into the material that follows, since it is a reflection on how much San Antonio had changed between Menchaca's youth and his last years.

my great-grandfather, Don Pedro Ocón y Trillo, and old Captain Menchaca and his wife. My great-grandfather had a grant for all of the land for his colony to settle given to him by Baron de Pegnia Flora, the representative of the king of Spain, and they chose this part of the country to locate. They had with them the following other families of Castilian descent, viz: the Arochas, Delgados, Granadoses, Galváns, Traviesos, Rodríguezes, Fernándezes, Leals, Casanovas, Cepedas, Courbieres, Calvillos, and Saucedos.[86]

They camped on the west side of the San Pedro River in that portion of San Antonio facetiously called "Chihuahua" and were joined by the following mentioned families who shortly thereafter came in from Mexico, viz: Pérezes, Floreses, Garcias, Cárdenases, Gonzálezes, Monteses, Sambranos, and Silvas. They intended to commence building the town there. The Indians who lived in the holes and on the rocky bluff on the banks of the San Antonio River near its head, where the large rock quarries where most of the rock used for building purposes is now obtained for the construction of houses in San Antonio, were very troublesome, however, and continually harassed them so that they were compelled to move on the eastern side of the San Pedro between that stream and the San Antonio River.[87]

86. This paragraph contains a number of inaccuracies. The sixteen Canary Islander families arrived in San Antonio in 1731. Although they came with the official recognition *primeros pobladores* (first settlers), they were not the first Hispanic inhabitants of San Antonio. The settlement had been founded in 1718 by Governor Martín Alarcón. Neither Pedro Ocón y Trillo nor Captain Menchaca and his wife were Antonio's ancestors, nor were they Canary Islanders. Moreover, no one ever received a grant for a colony during the eighteenth century. While the Arocha, Delgado, Granados, Travieso, Rodríguez, and Leal families were Canary Islanders, the Galván, Fernández, Casanova, Zepeda, Courbiere, Calvillo, and Saucedo families were not. Although it contains errors, the best published genealogical reference on San Antonio remains Chabot's *With the Makers of San Antonio*, where entries for all these families may be found, with the exception of the Fernándezes.

87. This is a confused retelling of the origins of the civilian settlement. When the Canary Islanders arrived at Presidio de Béxar, the Indians in the vicinity either had been incorporated into one of the missions or had fled the area. The commander, Juan Antonio Pérez de Almazán, judged the countryside too dangerous to allow the *Isleños* to establish a separate settlement because of Lipan Apache raiders. He had the Islanders housed among the presidio population and after a few months laid out and distributed the lands in the area of the Main Plaza, east of San Pedro Creek.

THE FIRST HOUSE BUILT IN SAN ANTONIO

These colonists commenced building then like beavers, making adobe houses. The schoolmaster, whose name I cannot recollect, succeeded in finishing his house, which is a house still standing on what is now the northern extension of Flores Street about 400 yards north of the Military Plaza. At the present time of writing it is occupied by Madam Antonia Cárdenas, a lady very nearly of my own age (a little over seventy-six years).

The Mexican and Canary settlers next laid off the Military and Main Plazas and built around them. Old Captain Menchaca's house is also standing and is situated on the corner of Flores and Rio Grande Streets[88] and is occupied by Mariano Rodríguez. On the northeast corner of the same streets, directly opposite old Captain Menchaca's house, on the east was old Angel Navarro's house. Angel Navarro was the father of young José Antonio Navarro, who became a colonel in the service of the Army of the Texas Republic.[89] Next to Menchaca on the westward lived Martianna Jaimes. Adjoining her place westward was Ignacio Lucero's place, which is owned by T. T. Tell, the attorney. Still next was the residence of José Manchaca, who was sent by Salcedo prisoner to Mexico and died in Chihuahua in prison at the end of ten years' confinement.[90] Jacob Lane Esq. now owns his property and also that adjoining it on the west, where Manuel Núñez's place was. Next to Núñez's place and where the Catholic padres are now domiciled, opposite the old courthouse and jail, on the north side of the Military Plaza, was Francisco Arocha's place.[91]

I will now take the western side of the Military Plaza in rotation. On the northwest corner, just in the rear of the city jail, now stands the old house of Salvador Rodríguez, which is at present owned by the heirs of the late Ignacio Pérez. Just to his right, on the south, was the residence of Luis Menchaca, old Captain Félix Menchaca's brother and also a brother

88. This is now the intersection of North Flores and Commerce Streets.

89. José Antonio Navarro was a civilian participant in the Texas Revolution, being one of two Texas-born signers of the Declaration of Independence. Made lame by a fall from horseback as an adolescent, he never participated in military activities. *Colonel* was a common honorific in the nineteenth century, and he was so referred to in a newspaper editorial of 6 March 1845 in regard to his imprisonment in Mexico as a member of the Texan Santa Fe Expedition.

90. See *Edited Reminiscences, Part 1*, n. 9 (p. 43).

91. This is a description of West Commerce between North Flores and Cameron (originally Camarón) Streets.

of Don José Menchaca.[92] Right next to him lived old José Flores de Abrego. Ignacio de los Santos lived next to him on the southwest corner of the Military Plaza.

I now take up the south side of the Military Plaza. On the west, opposite de los Santos, where the *monte pio* shop[93] is, was Romillio Pérez's place. Next to him lived Plácido Hernández. Old Don Pedro Travieso lived next door to him, and next to him on the southeast corner of the Military Plaza lived Francisco Travieso.

Opposite him, on the east side of Flores, at the corner of Ruiz Street,[94] was the property of Don Pedro Flores, whose heirs now own the property. Adjoining Flores on Ruiz Street, Vicente Cabrera owned the locality that is now occupied by the office of the San Antonio [text missing] and bounded on the east by the ditch which runs along the west side of the Main Plaza.[95] Adjoining on his right hand was Manuel Salinas. Next to Salinas, and where the Central Hotel kept by Mr. Baker stands, was old Clemente Delgado's residence. Next to him on the south side of the Main Plaza lived Tomás Delgado.

Where the livery stable next to Baker's Central Hotel is situated is the old site of Bartolo Seguín's residence, who was the great grandfather of my Captain Seguín, so often before mentioned in connection with the Texas service and the campaign against Santa Anna. Next to old Seguín lived Patricio Rodríguez, whose place formed the southeast corner of the Main Plaza. Where French's large stone building stood and the present U.S. Army headquarters of this division stands was the property of Francisco Rodríguez.[96]

We now take up the places opposite the Main Plaza on the eastern side. Opposite Francisco Rodríguez on the northeast corner of Ruiz and Soledad Streets[97] was the property of Francisco Charis extending to the next corner

92. The northwest corner of the Military Plaza was owned originally by the Urrutia family, which built what came to be known as the Spanish Governor's Palace. Luis Menchaca acquired the property through his mother, Antonia Urrutia, daughter of Joseph Urrutia, the presidio commander who built the house in the 1740s. José Menchaca, Luis's son, sold the property to Ignacio Pérez.

93. A *monte pio* shop is a pawn shop.

94. Ruiz Street is now Dolorosa Street.

95. Menchaca here refers to the Acequia Madre, the city's first irrigation ditch, excavation of which began shortly after the settlement's founding in 1718.

96. Because of changes to the area, what Menchaca describes here is no longer on the Main Plaza but slightly to the south, at the corner of Kallison Walk and Dwyer Street.

97. As above, the area to which Menchaca refers here is between Dolorosa and Market Streets, just below where the Main Plaza begins today.

or to Calavasa (now Market) Street. On the northeast corner of Calavasa and Soledad Streets stood the old Spanish Calaboose, or prison. Next to the Calaboose or Soledad Street, where Willie Adams, the government transfer contractor has his office, was the old "Corporation House." Next on the right stood the Governor's Mansion, the residence of all the old Spanish governors.[98] (The first whom I recollect to have seen was old Don Antonio Cordero, the first one mentioned in my narrative.) Next to the Governor's Mansion, at the southeast corner of Commerce (Main) and Soledad Streets, was the residence of the family of Granados. Directly opposite them, on the northeast corner of Commerce and Soledad Streets, was the property of old Manuel Barrera, which is now owned by Mr. Samuel Maverick and occupied as a clothing store by some Israelites.[99]

Now we come to the north side of the Main Plaza. On the northwest corner of Commerce and Soledad, where Jack Harris's barroom is, stood the residence of Don Tomás Arocha. The property is now jointly owned, I believe, by Messrs. Sweet and Sam Smith. Next to the corner was Vicente Travieso's property, now owned by Mrs. Elliott. Next to Travieso lived Don Simón Arocha, a very wealthy and influential citizen of the old first community of San Antonio who owned the remainder of the property facing the Main Plaza on the north, including the northeast corner of Main and Acequia Streets.[100] Opposite, on the west on the northwest corner of Main (Commerce or Rio Grande) and Acequia Street, which is also now owned by Mr. Maverick, stood the residence of Remundo Díaz. Next to Díaz to the westward of Rio Grande Street stood Fragosa Galván's premises, and next to him Antonio Navarro, who lived next to his father, Angel Navarro, whose residence has already been mentioned.

We now take the west side of Main Plaza. On the northwest corner of the plaza was the place of Don Francisco Barrera. His place is now owned

98. In Spanish, *calabozo* is the term from which *calaboose* derives. The Spanish colonial jail was part of the complex of buildings referred to as the *Casas Reales* (government buildings) that occupied the east side of the Main Plaza and that Menchaca refers to as the "Corporation House." Because by law the governor could reside in the Casas Reales in the absence of a separate residence, Governor Barón de Ripperdá, the first to have his official residence in San Antonio, began the custom of using the building as his residence.

99. That is, Jews.

100. The Travieso and Arocha families were related through marriage to the Curbelo family, all from the Canary Islands. Travieso, who was one of the original *Isleño* settlers, was named constable for life, and Simón de Arocha, a nephew, served as lieutenant governor and militia commander for a number of years.

by an aged Mexican widow, Doña Trinidad Soto. Next to him and where the Auction Mart of Mr. Frost is located, and already mentioned and the identical spot where David Crockett met James Bowie when he first came into San Antonio from Tennessee, was Don Toribio Fuentes's domicile. In the rear of these two properties and comprising the property in that locality at present owned by Mr. F. Guilbeau was the property then owned by Señora Tia Chonita. Next is the Catholic church, which will be hereafter more fully described. Opposite the south side of the church, on the corner of the small street and facing the Main Plaza and extending to a depth of about one quarter of the square opposite to the south side of the church was the property of Francisco Galán. Next to him, and where the "Plaza House" kept by Eugene Dietrich Esq. stands, lived old Don Ignacio Flores, who owned the whole square (with the exception of Galán's corner), facing the Main Plaza on Acequia Street next to Galán's, facing Ruiz Street, facing Military Plaza on Flores Street and the Catholic church on the little street on its south.

Mr. Juan Martín Veramendi, the former governor of the state of Coahuila and who became the father-in-law of the celebrated hero of the Alamo, James Bowie, had a residence in San Antonio situated on Soledad Street immediately opposite the post office, which was the house that is now used as a confectionary, and which very recently caught fire and was slightly damaged on the inside.[101]

Houston Street, where the iron bridge that now spans the San Antonio, and running in front of Sappington's stable, was not at that time laid out and is to me a modern street. Next to Veramendi and up to where Houston Street now crosses Soledad was Don Francisco Amangual. Adjoining him was the property of the lady Yficiaca Rodríguez. Beyond her, and where the property I now live in is situated, and where the old mill in its rear on the riverbank formerly stood, and where Bowie gave his grand ball on the eve of receiving the fatal tidings of Santa Anna's approach, stood the residence of Marcos Cepeda.

Where the livery stable is, on the same side of the street as the post office, and opposite diagonally to the northwest of where the new courthouse on Soledad Street is located was Manuel Delgado's place. On the northeast

101. The Veramendi "Palace" stood on the east side of Soledad Street near the corner of Houston Street. At the time it was built by Fernando Veramendi (Juan Martín's father) in the 1770s, it was the most elaborate house in town. After Menchaca's time, part of it served as law offices as well as a saloon and curiosities museum.

corner of Acequia and (new) Houston Streets was the residence of Francisco Casanova. Next to him, and including the corner of Obraje Street, was the property of the widow of Don Antonio Galván. Don Pedro Zambrano owned the property adjoining Angel Navarro on Flores Street extending from next to the northeast corner of Rio Grande and Flores Streets up to where the church now built on the corner of Houston and Flores Streets stands. Beyond and adjoining him to the north on Flores Street was Don Mariano Rodríguez. Opposite and adjoining Félix Menchaca's place lived Manuel Berbán, and next to Berbán lived Francisco Montes.

On Main Street, where the banking house of John Twohig Esq. stands, was the residence of Old Antonio Baca, who died of a sunstroke while on the road to La Bahía during the time of the difficulties and hostilities that were going on between Salcedo and Menchaca and Gutiérrez de Lara in 1812.

Waccine Lealles [possibly Joaquín Leal Goraz] owned the whole property fronting on Alamo Street, Alameda Street, or the Powder House Road facing the Menger Hotel, and facing Bowie Street. Some of this property is now owned by our fellow citizen Louis Edward Grenet Esq.

I have now mentioned the names and localities of all the prominent and influential citizens of San Antonio that I can recollect at present, and I will now say something about the old Catholic Spanish missions, which are such prominent historical landmarks that all who take an interest in historical topics and the sites of celebrated historical landmarks should pay them all a visit and study their history closely. I am only able to give a meager and brief general outline and sketch of their history, but I suppose the Catholic Father Superior here could furnish all of the details necessary to any who desire to be fully informed in regard to their history.

THE MISSIONS AND CHURCHES

My parents and the old citizens who were here during my boyhood have informed me that the missions were all of them built by the Indian Christian converts under the immediate supervision of the priests (missionaries who came here to convert and civilize them). The Catholic church in the city facing Main Plaza was built in the years 1745 and 1746, having been completed in the latter and commenced in the former year. It was then called the church of San Fernando de Austria. All but that old wall still standing, in the rear where the altar and sacristy is, was burned accidentally by a boy on 14 November 1828, and repairs were commenced on it in 1829 and they were finished in 1830. In the year 1873 it was enlarged considerably, and now its dimensions are much greater than formerly.[102]

The Alamo

The property of the present site of the Alamo and the buildings connected with it formerly belonged to two brothers named Alejandro and Vicente Gortari, who either presented or sold it to the Catholic missionaries (the former more likely). It was built several years after the church on the plaza, during 1750 or 1760, and used as a missionary church for the conversion of the Indians until it was occupied by the Mexicans in 1835, just the preceding year to the time when the Texans used it. Bowie, Crockett, and Travis used it for their barracks until they were massacred there in March 1836.[103]

After it became the scene of this horrible massacre no one used it for any purpose whatever and it was a shrine and visited only with a sort of dread by all until 1847, when the U.S. government procured it from the Catholic Church as a storehouse and quartermaster department and has been used as such ever since up to the present time. It was first called the Mission of San Antonio Valero, but both it and the other church on the plaza were called San Antonio de Béxar.[104]

102. What is now San Fernando Cathedral was begun in 1738. Principal construction was completed in 1755, when the church was dedicated. In the 1860s reconstruction of the nave in French Gothic style began; this work was completed in 1873, one year before the church was elevated to the status of cathedral with the creation of the Diocese of San Antonio. See *Edited Reminiscences, Part 1*, n. 1 (p. 41).

103. San Antonio de Valero was the first constructed of the five Franciscan missions of San Antonio that survive in various states of repair and use. Founded in 1718, it was relocated three times before settling into its present location in 1727. Menchaca's confusion about owner and construction is understandable. The chapel referred to as the Alamo today was begun in 1750 but was never completed. Hence, its construction dates to a few years after San Fernando Cathedral's. In 1793 the mission was decommissioned and its property distributed among the remaining Indians, some of the townspeople, and refugees from the abandoned post of Los Adaes. In 1803 the convent and chapel were occupied by a light cavalry company from San Carlos del Alamo de Parras, thus providing the name by which the mission is known today. In December 1835 General Martín Perfecto de Cos surrendered to the Texans at the Alamo, which was subsequently reinforced by the Texans and defended during Santa Anna's siege and assault of 1836.

104. After Texas independence the names of the various entities that had made up

The Concepción Mission was built in 1766, the San Juan in 1765, the Espada in 1769, and the San José in 1771.[105] The three first mentioned were first built without devoting as much care, time, or labor to their construction as the last. They are all made in a marvelously solid and substantial manner when you consider the qualifications of the builders, who were Indians who never knew what it was to build a house of any character before and who either lived in caves in the rock or in the open air without any shelter save the friendly shade of a neighboring oak tree.[106]

The capital of these missions was the last (San José). It seems that the missionaries succeeded in converting a very powerful chief and his tribe to Christianity and he took up his residence with them at the San José Mission as the ruler of the whole tribe and the five missions, namely, Alamo, Concepción, San Juan, Espada, and San José. I was told that he dressed as gorgeously as a peacock, with gold and silver all over him, and that he wore an *admiral's* hat and a Spanish red *capa*, or cape, and cloak. He was very celebrated among his tribe as a great man, and a mighty ruler, and was esteemed, feared, and respected by them, and he made them very useful

the Spanish and Mexican jurisdiction of Béxar underwent some changes. Mission San Antonio de Valero, which was fully incorporated into the city, came to be known as the Alamo, as it is today. The city changed its name from San Fernando de Béxar to San Antonio, while the county created by the Republic was named Bexar County (no accent mark). What Menchaca might be referring to when he says that the mission church and the one on the plaza "were called San Antonio de Béxar" is that both were part of the city of San Antonio. After Menchaca's death, in 1883 the State of Texas purchased the Alamo chapel building and presented it to the city for preservation. In 1905, after acquiring the remaining mission buildings, the state transferred custody of the site to the Daughters of the Republic of Texas, and in 2011 the state legislature turned oversight of the site over to the Texas General Land Office, which manages it in collaboration with the Daughters of the Republic of Texas.

105. Menchaca's dates correspond roughly with the actual dates of construction for the church structures. Although Mission San José was founded in 1720, and Concepción, San Juan Capistrano, and San Francisco de la Espada were all founded in 1731, their church buildings date from fifteen to sixty years later.

106. While neophytes (Indians in the process of conversion) may have provided the labor, the planning and direction of construction were in the hands of artisans brought in for the task from central parts of Mexico. San José had a decade's head start on Concepción, Capistrano, and Espada, having been founded in 1720. It also had both a better location and more concerted attention, as it was the only College of Zacatecas mission among the five until 1772, when all the existing Querétaro missions were turned over to the College of Zacatecas.

building missions and doing other light work of a similar character whenever he required it.[107]

How long this civilization and Christianity in the tribe lasted is a matter of history that I am unable to delineate. But as the successors of this tribe did not evince much of either, I fear that like in almost all other instances the efforts to Christianize and civilize "Lo the poor Indian" was a complete failure.[108]

The Alameda

Cordero, the first governor alluded to in this narrative as having cleared away the timber from the river to the Powder House Hill, in cutting the timber out by the property owned by Leal found a great many alamedas or cottonwood trees and hence the street got its name, Alameda, or the street of cottonwood trees. The Alamo also derived its name from the same source.[109]

Out beyond Leal's place on the right-hand side of the Alameda Road, the old Spanish governors used to have a sort of park where they went and attended fandangos and other dances, and this Alameda park became a very popular public resort for amusement, especially on Sunday, long before the park was made at the Springs at the head of the San Pedro, which is a modern resort very popular just at present.

The First Buffaloes Ever Sent to Europe Are Sent from San Antonio

One of the old Spanish ancestors, a settler from the Canary Islands,[110] when he came here captured some buffaloes, which were then very plentiful and

107. There is no evidence for any aspect of this story.

108. As in various other passages, here Menchaca reflects the generally condescending and derogatory view of the native peoples among his contemporaries.

109. *Alameda* means tree-lined boulevard, promenade, or walk, more specifically one lined with poplars or cottonwoods, both of which are called *álamo*. The powder house was actually built during Governor Manuel Muñoz's tenure. It was located near the intersection of what is now East Commerce and Monumental Streets. As noted earlier, San Antonio de Valero's nickname of "Alamo" came into use after the Alamo de Parras cavalry company took up residence there in 1803.

110. The individual in question was José Antonio Curbelo, son of Joseph Curbelo, who came to Texas from the Canary Islands with his parents, Juan Curbelo and Gracia Prudhome y Umpierre. In 1780, Governor Domingo Cabello assigned the task of getting the buffaloes to Spain to Curbelo, who had previously demonstrated his compe-

ranged in large herds around San Antonio. He took them over to Spain in the year 1760[111] and presented them to the king of Spain, who was much pleased with the interesting and odd present.

The monarch, to show his appreciation of the gift, asked Curbelo to name the reward he desired, but the latter was too modest to request anything beyond enough money to pay his passage back to San Antonio from the European continent and would not have asked that unless he had spent all of his means in taking the present to his sovereign. The king granted his moderate request and conferred on him also the rank of a lieutenant in the Spanish army and gave him his commission. Curbelo returned to San Antonio and gave up his hunting proclivities and became an industrious citizen.

An Old Legend

It was related to me in my youth as a very old legend[112] at that time that many years before, a missionary padre named Margil, with a small band of Christians, was crossing the plains and vast prairies between Nacogdoches and San Antonio, which at that time were completely filled with bands of hostile and nefarious Indians. One day the illustrious padre and his followers were resting in the afternoon of a very sultry day under a friendly and also shady oak when one of his adherents exclaimed, "See, Padre! We shall all be killed; there is a large band of savages coming to murder us!" The venerable padre raised his eye and looked and said, "My brother, I see nothing but a herd of peaceable deer grazing on the Plain." And Lo! Wonderful to behold! In the twinkling of a bedpost the savages were transmogrified into deer.

---

tence in public service. Curbelo managed to deliver two animals alive, which resulted in his receipt of a commission as a lieutenant of cavalry and generous travel stipends to get him and two assistants back to Texas. They did not make it back until 1785. The buffalo story can be found in various documents in the Bexar Archives at the University of Texas at Austin, including several references that mention José Antonio Curbelo as the individual charged by Governor Domingo Cabello to take buffaloes to the king. See, e.g., "Estado de la fuerza," 31 January 1783. A somewhat inaccurate representation of the story is found in Frederick C. Chabot, *With the Makers of San Antonio*, 155.

111. Collection of the animals began in 1779, and Curbelo did not deliver them to the king until sometime between 1781 and 1784.

112. A more literary version of this legend appears in Wright, *San Antonio de Béxar*, 127–128. See also Adina de Zavala, *History and Legends of the Alamo and Other Missions in and around San Antonio*, 145.

Another Legend

It is also said, either of the same or another padre, that he also with his band of pilgrims had been for several days traveling without any water to drink and they were very nearly perishing of thirst when they came to a grapevine that grew on the spot where the headspring of the San Marcos River is located (which, however, was not a river at that time).[113] They commenced to eat the grapes that grew on it and they then said their prayers. When the padre pulled up the grapevine by the roots, out burst the water from the base of the hill, and that was the origin of the river.

Mollie Moore,[114] the Texas poetess who was born on the banks of that beautiful stream near its romantic head, forgot in her beautiful poem describing it to insert this legend or was ignorant of it. Had she done so, in her sublime verse the poem would have been much more charming than it is.

113. Barnes, in *Combats and Conquests of Immortal Heroes*, 76–78, provides an extensive version of this story, but with the major difference that it is in regard to the San Antonio and not the San Marcos River. Barnes claims that Menchaca told him the story with regard to the San Antonio in 1875. In Wright, *San Antonio de Béxar*, 119–122, this legend is tied to the head of the San Antonio River. For further details see J. Frank Dobie, ed., *Legends of Texas*, 204, ed. note.

114. In fact, she was born in Alabama in either 1847 or 1852 and with her family moved to Texas as a young girl. She spent part of her childhood on her father's property on the San Marcos, which was the inspiration for her poem "The River San Marcos." She later moved to New Orleans, where she died in 1909. This last paragraph of the manuscript is obviously a gloss by the collaborator.

THE MEMOIRS OF
CAPTAIN MENCHACA

Being an Unpublished Manuscript Detailing Events in
San Antonio from 1807 to the Battle of San Jacinto

I was born in 1800, was baptized in the church of San Fernando de Austria on the 12th of January same year; was raised in San Fernando de Austria. From the year 1807 I remember events clearly; when came the express order from the king of Spain to the Lieut. Col. Antonio Cordero to select two hundred and fifty men from the king's service to go and establish the Spanish line on the Sabine River. He did so and went to "reconocer." Having returned from the Sabine river, he left at Nacogdoches one hundred men for the safeguard of the Spanish law—that it be respected and obeyed. When he had concluded his military business at Nacogdoches he returned to San Fernando de Austria.

Having arrived here he took upon himself the task of improving the city. He straightened the streets, Main street, so called now, was at that time very crooked, running straight from the Plaza up to where the street from Lewis' Mill intersects it, thence to the mill. He cut the street straight and built bridge . . . He also straightened Flores street and built a powder house. While he was governor he was very good and kind, doing many things for the welfare of the people.

In 1811 Manuel Salcedo, lieutenant colonel of the royal Spanish armies, relieved Cordero, Salcedo, being governor, secret letters were received here by parties who desired to throw off the Spanish yoke from parties in Mexico, from Ayendes, Hidalgo, Ximenes, and El Pachon, inviting those here to join them in their enterprise. Many of these answered that they could rely upon help from here. That there were a great many here who would willingly enter into the plot. These parties here, while considering the measures they were to adopt to secure their ends, were suspected, and from fifteen to twenty of the leaders were arrested; some were shot, others remained here in prison, others were sent to Chihuahua prison. Among those sent to Chihuahua was Captain Jose Menchaca, who remained in prison until his death in 1820. The principal leader of the revolutionists,

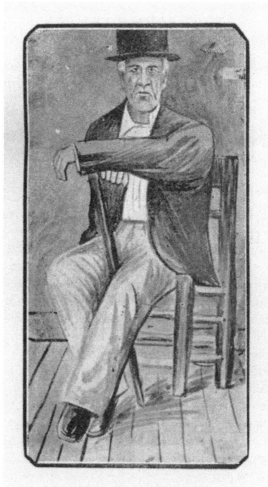

Captain Antonio Menchaca

FIGURE 7

In this sketch of Antonio Menchaca by an unknown artist, the grandfatherly pose of the storyteller is faithful to the available portraits, although the drawing, which accompanied "The Memoirs of Captain Menchaca," published in the Passing Show *in 1907, was almost certainly made twenty or more years after his death.* Courtesy of the San Antonio Public Library— Texana Collection.

Juan Bautiste Casas, remained here in prison for awhile, was then taken to Monclova, where he was shot, his head severed from his body, placed in a box, sent here and put in the middle of Military Plaza on a pole.

At the same time that Casas was killed, Ayendes, Hidalgo, Ximenes and El Pachon, who were on their way to San Fernando de Austria with $3,000,000, were apprehended, killed and all the property taken.

On the 11th of March, 1811, an order was received from the vieroy, Felix Maria Calleja, that San Fernando de Austria and San Antonio de Valero should be incorporated under the name of San Antonio de Bexar.

In 1812 Juan Manuel Zambrano, a citizen of this place, he being a man who owned a great many sheep, having 77,000 sheep, determined to put four droves of mules loaded with wool on the road to Nacogdoches. He accompanied his train to Nacogdoches, and upon arriving there some of his friends informed him of a plot to assassinate him, and that Miguel Menchaca and Bernardo Gutierrez were the ones to kill him; they were at that place recruiting men for the contemplated insurrection. As soon as Zambrano ascertained that Gutierrez and Menchaca had three hundred men, he left Nacogdoches through the instrumentality of some of his friends, having lost all his wool, and returned to San Antonio; arriving here towards the latter part of August and immediately advised Governor Salcedo of what was going on at Nacogdoches.

The Governor immediately sent couriers to the City of Mexico and Chihuahua, notifying the authorities of what was expected. By the month of November about four thousand troops had arrived here from different parts of Mexico. At this same time an army of Americans were advancing upon Goliad, [the Mexican troops started from here to Goliad][1] where they took possession of the Mission del Rosario and the Mission del Espiritu Santo, to consider their action. There they skirmished frequently with the Americans, but were always defeated. They put pickets out every night. They remained keeping up a siege during the months of December, January and February, 1813.

THE AFFAIR OF CORDERO, THE COMANCHE.

Captain Cordero, a Comanche Chief, arrived at San Antonio with fifteen hundred Comanches and presented himself to Jose Flores de Abrego, who

1. Underlined bracketed phrases represent insertions from Frederick C. Chabot's 1937 published version.

was in command here in the absence of the Governor, asking him for a "regalo." Jose Flores de Abrego told him that he could give him nothing, that the Governor was at Goliad in the war. Cordero then said that if he had nothing to give him, he wanted to speak with the Governor and started for Goliad arriving there with all his followers, presented himself to Salcedo, insinuating to him that he wanted "regalo." Salcedo told him that he had no "regalo," but that he would furnish him with powder and lead for him to assist him in fighting the Americans; but the Indian chief answered that he did not want to fight the Americans, that they were too brave and would kill too many of his men, and that if he did not give him "regalo" that he would come and destroy all the ranches and take off all the horses.

The Indians remained in camp there three days. Salcedo, as soon as he found out their intentions, sent an express to Flores directing him to have all the horses in the country brought into San Antonio and the town fortified. So that when the Indians returned they found all the ranches abandoned and the horses within San Antonio. The horses, about 7000 head, were kept here, being herded by sixty men for fifteen days, at which time about two thousand Indians came and took them all away. During all this time the Mexicans and Americans were fighting at Goliad and continued through the most of March, on the 10th of which month the Mexicans, finding they could not whip the Americans, started for San Antonio.

AMERICANS CAPTURE SAN ANTONIO.

The Americans gave them time to arrive at San Antonio, when they advanced and encamped on the Rosillo. The Mexicans sallied from San Antonio and a fierce battle ensued, in which the Americans were victorious, killing about 200 Spanish soldiers, besides leaving a great many wounded. The Spaniards retreated in bad condition, the Americans remained on the field. Three days after the battle, the Americans moved up and encamped at Concepcion Mission. On Friday, Bernardo Gutierrez and Miguel Menchaca sent a herald to Manuel Salcedo, stating that by next day at ten o'clock they wanted the Military Plaza evacuated. The answer was sent through J. M. Veramendi that at any time they choose to come in no resistance would be offered. At the appointed hour, on Saturday, the Americans entered the city. At three o'clock of the same day the Americans imprisoned Miguel Delgado, Santiago Menchaca, Francisco Riojas and twenty-one others of the American side, and Manuel Salcedo, Simon de Herrera, Geronimo Herrera, Francisco Povola, Miguel de Arcos and old

Captain Gravielde Arcos, son of Captain de Arcos, Miguel de Arcos, Jr., Miguel Pando, Juan Francisco Caso and four others of the Mexican side, who were all taken to the Salado and arrived at the Rossillo the same evening, the prisoners were beheaded, and by eight o'clock next (Sunday)[2] morning the twenty-five Americans were in the city and said that they had started the Americans to ship them to New Orleans, though they were infamously butchered as before stated.

THE FIRST CITY COUNCIL IN SAN ANTONIO.

Then Bernardo Gutierrez determined to establish good order in the city of San Antonio. He called a council, president of which was Don Francisco Arocha, Thomas Arocha, Ignacio Arocha, Clements Delgado, Miguel Delgado, Manuel Delgado and Antonio Delgado being the council; all gentlemen of the city of San Antonio, and descendants of the first families who migrated from the Canary Islands in 1730, and all adherents of the American government.

A MEXICAN ARMY MARCHES AGAINST SAN ANTONIO.

In the same year (1813) on the 11th of June, at night, appeared here fifteen hundred Mexican soldiers under command of Ignacio Elizondo, a superior Colonel, and Ignacio Perez, Lieutenant Colonel. On the morning of the 12th of June they were within one and a half miles of the city on the Alazan Hill. The Americans seeing that they were there took one of the old Spanish guns that was here, a twelve pounder, placed it upon the old powder house which was built on the west side of the San Pedro Creek, and saluted the Mexicans with five shots. Gutierrez let them rest four days, while he rested his troops. On the fifth day at 8 o'clock A.M. he took his troops out and attacked the Mexicans with such force and effect as to entirely rout them in about a half hour's engagement, killing forty to fifty, taking fifty to sixty prisoners and the balance put to flight. Gutierrez brought the prisoners into the city and treated them very well.

June passed, July came, on the 15th of which month, the American spies who had to reconnoiter in the vicinity of Laredo, returned and gave the

2. Parenthetical words or statements, unless otherwise noted, appear as such in the original manuscript.

intelligence to Gutierrez that Arredondo was raising a great many troops for the purpose of attacking San Antonio. On the same day that this news reached here, General Toledo, from New Orleans, arrived and relieved General Gutierrez from the command of the troops; upon being relieved General Gutierrez left for Natchitoches.

THE AMERICANS GO OUT TO MEET THE ENEMY.

The American spies were incessantly on the lookout lest they should be surprised, watching Arredondo's movements, until he got this side of the Atascosa, when the spies came in and told Toledo that the Mexican army was on this side of the Atascoso and advancing. Then Toledo prepared to meet them. Starting from here in the direction in which Arrendodo was approaching; he camped at Laguna de la Espada the first night and the next day crossed the Medina river, and on a hill a short distance the other side he thought a convenient place to take the enemy at a disadvantage.

Arredondo also coming to a place he considered advantageous to his purpose, stopped at the water holes called "Charcos de las Gallinas," on the hill this side of the Atascoso creek, about five miles from the Medina river. On the day following Arredondo's occupation of the waterholes, he sent a detachment of men of about four hundred strong, cavalry, with two pieces of light artillery, to try and engage the Americans. The detachment was under the command of Ignacio Elizondo and Ignacio Perez. They came up to the American troops and trying to engage them, upon seeing which Miguel Menchaca, the second in command on the American side, came up to Toledo and asked him what his intentions where. Toledo remarked that the manoeuvering was only intended as a decoy to ascertain the strength of his troops, that he, Menchaca, might take some of his men and engage them, but under no circumstances to follow them far if they retreated; that Arredondo merely wished to get him out of his position in order to take him at a disadvantage.

THE BATTLE OF THE MEDINA.

Menchaca went to attack them and did not return. He followed the detachment of Mexicans, killing all he could, until he got up to the main body. He took two guns from the cavalry, but was attacked by the artillery and he retreated about half a mile from where he sent word to Toledo to advance with his troops, for he, Menchaca, would not turn back.

Toledo then sent word to him that it would be worse than madness for him to attempt to move forward and leave his position, for he would be sure to be defeated if he did. Upon receiving this word, Menchaca, infuriated, himself came over to where Toledo with the balance of the forces was and told the troops that the fight had commenced, that under no consideration would he quit until he and the men under him had either died or conquered; that if they were men, to act as men and follow him. Whereupon all the forces became encouraged and moved in a body to follow Menchaca.

Toledo, though unwillingly, followed. They started to meet Arredondo, and having no water, also having to pull the guns along by hand, by the time they came to where Arredondo was, and were placed in battle array, the troops were nearly dead from thirst.

The battle began with great fury. As soon as it commenced Menchaca, who commanded one wing of the cavalry, [and Antonio Delgado, the left wing,] pushed their men up with such vigor as to compel the cavalry, which opposed them, to retreat to the center of the main body of Arredondo's infantry. The Americans were so thirsty that they even drank water in which the rods for loading the cannon were soaked.

The battle had almost been declared in favor of the Americans when by an accident Colonel Menchaca was struck by a ball on the neck. He fell, and there being no one to cheer the troops on, they became discouraged and then frightened, and disorder commenced. The Mexicans under Arredondo seeing this, took courage and charged with fury, got into the American line and killed a good many of them. Though Menchaca was brought with them he died on the way and was buried on the Seguin road at the place called Menchaca creek or Canada de Menchaca. Arredondo having come off victorious, advanced as far as the Laredo road crossing of the Medina, camped to cure his wounded soldiers, have their clothes washed and at the same time to dispose of the prisoners he had taken, which he did by shooting them. The number of prisoners killed were about two hundred and fifty.

After murdering his prisoners and resting his army, Arredondo marched into San Antonio. It was about ten o'clock P. M., the 15th of August, that he arrived the town. The Catholic church was filled with poor men praying that their lives should be spared. All were taken out, some were placed in the old Spanish guard house, and others were crowded into the house of Francisco Arocha. Of those imprisoned in the latter place, it being so crowded, eight men suffocated to death by the next morning.

On the following day they were all taken out and drawn up in line to ascertain which of them deserved to be put to death and which to be put to hard labor. Arredondo asked Ygnacio Perez, a native of San Antonio, to name two persons of the natives that they might call out all such persons as were deserving of death and to also name such as should be put to hard labor.

Ygnacio Perez nominated Louis Galan and Manuel Salines, who, though natives of San Antonio, answered that they knew no one. Upon hearing this, Arredondo selected forty who should be put to death and the balance, one hundred and sixty, were handcuffed in pairs and put to work upon the streets.

Of the forty who were selected to die, every third day three would be shot, on the north side of Main Plaza, until the entire number were disposed of.

The wives of these unfortunate men were placed inside the "quinta" to make "tortillas" for the soldiers; they had to make 35,000 tortillas daily.

Six days after Arredondo's entry into the city, he ordered Ygnacio Elizondo and Ygnacio Perez, with two hundred and fifty men, to follow the fugitives who had started for Nacogdoches.

After the expedition under Elizondo and Perez had departed, Arredondo displayed still further his cruel nature; he seemed furious to punish all those who had taken any part whatever in the revolutionary movement; the result was that whosoever chose to have any one punished would merely complain to the officers and the chastisement would be inflicted by whipping them on the public square.

This punishment was seldom relented or excused; though there is an instance. Mariano Menchaca was accused of some trifling thing. The soldiers at dead of night went over to his house and took him and his wife out of their bed. The wife was taken to the "quinta" and Menchaca was to be publicly whipped, when his son, Antonio, who was about fourteen years old, and had become a favorite of one of the ranking officers, Cristobal Dominguez; seeing that they were going to whip, ran into this officer's bedroom, where the officer was in bed, and going up to him, told him that his father was about to be whipped and begged him to intercede in his behalf.

The officer at first told him to go away, but the boy would not thus be put off. He begged for all that was dear to him to save his father. The officer relented, and stepping out he spoke to the men who had charge of Menchaca and made them turn him loose. The boy then asked to please have his mother liberated; the officer gave him an order for her release, which he took to officer in command of the "quinta" and got her released also.

Elizondo and Perez overtook the fugitives on the Trinity river, which had swollen from heavy rains and had fallen. All the men of note had already crossed the river; only the women and inferior men were remained on this side. The Spaniards had along with them a priest named Esteben Camacho. When the Spaniards arrived at the river the men who had not crossed presented [themselves to the commanders. The commanders] asked them why they had rebelled, that they would hurt nobody; as the fugitives would see, that they would be kindly treated, and that the soldiers' only object in following them was to bring them back to their homes. Elizondo ten asked if there were any man present who would cross the river and tell those on the other side that if they came over to this side a full pardon would be granted them.

One of the men who had not crossed over, agreed to go over and take the letter, in which was guaranteed to the fugitives, in the most sacred terms, a full and complete pardon if they would but give themselves up. He went; the letter was presented, and after considerable debate, the terms being so moderate and couched in such plausible language, they consented to come over and give themselves up.

They did this, the Spaniards taking the precaution to tie their hands as they crossed over. All of them crossed that same evening and slept tied and next day were unmercifully slaughtered. The whole number thus so cruelly killed was two hundred and seventy-nine.

Having killed all the men fugitives, Elizondo and Perez started to return with all the families afoot.

On the second day thereafter, Don Manuel Serrano, captain under Elizondo, who felt deeply grieved at the barbarous manner in which the men had been killed, deliberately walked into Elizondo's tent, shot him dead and started towards Perez' tent with the same end in view, shot at Perez and missed him, was arrested and prevented from doing further harm. They tied poor Serrano and brought him to San Antonio a raving maniac.

[They arrived here about the 22nd of September, about 10 A.M. and formed all the captives, women, in a line on the main square. The line being formed, Arredondo in full uniform, with his staff, came in front of the line of captives and asked who was the Mexican Aunt. When he said this, Da. Josefa Nuñes de Arocha, wife of Francisco Arocha, answered "Here I am Nephew." Arredondo then said, "So you have offered $500 for my paunch to make a drum with?" "Yes, I have and would have made it, had I got it," she answered. "You could not obtain my paunch," said he, but now I can punish you as you deserve. You can go and rest at the Quinta, to make tor-tillas for my men and me. "I would rather you would give me fifteen shots, than that it should come to this," said she. Upon this Arredondo gave the order that the captives should be taken to the Quinta. Arredondo [was] kept in command in San Antonio, until the month of November, when he was called to Mexico.

On the 8th of December, 1813, the Estremadura regiment, 800, under the command of Col. Benito de Armenan entered San Antonio. They did not seem to be other than devils. They stole and committed many things. Armenan remained in command here until November, 1814; when he was ordered to Chapala, where his regiment with the exception of about thirty-five, were killed; Ygnacio Perez remaining in command here. In 1816, Manuel Pardo relieved Ygnacio Perez. In 1817 Manuel Pardo was relieved by Antonio Puertas. In 1818 Antonio Martinez relieved Antonio Puertas. In 1819, on the 5th of July San Antonio was inundated by a flood, in which twenty-eight persons were lost. On the 25th of same month, Antonio Menchaca, being a soldier of the King of Spain, took the message to Col. Galica that Mexico was independent of Spain.]

On account of the fact that the city was surrounded by Indians, the pri-vations were such in 1814 that a peck of corn cost three dollars and a half; sugar a dollar fifty a pound, and tobacco a dollar an ounce. The people being under such pressure for food, would go out into the country at the risk of their lives to kill deer, turkey, and other game, and to find herbs for the support of their families.

At planting time, 1815, there was not a single horse belonging to the military service in San Antonio. Detachments or squads of fifteen soldiers had to be sent afoot as far as the Leona to receive the mail from Mexico. The persons engaged in agriculture, had also to go in parties of fifteen or more to look for their oxen; and, while working in the fields, had to keep their arms with them.

There were so many Indians around the city that one evening, while it was yet light, a lady, sitting at her door, was killed by a Twowakano, who walked right up to her and shot her in the head. In the same month another lady was killed at the Alamo, also by a Twowakano, and Domingo Busti-llos, who was coming from the Alamo Labor in company with three others, was shot in the shoulder. It may well be counted as a miracle that no more deaths occurred than there did; for the Indians would dress themselves in the clothes of their victims and promenade the streets at will.

The people lived with this dread until 1820, when the Comanches and other tribes of Indians, came to make peace. Peace was made with them;

but, notwithstanding, they still continued to kill and rob, and the settlers had to be constantly on the alert. Very few people had milch cows, for the Indians had not given them a chance to raise cattle; but, when the peace was made, a good many bought horses from the Indians.

GOOD TIMES HERE UNDER A CAVALIER GOVERNMENT.

In 1822, Jose Felix Trespalacios relieved Antonio Martinez from the command of San Antonio, and during the command of Trespalacios, this place, underwent a great change for the better. Money circulated more freely until 1825, when a provincial government, composed of six cavaliers, was established until it was decided that a political chief should be named. The nomination fell upon Don Antonio Sancedo, who governed as political chief for two years. He was succeeded by Ramon Musquiz.

In 1826, the regiment of Mateo Aumado, a Mexican, arrived. Aumado remained as military commander until 1828, when General Anastacio Bustamante, and General Manuel Theran came. On the sixth day after their arrival, General Theran, at the head of Aumado's regiment, started for Nacogdoches to suppress the Americans who were reported to be making preparations for fighting. Arriving at Nacogdoches and finding everything, to all appearances, quiet. Theran left Aumado in charge of the troops and then he proceeded with a body guard to the Sabine River. Seeing that all was quiet there also, he returned to Nacogdoches.

In 1830 Theran left Amuado in command and came to San Antonio

In the month of March, 1830, James P. Bowie of Kentucky came to San Antonio in company with George Wharton. From here Bowie went on to Saltillo.

In the same year M. Veramendi was appointed Lieutenant Governor and proceeded to Mexico to qualify. There he met and became friendly with Bowie and, when he returned to Texas with his family, Bowie accompanied him. It was then that Ursula Veramendi, the Governor's daughter, and Bowie became engaged. Upon their arrival in San Antonio, Bowie asked Veramendi to give him time to go to Kentucky for funds, as he did not have enough to justify his marrying. The request was granted, and so, in March, 1831, Bowie went to Kentucky. He returned in the same month and was married.

Bowie remained in San Antonio three months before starting for the interior of Texas to recruit forces for the war.

He returned in 1832, but went away again in search of the old Spanish

San Saba mines. He came back for four months and then made another trip to look for the mines. (It was during the search for the mines that Bowie did some fiercest fighting with the Indians.) During this second search, news reached San Antonio that Letona, the Governor of Mexico, had died.

This made it necessary for Veramendi to go to Mexico to take charge of the government.

While Bowie was on the Colorado he received a communication from Austin at San Felipe, directing him to repair immediately to that place, as his services were greatly needed.

Upon receiving this news, Bowie wrote a letter to his wife, telling her where he was going, and upon what business, and adding that it was hard to tell when they would meet again.

VERAMENDI BECOMES GOVERNOR.

Veramendi, having heard of Letona's death, repaired at once to Saltillo, arriving there on the eleventh of the month, 1832. He received his commission as governor as soon as he reached there, and he performed the duties of his office until the seventh of February, 1833, when Bowie, with several other Americans, arrived there also.

BOWIE'S UNEXPLAINED MISSION — WAS THIS
A PLOT FOR INDEPENDENCE OF TEXAS?

On the following day, Bowie had an interview with Veramendi and was introduced to the members of Congress.

As soon as his acquaintance with the leading members became such as to warrant it, he told them his object, and he received the assurance of Marcial [Borrego and Jose María Uranga that they would aid him his enterprise.] sent ten thousand dollars to Musquiz, to they would aid him in his enterprise.[3]

3. The fragments here in brackets and following the brackets represent a copyediting mistake on the part of the *Passing Show*. Obviously, instead of the text omitted there (the section here in brackets), the typesetter put in some incorrect text that was then correctly inserted just below, in the next section, in connection to Veramendi's business in New Orleans.

He also succeeded in making them move Congress from Saltillo to Monclova and, when it was established in the latter place, he returned to Texas.

CHOLERA SCOURGE VISITS MONCLAVA — THE DEATH OF THE VERAMENDIS AND BOWIE'S WIFE.

In July of the same year Veramendi sent ten thousand dollars to Musquiz, to be forwarded to New Orleans.

In September, Veramendi's family, including Bowie's wife, with twenty-five thousand dollars worth of goods, were taken to Monclova They reached there on September 27th, and that same day cholera broke out in Monclova.

Madam Veramendi was the first victim of the disease and, after her, Governor Veramendi and then Madam Bowie died.

The rest of the family stayed in Monclova until the first of November, when I brought them back to San Antonio.

BOWIE AND COL. TRAVIS FORM A COALITION TAKE MENCHACA INTO THEIR FELLOWSHIP AMERICANS HOLD THE ALAMO

[The year 1834 passed; also 1835, in which year in July, Col. Nicholas Condelle, with 500 Infantry and 100 Cavalry, arrived here; for it was reported that the Americans were gathered at S. Felipe. With these last troops there were here 1,100 soldiers, 1,000 Cavalry, and 100 Infantry.]

On October 20th I, Antonio Menchaca, received a letter from Bowie in which was enclosed a note addressed to Marcial Borrego and J. M. Uranga; the letter told me to deliver the note in person, to trust no one and to be a quick about it as possible. I went and delivered the note, while it was reported here that the Americans were at Gonzales; and, on my return, got as far as San Fernando de Rosas, where I was detained and not allowed to pass. My liberty was finally granted me upon my giving bond.

Six days after the capitulation of San Antonio, Pedro Rodriguez, a friend of mine, furnished me with two men and horses to bring me to San Antonio. I crossed by night, at Eagle Crossing, and reached here on the 20th of December. The companies which had assisted in the siege were still here.

I sought Bowie as soon as I arrived.

When Bowie saw me he threw his arms around my neck and wept to think that he had not seen his wife die. He said, "My father, my brother, my companion, and all my protection has gone! Are you still my companion-in-arms?"

And I answered him:

"I shall be your companion, Jim Bowie, until I die."

"Then come this evening," Bowie said, "and I'll take you to meet Travis at the Alamo."

That evening he introduced me to Travis, and Col. Neil.

On the 26th of December, 1835, Don Diego Grau left San Antonio on his march to Matamoros, with about five hundred men, Americans and Mexicans, of those who had assisted in the siege. They here kept up guards and patrols by night, while here. Two hundred and fifty men went from here to keep a look out on companies[4] who had gone to Mexico and returned here on the 5th January, 1836.

ARRIVAL OF DAVID CROCKETT.

On the 13th of January, 1836, David Crockett arrived at the old Mexican graveyard on the west side of the San Pedro Creek, and had in company with him fourteen young men who had accompanied him from Tennessee.

Shortly after arrival he sent a message to Bowie to come and receive him and conduct him into the city.

Bowie and I went and he was brought in and lodged at Erasmo Seguin's house. Crockett, Bowie, Travis, Niel and all the officers joined together to establish guards for the safety of the city, fearing the Mexicans' return.

BALL GIVEN IN HONOR OF CROCKETT.

On the 10th of February, 1836, I was invited by the officers to a ball to be given in honor of David Crockett, and I was asked to invite all the prin-

---

4. In Chabot's edition, *Cos* appears instead of *companies*. The comma following *Cos* must look like a period in the original manuscript for Newcomb to mistake it for the abbreviation for *companies*. Chabot only partially corrected the problem, changing the text to "Cos" but leaving the punctuation mark a period.

cipal ladies in the city. On the same day invitations were extended and the ball given that night.

ARRIVAL OF THE COURIER.

While the dance was still going on, at about ten o'clock[5] of the eleventh, a courier sent by Placido Benavides arrived from Camargo, with the intelligence that Santa Anna was starting from the Presidio Rio Grande with 13,000 troops, 10,000 infantry, 3,000 cavalry, with the view of taking San Antonio.

The courier arrived at the ball room door and inquired for Colonel Seguin. He was told that Colonel Seguin was not there. He then asked if Menchaca was there and was told that he was.

He spoke to me and told me he had a letter of great importance, which he had brought from Placido Benavides at Camargo. I seated my partner and came to see the letter; opened it and read the following: "At this moment I have received the very certain notice that the commander-in-chief, Antonio Lopez de Santa Anna, marches for the city of San Antonio to take possession thereof with 13,000 men."

As I was reading the letter Bowie came up to me to see it, and then Travis came by, so Bowie called Travis to read it also. Travis declined, saying that at that moment he could not stop to read the letter, for he was dancing with the most beautiful lady in San Antonio. Bowie replied that the letter was one of grave importance, for him to leave his partner. From this reply, Travis came and brought Crockett with him. Travis and Bowie understood Spanish; Crockett did not. After reading the message, Travis said, lightly: "It will take 13,000 men, from the Presidio de Rio Grande thirteen or fourteen days to march to this place. This is the fourth day. Let us dance tonight and tomorrow we will make arrangements for our defense." The ball continued until seven o'clock in the morning.

5. The ten o'clock time does not make sense in the context of the previous statements regarding the invitations and actual date of the dance, which Menchaca claims to have taken place on the tenth. If the courier arrived on the eleventh, then the dance must have extended beyond midnight. Chabot corrected the time to one o'clock a.m., and we must assume he did so on the basis of the original manuscript.

TRAVIS CALLS COUNCIL OF WAR — MENCHACA
RETREATS TOWARDS HOUSTON'S ARMY.

After the ball, Travis invited officers to hold a meeting to consult as to the defense of the place. The council assembled and many resolutions were offered and adopted, after which Bowie and Seguin made a motion to have Antonio Menchaca and his family sent away from here, knowing that they would receive no good treatment at Santa Anna's hands.

I left here and went to Seguin's ranch, where I remained six days, preparing for a trip; started from there and went as far as Marchelino, then three miles farther on the east side of the Cibolo, at an old pond. At sun-up the next morning, Nat Lewis passed afoot with a wallet on his back, and I asked him why he was afoot, and he answered because he could find no horse, that Santa Anna had entered San Antonio the day previous. I ask him what the Americans had done upon the entry of the Mexicans and he answered that they were in the Alamo, inside the fortifications. I then asked why he did not remain there and he said that he was not a fighting man, he was a business man.

MENCHACA CONTINUES HIS JOURNEY.

I continued my journey to Gonzales and arrived at the house of G. Dewitt and there met up with Gen. Edward Burleson in command of 73 men, who had just arrived there.

I slept there and on the next day attempted to pass to the other side of the river with my family, but was prevented by Burleson who told him that my family might cross but not me, that the men were needed in the army.

There I also met fourteen Mexicans from San Antonio and they united and remained until a company could be formed. The Americans were gradually being strengthened by the addition of from three to fifteen daily.

ARRIVAL OF SEGUIN WITH MESSAGE FROM TRAVIS —
ORGANIZATION OF COMPANY OF MEXICANS.

Six days after my arrival at Gonzales, Colonel Seguin, sent as a courier by Travis, reached there and reported to General Burleson, who, upon receipt of the message from Travis, forwarded it to the convention assembled at Washington, Texas.

On the following day, a Mexican company was organized with twenty-two men, having for captain Seguin, first lieutenant, Manuel Flores: second lieutenant, Antonio Menchaca.

On the fourth of March the news reached us that Texas had declared her independence. The few that were there, three hundred and fifty, then swore allegiance, and two days later Gen. San Houston arrived there and took command of the forces.

When Santa Anna took the Alamo and burned the men he had killed, he addressed[6] Madame Dickinson, Travis' servant and Almonte's servant, a lady whose husband had been killed in the Alamo, with propositions to Americans or to those desiring to make Texas their home. The propositions were in these terms: All American Texans desiring to live in Texas, by presenting themselves to Gen. Santa Anna and giving up their arms, would be treated as gentlemen.

When the Americans heard what was proposed, they in a voice cried: "Gen. Santa Anna, you may be a good man, but the Americans will never surrender; go to h—l and hurrah for Gen. Sam Houston."

On the following day the Texan spies brought the news that the Mexicans were on their way to Gonzales and were encamped on the Cibolo. On the same day the Americans started for the Colorado and slept on Rock Creek. On the following day, at Lavaca, where Colonel Hawkley reported with 160 men to General Houston for orders. The following day they camped on the San Antonio and there General Summerville reported with 250.

From thence they started and arrived at Mr. Bonham's on the Colorado, and there remained ten days. On the 6th day after they reached there, General Ramirez y Sezma, of the Mexican side, approached with 400 men. There were 900 Americans in camp. As soon as the Americans saw that the Mexicans were trying to draw them into an attack, the Americans prepared themselves to attack. But Houston told them that not a single man should move out, that the Mexicans were only trying to draw him out and ascertain his strength, which he did not intend to let them know.

The Americans murmured, whereupon Houston told them that such was his determination, and that nothing would tempt him to depart from it; but, if they were determined to do otherwise, all they had to do was to

6. The phrase makes better sense if the word that appears here in the Yanaguana Society version is used, "ordered," since it is obviously including more than just Dickinson. Chabot completes the correction by placing the phrase "Travis' servant and Almonte's servant" in parentheses so that the identification of Dickinson is continuous.

choose some other commander, for he would not take the consequences upon himself. He then would fight as a private, but never as a commander.

Upon hearing this, the soldiers saw that it was useless and gave in. They then started for the Brazos River with the intention of crossing at La Malena, the Nacogdoches road, about eight leagues above San Felipe de Austin. They arrived there in two days and took a position in the bottom on the west side.

Houston sent M. Baker in command of 250 men to go to San Felipe and take all they could in stores and burn the balance. Baker with his men went to San Felipe, crossed the river, encamped in the bottom, and then commenced to haul all he could away from San Felipe and hide it in the bottoms until he could wait for them no longer, when he burned the stores.

While the stores were being burned a great many barrels of liquor that had been brought over, were ordered to be broken, which was done. American spies came on the other side and told Baker that Houston wanted him to come back; that the Mexicans were on the march and were then at San Bernardo. Baker immediately set out to join Houston: he arrived at Groos' house on the following day and there received word to remain until further orders. On that same day, the steamboat Yellow Stone, L. G. Grayson captain, came up the river and Houston stopped it and told the captain that on his return he should stop there and await his orders, which he did, and remained there twelve days.

The Mexicans, the greatest part of them, turned to Fort Bend, only five hundred going to San Felipe crossing. On the 18th when Houston was in camp, Santa Anna, with 700 men, crossed at Fort Bend in the direction of Galveston. He was seen by an American, who took the news to Houston. The American arrived at Groos' at about 5 o'clock p. m., his horse very much fatigued. He had ridden two other horses to death. He gave Houston the news and on the following day Houston began to cross his troops on the steamboat.

After crossing, the Americans marched as far as Isaac Donoghue's house. On the following morning at about 8 o'clock, Colonel Bell, Colonel Allen and Mirabeau Lamar, with fifty-four men, reported to General Houston for duty. From this point they marched to the edge of the pine woods and camped. On the following morning an old man in company with a young one arrived at camp the word from Santa Anna asking where were the Americans; that he had heard every oak produced six Americans. Houston replied that though he did not have many men, with what he did have he would surely call upon Santa Anna.

The head waters of Buffalo Bayou was the next halting place, and on the west side the camp was pitched. As soon as camp was established, General Houston sent twenty-five horsemen to reconnoiter and ascertain what was going on. The horsemen found that Santa Anna had crossed towards Harrisburg; they captured two couriers, one from Musquiz of San Antonio, and the other from Mexico. They were taken before General Houston.

General Rusk called the Mexican officers to read the message. It happened that I opened the official dispatch from General Filizola to Santa Anna in which the former said that he sent Santa Anna eight hundred choice men, as he had heard from a reliable American that the Americans were six thousand strong and that he awaited instruction from Santa Anna in order to know what to do.

As soon as General Houston heard the contents of the dispatch, he remarked that he did not care a cent for the Mexican disposition, that all he wanted to know was where Santa Anna was; that as Santa Anna was separated from the main body of the army, he felt confident he could defeat him. He then gave orders that two hundred men should be placed under the command of Captain Splinn to guard the horses and equipages, which was to be left there by the Americans, who were to march next day to meet Santa Anna. General Sherman then said that his orders would be obeyed and he immediately proceeded to select the company that was to remain.

MENCHACA PROTESTS TO HOUSTON.

Houston ordered Sherman to have the Mexican company left at camp, that they knew but little about fighting, but were good at herding. General Sherman went to the Mexican company and asked for Captain Seguin and was told he was not there. Then General Sherman instructed me that as soon as Captain Seguin came to tell him that his company was ordered to remain and guard horses and equipages.

I asked General Sherman why this company was ordered to do this duty. The General explained that those were his orders. Seguin came and I told him what Sherman had said. Seguin asked me what I thought about it; I replied that I wanted to see General Houston, and we both went.

We reached General Houston and saluted him and the general asked what was wanted. I answered that Sherman has given me orders to remain in camp and I wished to know why it was.

Houston replied that as a general he had given that order. I then told him that he could not deprive me of my commission; that when I joined the Americans I had done so with a view of aiding them in their fight and that I wanted to do so even if I died facing the enemy; that I did not enlist to guard horses and would do no such duty. That if that was the alternative I would go and attend to my family, who was on its way to Nacogdoches without escort or servants.

Houston answered that I spoke like a man. I answered that I considered myself one; that I could handle all kinds of arms, from a gun to an arrow, and that having a willing heart, I did not see why I should not be allowed to fight. [Houston then told me that he would gladly let me and my company go to fight.]

HOUSTON AND RUSK ADDRESS THE TEXANS.

On the following day, after breakfast (19th April, 1836), the army was marshalled and addressed by General Houston and General Rusk. Houston spoke very eloquently; he dwelt long and pathetically upon the suffering of those who had fallen at the Alamo and of those who fell at Goliad under Fannin. Houston concluded and Rusk addressed the troops with such force and effect as to make every man, without a single exception, shed tears.

When General Rusk concluded speaking, provision was made for crossing the bayou, which was done by making rafts on which the guns, two four-pounders, were crossed, and also the horsemen.

SKIRMISHES BEFORE THE BATTLE.

It took until five o'clock of the 19th of April to get over. The march was continued until ten a. m. of the 20th. The men slept on their arms and proceeded very early the same morning to bridge at Harrisburg, and at 7 o'clock a. m. crossed it. We halted on a hill to await reports from spies. The spies came and reported that Santa Anna was within one and a half miles from there. Upon hearing this, General Houston ordered that the troops should discharge their arms and clean and reload, for, he said, the time was close at hand when they would be needed.

After this order was compiled with, the Americans moved forward to a bend in the bayou, where they were halted in line. They were ordered to lie down and cautioned not to shoot a shot until ordered to do so.

Shortly after the Americans were on the ground, three Mexican companies came in sight, shooting scattering shots to draw the Americans on, for they could not see the Americans.

When the Mexicans saw that no one answered their shots they halted and an officer came and ordered them back.

They remained about half an hour without shooting and General Houston ordered General Sherman to advance with cavalry and ascertain what the Mexicans were doing. Sherman did so. As soon as he reached the spot indicated the Mexicans attacked and wounded two of his horses badly. Sherman ordered that those men whose horses were wounded should be taken up behind two others, and he retreated in good order.

The Mexicans, about forty, followed the Americans, and when they came in good range a gun was fired at them which killed some eight or ten, and they retreated.

When they reached the mott they commenced to shoot at the Americans with yangers.

DEER HUNTERS DO EXECUTION.

Houston gave orders that those men who lived upon the Navidad and Lavaca and killed deer at a hundred paces offhand should come forward and take a shot at the Mexicans. Immediately about fifty men were formed in line and went to a good distance from where the Mexicans were, fired one volley and hushed them.

General Houston, seeing that the Mexicans fired no more, after some time elapsed, sent some men over to find out if the Mexicans still occupied the mott and they found no one there. As soon as this report was brought to the general, he sent a detachment of one hundred men to occupy the place and to let a man climb a tree and see what the Mexicans were doing. The sentinel on the tree reported that they were cutting timber and fortifying from point to point the space upon which no timber grew.

The hundred men were relieved by another hundred men until three o'clock of that day, at which time Houston ordered the line to be formed where the troops had first lain down. He then gave Sherman command of three companies of infantry and Lamar the command of the cavalry, with orders to advance and ascertain what the Mexicans were doing.

When Sherman got to the edge of the prairie he ordered his companies to fall flat, the cavalry going out. The Mexicans, upon seeing the American horse coming out with his cavalry engaged them. When the Mexicans observed that the Americans would not retreat, they sent some infantry to

FIGURE 8

Archeological work in and around the San Jacinto battlefield supports Menchaca's (and others')
descriptions of the Mexican camp being overwhelmed by the Texans. According to archeologist
Douglas Mangum, the area depicted in this photograph represents the likely site of Juan Almonte's
surrender. Courtesy of Douglas Mangum and NRG Energy, Inc.

support their cavalry. Upon this, Sherman ordered his men to the relief of the horse, upon which the Mexicans retreated. In this skirmish three Americans were wounded, Colonel Neil and two others.

The Americans under Sherman and Lamar then came over to where Houston was. Fifty men were placed on guard on the American side that night.

On the 21st, early in the morning, about ten or twelve Mexican mules were in sight of the American camp and were driven in by the Americans. At about ten o'clock the spies came in with their horses very tired and told General Houston that Coz had crossed with eight hundred men and had burned the bridges; that if he wanted to trouble them he could do so, as they were then close by; but Houston said no, that they were his anyhow; to let them rest.

THE BATTLE OF SAN JACINTO.

About 2 o'clock of the same day Houston ordered the troops to fall in line in three divisions, the right wing under Rusk, left under Sherman and the center under himself. When they were so arranged he called the officers together to give them his instructions and after having done so, ordered that the whole front should move at the same pace he did. He then ordered Sherman to advance with his division to Santa Anna's right and that Lamar should march with him.

The attack was made, the battle begun. The Mexicans were taken by surprise — so much so that eleven rows of stacked arms were not touched. The fight lasted two hours and a quarter, when those Mexicans who were not killed, taken prisoner or wounded fled in great disorder.

On the following day Santa Anna was brought in by two Americans, a lieutenant and Louis Robinson of Nacogdoches. He was found in the woods under care of two mulatto girls. He was taken to General Houston and many were in favor of putting him to death, but as he was a Free Mason and the most of the officers were Masons, he was protected.

Next day, a steamboat from Galveston arrived with three hundred men, four guns and provisions. Houston ordered that the provisions be divided into two equal parts, one for his troops, the other for prisoners and wounded, which was done.

On the next day Don Lorenzo Zavala arrived and spoke to Santa Anna, abusing him severely.

Orders were given that Sherman and Burleson, with two hundred and fifty men, should march down to Fort Bend, to see what Felizola, who was with the main body of the Mexican army, determined upon. When they reached Fort Bend, they found that Felizola had left for Matamoras. They then crossed the river and arrived at a lake and halted for the balance of the day.

At about 3 o'clock p. m. General Ampudia came into the American camp and asked permission to take all the wounded and sick away. He was told that he could do so and would not be molested. Two men with two horses loaded with roasted meat and gourds of water for the wounded and sick were sent with Felizola. He took them with him and overtook the main body at Colorado river.

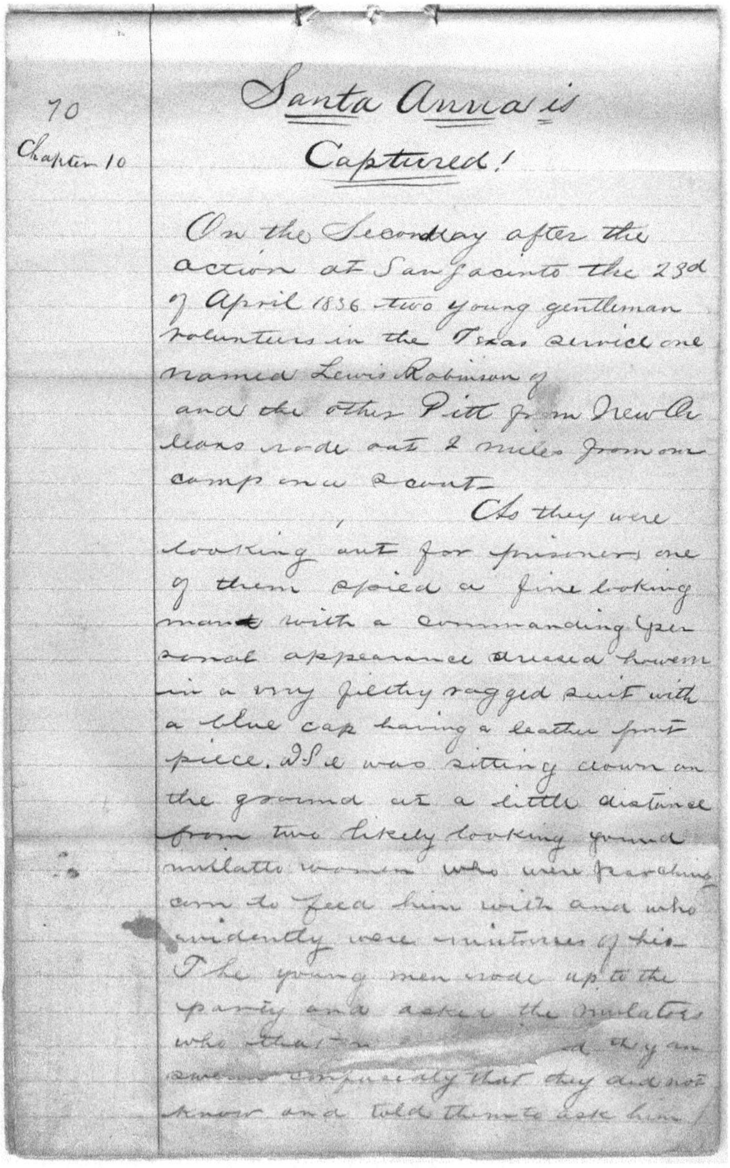

FIGURE 9

The first page of Menchaca's unpublished manuscript picks up the story of San Jacinto midsentence. In the absence of the original manuscript of the first half, but with its rather abrupt ending, it seems likely that when Menchaca picked up the story at some point after turning over the first half to James Newcomb, he did considerable backtracking. Just how much, however, is a matter of speculation. From the Antonio Menchaca Papers, di_07955, courtesy of the Dolph Briscoe Center for American History, University of Texas at Austin.

THE UNPUBLISHED SECOND PART
OF THE MENCHACA MANUSCRIPT

Jacinto & Buffalo Bayou Banks drawn up into a line, Among them was Genl Almonte and col Bringas who surrendered to me. I found among them a great many badly wounded men and I made those who were not wounded make bridges with their hands & carry the wounded on them to our camp many of whom did not live to reach it — It was now growing dusk — Rusk Allen and Morelavecka asked me to take the well prisoners and make them cut wood and build fires as it was cold and I made them make 3 fires about 50 yards long in a line and we laid down the wounded beside them. We had about 50 Physicians and surgeons mo. or less skillful in their professions and Houston sent for them and told them to dress the w[. . .] men and the Mexican prisoners. These surgeons got us to light about 400 candles for them to see how to dress the wounds — We had lost in the battle only 7 men and about 30 were wounded —

On the next day we went to the battle field and found it covered with dead Mexican soldiers. We dug trenches and buried them with our own 7 dead and returned to our camp where I found General Sam Houston surrounded by his Staff and they were all in high glee over the brilliant victory of the day previous and all the army were in fine spirits.

The battle of San Jacinto was the most brilliant feat of arms I have ever witness and has Immortalized Houston his brave staff and the army who participated in it and makes a beautiful page not only [. . .] of the then Republic of Texas but also in the History of the United States

CHAPTER 10
SANTA ANNA IS CAPTURED!

On the Second day after the action at San Jacinto the 23rd of April 1836 two young gentleman volunteers in the Texas service one named Lewis

Robinson of and the other Pitt from New Orleans rode out 2 miles from our camp on a scout—

As they were looking out for prisoners one of them spied a fine looking man with a commanding personal appearance dressed however in a very filthy ragged suit with a blue cap having a leather front piece. He was sitting down on the ground at a little distance from two likely looking young mulatto women who were parching corn to feed him with and who evidently were mistresses of his—The young men rode up to the party and asked the mulatoes who that [. . .] they answered confusedly that they did not know and told them to ask him who he was. They did so and he said he did not understand them they then repeated the question and he said "I am Carlo General Santa Anna's private secretary"- The told him he was a liar that Carlo was a prisoner at that moment in General Sam Houstons camp. They then told him to get and follow them they did not care who he was they intended to take him into the camp to their General—They were on horse back he was on foot and after he had walked about 50 yards they saw that he was very much fatigued and Young Robinson got down off his horse and ordered him to get up into the saddle. The man did not as he pretended understand him but Robinson said I'll make you understand and he caught hold of him by the slack of his trousers [. . .] made [. . .] got up behind him and the 3 rode into camp As they rode in one of the Mexicans who knew the prisoner said:

<u>There is Genl Santa Anna!</u> and when the news which seemed to spread over the army by electricity was known the whole army cheered the 2 young men and their distinguished prize—

They rode up near General Houstons tent—and dismounted and Santa Anna took a seat on a trunk and crossed his legs and kept his sharp bright eyes occupied in watching the army who crowded up close all around him in a circle and those in the rear got up on the shoulders of the men in front of them to get a look at Santa Anna who sat like a lion at bay. He sat thus silently for some time and his eyes seemed every now and then to single out the the officers whom he distinguished by the difference [. . .] from their subordinates but their authoritative appearance.

Finally he said: "I am very thirsty will not some one bring me some water"—one of the Texans went down to the Bayou and returned with a large tin cup filled with it and Santa Anna took the cup and as he was about to drink it, <u>he made the Masonic Sign of distress</u>.

As he did so all the officers and men of that fraternity drew their weapons and closed around him General Houston among the rest to protect him.

Just at this Juncture General Sommerville who was not a mason and who was Just beyond the Circle of men around Santa Anna came up cursing and swearing that he was going to kill Santa Anna he had a bowie knife in one hand and a pistol [in] the [other]

Houston said to him "Sommerville your blood is too warm, go down to the Bayou and take a bath and that will cool it off"—Summerville answered I dont care what you say I intend to kill him—and became still more excited. Houston then told General Rusk who stood beside him to go and take Summerville away and make him promise not to harm their prisoner and if he did not <u>to kill him on the spot</u>—Rusk went with Morelavecka Sherman and Lamar up to Summerville and they each had a pistol in one hand a bowie knife in the other just as Summerville had—They told him to follow them and come away from there or it would not be well for him. Summerville referred rusk to the Devil and said he was still hungry and want to chaw up Santa Anna—Rusk then went close up to Summerville and Said General Houston has [. . .] orders to [. . .] off and make you promise not kill or hurt his prisoner and if you do not instantly comply with those orders I shall kill you here—Summerville did not weaken until Rusk took his bowie knife and <u>Stuck it into his flesh a quarter of an inch deep just over his heart</u> and then he said I will accede to my commanders orders Rusk Said "will you give your sacred word of honor to not molest Santa Anna in any"—Summerville said "Yes" and he then put up his pistol and Bowie Knife and marched away with them—to his quarters—

Santa Anna speaks

Santa Anna then drew a long sigh of relief as Summerville was led off and said after a short pause: "Is there not some one who speaks Castillian and English"—he asked this question in Spanish and Houstons own interpreter answered him in the same tongue and said "I do [. . .]" you can tell y[. . .] in chief that <u>I am Don Lopez de Santa Anna President of the Republic of Mexico.</u>"

Hallet complied and Houston who was lieing down near him suffering from a painful wound in his foot politely arose and shook his hand and at the same time bade Hallet ask Santa Anna to tell him why he had not told to the young men who had taken him prisoner. Santa Anna answered with much confusion that he feared if he did so the 2 soldiers would have killed him.

Houston then said tell santa Anna that I have no <u>soldiers</u> all of my brave me are honorable gentlemen who are above such brutality and if not they fear me too much to do a thing that I would not countenance on account of its barbarity—

Santa Said give me another interpreter Dr. Ald[. . .] but neither he or [. . .] who came up to interpret pleased Santa Anna who had Spied General Almonte and asked that he be permit to act as his mouth-piece Almonte was called and came up—He Houston and Santa Anna then had a General and plilical conversation which lasted some time and Houston then said "I see General Santa Anna that you are extremely fatigued & I will have you a tent erected close to my own and have a bed prepared for you to rest upon" and he gave orders to that effect which were promptly executed.

Santa Anna then asked Houston through Almonte if he did not have some Mexican gentleman among his command. I, who had been standing close during the whole conversation which had occurred since Santa Anna first asked for water, stepped forward bowed uncovered my head and put my left [. . .]y bosom and then [. . .] Santa Anna thus "You see before you General Santa Anna a Mexican your humble servant and ready to do your bidding." He said: "you are a very fine looking fellow and your face seems familiar to me. What is your name"?

I answered "my name, General Santa Anna, is Antonio Manchaca."

He said "You are from San Antonio are you not Manchaca"? I said "I am sir—

He then replied "Manchaca I know you very well"—

I said "I know you also very well General de Santa Anna and I remember you when you came to San Antonio with General Arrerondo and you were then a young cadet fresh from school."

He then told me that when he was in San Antonio last he had heard me very highly spoken of—

I said to him [. . .] prisoner I s[. . .] by treating you kindly that my good repute in San Antonio may not be undeserved. Please tell how I can be of any service to you."

He replied to me "Major Manchaca I have not tasted any food for 3 days but parched corn and I have not had more than enough of that than barely to keep me alive and I am very hungry indeed will you get me something to eat"

I said "General de Santa Anna the provisions in the American army are very low and we fare but little better than you have done but I will get what I can for you"—He said "please get me some meat and roast it with your own hand as some of the rest of the men might try to poison me" Then Santa Anna and Almonte were conducted to the tent prepared to receive them and Rusk with a picked detachment of 25 men most of [. . .] and all rel[. . .] Cannibals like Sommerville might feel hungry and wish to feast on Santa Annas bones.

Santa Anna was strongly hated by Texas Volunteers on account of his brutality in murdering the men who were in the Alamo when it was carried by storm—During the battle of San Jacinto the battle cry of the Texans was "remember the Alamo" and they made me take my men who were Mexicans and put large pieces of white paste board on their hats and breasts lest they should be mistaken for Santa Annas men and killed—

I as I before stated started of in quest of some food for Santa Anna. As I got to my camp 4 companies of men from Galveston sent to reinforce General Houston arrived (They were "just behind the battle Mother" and the fighting was all done when they came in) and they marched in front of my c[. . .] As they were passing I went out to met them and when the halted close by I went to one of the men and asked him if he had any green Coffee to sell and he said that he had. I asked him what he charged me for it and he said $5 a cup full—I bought a cup of it and also 2 cups of sugar for $5 more and also 14 cups of flour for the same price and paid him in bills of a Bank in New Orleans of which I had $7.000 in my belt and they were at par with gold or silver with us and even at a premium with the latter as they were so much easier to carry in large quantities without danger of losing them—

These provisions I conveyed to my camp and asked one of my men named Flores who was an excellent cook to parch the coffee and drip some of it make some bread with the flour—boil some of our mess beans, roast some meat ala mexicana, and fry some in the same mode which he set himself at work to do and when Flores had finished cooking it I saw to having it dished up in some tin pans.

In the mean time however while Flores was cooking this supper A court Martial was being held at head quarters in front of General Sam Houstons tent—and I went to ascertain what they intended to do—

Santa Anna was looking on at the court from where he was standing at the front opening of his tent which was about 10 or 15 paces distant from the place where the tribunal was in session. The court was discussing what they would do with Santa Anna and whether they would execute him or not—The court finally concluded not to kill him but to Send him as a prisoner of war to the National Capital of the United States Washington City and present him before the President of that Government to answer for the wrong he had done some of its citizens who were murdered in the Alamo—After this decision had been reached I thought I would go and see about Santa Annas supper which I found ready I made 4 of my men take the pans and coffee pot and follow me over to Santa Annas tent. When I reached it the guard halted me and would not let me pass—I told him prisoners were human beings with appetites like other men and it was a shame not to permit me to feed them Houston heard me remonstrating with the guard and immediately gave me a written pass to go at any hour day or night into the quarters of Santa Anna and the Mexican prisoners—I was then admitted and I got my 4 men to go and cut branches and bougs and spread them as even as possible to mak a table in the tent—When this had been done and a cover was spread on them I took 3 cups of coffee and made places for the 2 Generals Santa Anna and Almonte and their Col Bringas and when Santa Anna Sat down to eat I took out my knife & scraped all of the mud that I could get of his trousers and the breeches of the other two officers—

Santa Anna was so ravenously hungry and thirsty he drank two cups of coffee one right after the other without intermission and called for a 3d cup to wash his supper down with—

He ate like a wolf and did not look around until he had finished his supper—After his supper had been eaten he then commenced to talk to me and ask me why the Americans hated him so why they wanted to kill him and if the Court martial had ordered his execution yet—I told him the cause of the hatred the Texans bore for him but told him he was not to be killed but sent to the President of the United States as a prisoner of war and his fate would be termined there—He told me he thought that I was deceiving him that this information was almost too good to be true.

I told him that I gave him my word as gentleman of honor that it was as I told him he then put his hand in his belt and pulled out a splendid watch which he had concealed there and offered it to me—It was a wath that cost $3.700 and was presented to Santa Anna by the Government of Mexico as a token of appreciation of his services as its President.

As he extended his hand to give it to me I motioned to him to put it back in his belt and asked him why he had offered it to me.

He said "to pay you for the splendid supper you have given and the good news you have told me"

I said to him "General Santa Anna would you insult me by saying this and offering me that watch—You are my prisoner were you free you should fight for this." I then saw tears come to his eyes and he cried like a child I then said General Santa anna I do not need your watch which is the only thing of any value that you have about your person but you who are a prisoner do need some assistance I have in my belt nearly $7.000 in the bills of a New Orleans bank take it it may be of some service to you to pay for your servants and living when you are taken to Washington"—

(**It showed the goodness of heart of Manchaca to be sorry for hurting

Santa Annas feelings and offering to rob himself of his last cent to give to Santa Anna*)[1]

Santa Anna Said I was mistaken in believed he needed any assistance pecuniarily. He informed me that he had the incredibly large sum of $33,000,000.00 in gold in Mexico and his check for that amount at any time he saw to draw it would be paid. I then left him to retire as it was late and I saw the men who had been left <u>to guard baggage during the battle come in</u> with it as our camp was not at the same place where we had it when the battle was fought—My wallet and other baggage that had been among it turned up missing and I lost all of my changes of clothing and linen.

Sunday morning Just exactly a week after the battle I took one of the members of my company down to the Bayou to wash out the shirt that I had on. As I sat on the banking waiting for it to dry I saw a skiff coming up Buffalo Bayou in the direction from Galveston and as it came close to me and the person spoke to me His face resembled the countenance of young Savallo so closely that I knew it must be his father and Said to him how do you do Don Lopez Savalla and he replied I am very well.

It was Savallo Sr who had been the vice President of the Mexican Republic but he had been (banished by Santa Anna from Mexico[2] and had to work on the streets of London and Paris when he reached those cities he was sent off in such destitute circumstances) Savallo though was a Statesman and a scholar and was warmly welcomed by the Texans because he espoused their cause. Sam Houston fired a grand salute with his cannon when Savallo landed and went down with his officers followed by Santa Anna to the side of the water to meet him—

Savalla and Santa Anna were of course bitter enemies but the latter thought it Just as well to be polite as their fortunes were now reversed and so he went to the Bayou with the rest who went welcome Savallo—

After Houston and his officers and also Santa Anna had held a long conversation with Savalla—the latter asked to see the documents which contained a record of the proceedings of the Congress of the Republic of Texas.

---

1. This statement is set off in the original to clearly indicate that it is not Menchaca's words.

2. The following note appears in the margin of the text at this point: "This is not quite correct as Zavala was in Paris at the time Santa Anna usurped the supreme power and Zavala wrote and denounced him and refused to serve under him longer. That letter is still in existence. He was Minister to the Court of St Cloude at the time." See *Edited Reminiscences, Part 2*, n. 27 (p. 87), for further explanation.

Rusk told him that I had them and asked him to accompany him over to my quarters—when they reached there I had not returned and they asked where I was and sent after me—My shirt had not yet dried sufficiently for me to put it on so I went back without it—When I came into the presence of the august ex vice President of the Republic of Mexico I had no shirt on and both he and Rusk looked a little surprized and smiled <u>audibly</u>—

Rusk asked me to explain why I came on dress parade before one of the Generals of the army with such a pretty <u>brown</u> shirt that fit me so tight. I told him all of my other shirts but one had been stolen by one of his own men who were guarding some of the baggage & that one was drying on the Bank of the Bayou he then said he would make me a present of a shirt—and sent to his tent by one of my men to bring me one.

He after I got inside of it asked me to show vice President those papers already alluded to—

As he was looking over them his soon young Savallo came in to my tent with a large official paper in his hand which he handed to me. I could not at first imagine what it could be but I found on reading it that it was a commission as Quarter Master General of the Army of the Republic of Texas to which position the Court Martial had Just appointed me—

While I was looking at it Seguin my old Captain passed and he saluted me saying You have just been made a high officer without any more fighting to do and I will have to leave you now Major—I said Seguin have you got orders to leave here and he said yes he was to go with Burlesons division which Houston had then ordered to march to Atascosita crossing I handed the commission back to Young Savallo and told him to go for me to the court martial and say for me that I was deeply grateful for the high honor they desired to confer me but that it was my intention to stay with my command as long as there was a bit of fighting to be done and that I would be compelled to decline the high position of Quarter Master General. I then ordered my boy to go and saddle my Horse and I rode off without telling either Santa Anna Almonte Savalla Houston or any one else good bye. And I never saw Santa Anna afterwards.

I had some money then and had I accepted the position of Quarter Master General and stayed with Santa Anna I might have been very wealthy to day but in my old age I do not regret going off and losing those opportunities when I reflect that I was doing my duty to my country in its strictest and best sense and this is a great consolation to me now though I am a very poor man with but a meager subsistance

After I had gone some distance I waited for Burleson and his command to come up.

Sherman was with him and they both took the direction of Fort Bend and marched at easy stages until they got within about 5 miles of that place when they discerned a troup of 6 horsemen with 5 small red flags which they knew to be Mexican standards—The party we soon ascertained to be General Bull one of Santa Annas Generals. He rode up very close to us and must at first have mistaken us for Santa Annas men as I with my Mexicans marched at the head of the column—

When we rode close to us we halted him and Burleson asked Sherman to accost him which he did—asking who he was and where he was going he Said I am Generall Adrian Bull of San Annas Mexican Army and in search of my Chief can you tell me where to find him—

Sherman told him of Santa Annas capture & where abouts and then asked him why he rode up to us with such sang froid and if he was not afraid that we would kill him—He said no I am a Frenchman & do not fear death neither am I afraid that the Americans would kill me. Sherman asked him how he knew this and he said because they were not in the habit of shooting prisoners—

He then gave his parole of honor that if Burleson would give him a passport to Houston guards and pickets to protect him that he would ride on to meet Santa Anna whom he particularly desired to find. Burleson wrote him the safe conduct for himself and his body guard and parted company Burleson with his command going on into Fort Bend and Bull going to Houston's camp on the San Jacinto—When Bull reached there I am told that Houston was very indignant with Burleson and Sherman for giving him this safe conduct and for not taking him west ward with them and send him on his parole back to Mexico—

CHAPTER 11TH
SMUGGLERS SINK

Our Command marched into Fort Bend and after a short rest we marched onward and at the end of the after noon of the 2nd day we stopped at some holes of water in a lane called Smugglers Sink. Here we overtook a party of Mexicans with their General Ampudia—We halted and made our camp here and Ampudia struck up a conversation with Sherman and as he was a quarter master General in Santa Annas army they (Burleson and Sherman) might have known that he had a camp of with supplies around somewhere close in the neighborhood that night Ampudia stole off and made good his escape—

It was ascertained next morning that he had a camp with in 2 miles of us and had there 150 mules and horses a large number of wagons loaded with all sorts of military supplies and 2 wagons loaded with cannon balls and other artillery charges—One of our men Fillippe Hiemee who was captured as a courier for Santa Anna and who had taken allegiance to the Texas Government and was acting as one of our scouts at the time stumbled over a lot of sick and wounded 21 in number with the 2 wagons loaded with ordinance left who communicated the fact of Ampudia having escaped from the Texans and then coming over to his own camp and gathering up all of his stock took them with all of the supplies and provisions and left only the 2 heaviest wagons with the cannon balls and ammunition in them— They said he had left them not a morsel of food and that they were very hungry—and likewise implored them to go and bring them food from his camp—He went and told his superior officers Burleson & Sherman this in and they both felt sheepish at letting themselves be caught napping but they ordered Hyiemee to take them food which he did—

He was sent back on the following morning with more food for the wounded and to do all he could for them as the officers of the Texas army did not like to leave their wounded enemies to starve like their own officers had done but lo and behold when Hieméé went to the place where the wounded had been he found the 2 wagons that had contained ordinance as well as all of the wounded gone and nothing left but the cannon balls shells etc thrown promiscuously out on the ground—When he went back with his news to Burleson & Sherman they again opened their eyes very wide and looked very suspiciously and then laughed at the smartness of the Mexicans The supposition is that the first food sent by Hiemee strengthened some of them so as enable them to get out and capture some mules or horses on the prairie that night and they came back with them pitched out the loads of artillery ammunition and hauled of their wounded companions in the 2 wagons that had contained it—

Burleson & Sherman now sent forward scouts to the Colorado to reconiotre and report if they came up with the Mexican army either there on this side, as they rightly conjectured that they were then getting tolerably close upon it.

Some of the scouts returned very soon afterwards and informed us that Ampudea with his train and the wounded men had both crossed the Colorado and formed a junction just on the west banks of the river with General Felisseola who with his division was camped within a hundred yards of the rivers bank.

We were then within about 8 miles of the Colorado then and we reached it that night That night people were crossing the river in both directions unmolested by either army.

"Boots and Saddles!!"

Next morning at daymark we heard Felisolas buglers play playing boots and Saddles air on their bugles and Sherman ordered his own Buglers to play the Same strain—When we crossed the river and came up on his camp which was just as the sun rose it was deserted and nothing but the ashes of his camp fires were left—They could not have been very far ahead of us but we were marching a little more leisurely behind them than they were in front of us. Houstons orders to Burleson & Sherman had been to avoid bloody battles as long as their enemy retreated in the direction of his Own Country. And to follow him with out pressing him to close—

At 10 oclock Sherman ordered a detachment of 10 scouts to ride ahead and see how far off the enemy was—They rode about 2 or 3 miles and found 1.000 head of beef cattle lying almost exhausted in the road from hard driving and they concluded correctly had been left behind by Feliseola in his hurry to get beyond the reach of Texas powder and lead.

The next days march brought us to the San Antonio creek 12 miles west of the Colorado river where we halted a week From here we took up our march to Victoria and below the town about a mile and a half.

We remained at Victoria 18 days and in the mean time during our encampment there we were joined by General Rusk who came up from San Jacinto with 800 men—After Rusks arrival a short time he asked me if I would like to go with my men and Seguins to San Antonio and I told him I would—he Said there is some risk attendant upon the venture as General Andrade with 2500 men and 30 pieces of artillery is marching in the direction from San Antonio on his way to Mata Moras—I told I did not feel a bit afraid. He said if you fall in with him and get captured let me know as soon as possible by a courier and I will come to your assistance I have orders not to fight unless it is necessary but I would like very much indeed to pitch once more into the Mexicans—On the road to New Golliad we met Col Ugartachea with an escort of 5 men on his way to get supplies for Andrade's army—He asked Seguin and I which way we were going with our men and we said to San Antonio he said "I wish to see General Rusk who is at Victoria and if you will give me a pass port and and an interpreter through to him I will give you one through Andrades lines to San Antonio"—Seguin wrote him a passport and called one of my men Pedro Flores and sent him with Ugartachéa and he left us a written passport to

Andrade and his Mexican Corporal and we separated going in different directions. Our companies halted to prepare their dinner at a little house by the road side about 9 miles from Goliad—And very shortly after we had stopped the Mexican Corporal left by Ugartachea came to Seguin and I and informed us that Andrade's Command were marching toward us— As Andrades advance guard came up some of the officers in front accosted the Corporal and asked what he was doing among those Texans. And he explained to them. In the mean time Andrade and his staff rode up and Andrade asked "who commanded those troops" Sequin answered I do sir." Andrade then said my corporal informs me that you have a pass port from Col Ugartachea let me see it—Seguin handed it to him and he read it and Said you and your command can march on ahead to San Antonio undisturbed—Andrades Army marched then by us in silence and our men kept perfectly silent too as the passed on in a regular slow and orderly manner the came to a halt a creek about a mile beyond us and about an hour afterwards we took up our march

CHAPTER 12TH
BACK TO SAN ANTONIO

After 3 days more marching we got into San Antonio and made <u>Musca's</u> house head quarters of our division. We found the city almost deserted a great many families who sympathized with the Texas cause moved East and a great many Mexican families who either from choice or compulsion aspoused the Mexican cause went to Mexico—

We had returned and remained in town about a week when 6 Comanchei Indians with their chief Cassamiro rode into the town.

They were all horribly filthy and as lean and gaunt as wolves. The asked some of the Mexicans who was in command here and they were told Seguin and Manchaca. Cassamiro said he did not know Seguin but he did know Manchaca and he came to me and asked me how I came on and I told him very well. He then informed me that he was very hungry (all Indians always are) and wanted something to eat and also asked me if I did not have some thing to give him. I told him I would give him a plenty and I took the key to one of Santa Annas Store houses which was full of provisions and told him to follow me there. I unlocked the door and told him to pitch in and help himself—He ate like a hungry hound with his men and after they had satisfied the immediate ravings of their appetites Cassamiro began to look around the store house—He spied a large sack of bread cooked with lard

& Seasoned with Salt and he asked to be permitted to take it with a sack of beans and 3 strings of peppers—which I agreed to—

He then turned to go but before he left he looked at me in a very strange pitying manner and said to me Manchaca I feel a great deal of compassion for you and am truly sorry for you—

I asked him why this sudden out burst of pity and compassion and if there was any danger over hanging me—

He told me that the Indians intended to come into San Antonio burn the town and kill all of the people I said Cassimiro this is the worst piece of barbarous ingratitude that I ever heard of. The people of San Antonio have never yet harmed the Commanchees & have always fed them when they came and asked for some thing to eat.

He said Manchaca I have 20 horses 2 mexican prisoners to wait on me and 4 wives. If you will come and live with me and my band I will devide equally with you each of these articles—

I told him I was not quite as well fixed with wives as he was but still I was satisfied to remain where I was He says do you intend to stay in San Antonio I said I live here Cassimiro and I am going to get my family who left during the war and bring them back—

He said how many moons will you be gone? (Indians reckon time by the number of new moons) I told him I thought it might take me 5 or 6 moons to go & return—

He grunted Umph! Good! and asked me if I had any muscal and told him a little and I would him 6 bottles He then wanted polonciers (sugar) and I gave him 50 of them And then I said Cassamiro recollect what I have told you about killing people of San Antonio and think of my kindness to you and do not harm them He and his men then went away—and on the 10th of June 1836 I left San Antonio to go to get my family who were then at Nachadoches—and I arrived there on the 20th of July—I remained there with them until the 15th of August and Started with them back to San Antonio While we were on the road I heard that 1500 Commanches on the 15th of August had been into San Antonio & killed a Mexican woman and 2 girls and then gone down to the San Jose Mission and their killed two very good men and a lady—On the 16th they came back to San Antonio— and dismounted in the Cibollo Square and said they wanted to kill all of the people Cassamiro was their Chief and after a while ordered them to ride out of town. He was the last to go and before he left told a Mexican to tell me that he had been into town and staid all day with his band who wanted to kill every body in town and that he had ordered them of without let- ting carry out their threats—He asked the Mexican if I was in town and he told him I had gone to Nachadoches. One of Cassimiros men said it was so because he had seen me when I got to Nachodoches—

Cassimiro then left town—I did not reach home until November 1836 from Nachodoches—

Soon after my arrival here General Rusk who with 4.000 men near Lavacca sent 300 of them to Seguin & and I to protect San Antonio from the Indians Squads of whom we sent out on scouts to fight them—Seguin & myself were the Commanders of this post as officers of the Texas Republic from Nov 1836 to 1838—Early in the latter year a Colonel Kans was sent by the President of the Republic to relieve us who commanded until 1839. Kans always kept a guard to watch the horses at the San José Mission but in March 1839 a band of Indians from Presidio del Rio Grande captured all of the horses and the 2 guards who were watching them and took them away—

In September 1839 Col Kans was Superceded by Col Fisher who moved his quarters to the San José Mission—A short time after Fisher was placed in command a band of 7 Indians (Commanchees) and their Chief and wanted to make overtures for peace—Fisher told them they would first have to go and bring him all the Mexicans or American prisoners they had—And they told him they would go and return with the prisoners in the course of 20 days—He told his interpreter to tell the Chief if he caught him telling a lie he would kill him and all of the men he caught with him—The Indians left and returned at the end of 20 days and camped at the Spot where the market near main plaza now stands—There were about 20 of them including 5 women & some children. But they did not bring any of the prisoners with them—

Fisher was very indignant when he learned that they had returned without keeping their word to bring the prisoners and so he determined to teach them a lesson—He took his command and surrounded them and killed every man but one among them who escaped badly wounded by running down to the river Swimming across and following down the timber—He did not kill the women and children but kept them as prisoners. At the end of 3 months a Commanchee Chief came in unattended by his band his name was Poochaynaqua and he offered to exchange 5 prisoners Mexicans for the 5 commanchee women & children in the custody of Fisher to which the latter agreed and Poochaynaqua brought in his prisoners delivered them up effected the exchange and retired with his women & children—

In the Year 1840 while General Lamar was President of the young Republic he had an expedition fitted out which marched under General

McCloud assisted by the young Antonio Navarro whose father has already been mentioned as one of the former Governors of San Antonio under the Spanish regime The expedition numbered 400 men and was sent to attend to some troubles that were going on out on the Texas border near Paso del Norte.

They went out there and crossed the Rio Grande river and marched into Chihuahua but were attacked and captured after a short engagement by The Mexican General Armillo with 3.000 men and taken prisoners to Veracruz In September of the same year Kans was sent back to San Antonio to organize another expedition to fight the Indians who were then very troublesome—They went to San Sabba and had fight with the Indians in which they killed 20 of the Indians and took from them over 100 horses without losing a single The Army then of Texas in this place was disbanded and the discharged soldiers permitted to go to their homes as the Government was considered to have been established on a firm basis—

But while their were only 60 able bodied American & Texas men mostly lawyers and professional men and a great many treacherous mexicans in San Antonio we learned that The Mexicans under a Mexican General Vasquez were coming into San Antonio from Mexico—The 60 Americans who organized and were commanded by 2 lawyers Barnes & John D Morris prepared to defend the town Vasquez came in to the edge of town with 1500 men in March 1842 and sent word to Barnes & Moris if they would surrender the town without fighting that the people who chose to leave might be permitted to depart unmolested but if they did not surrender without firing a shot he would kill every soul among them—

Barnes and Morris held a consultation with the people and finally all agreed to accept the terms offered by Vasquez—

Vasquez marched in to town and the Texans and other American people all marched out via the Seguin road—

Vasquez remained here 12 days and then retreated on hearing that 1500 Texans were after him who passed through here the following day after his departure in hot pursuit after him—They however did not overtake him and gave up the chase very soon because Vasquez distanced them so badly—He was in a terrible hurry to get back across the Rio Grande and never stopped longer than necessary before reaching its opposite Bank And the Texans returned through San Antonio to the place from whence the came—

CHAPTER 13TH
ANOTHER 'BULLY' BOY; WHO CALLS
HIMSELF GENERAL ADRIAN BULL—COMES TO
TOWN AND IS TAKEN BY THE HORNS:

San Antonio was a very quiet place from the time that Vasquez left until the next September—On the 11th of that month the Same General Adrian Bull who was met by the roadside By Burleson and Sherman near Fort Bend Marched into San Antonio at the head of a force of 1500 men—He took 54 Americans and myself prisoners & put us in the Calaboose and I staid locked up 3 days when on the 3d Day Bull sent an interpreter named Martinez to bring me to his presence and he said you are Antonio Manchaca the greatest traitor to your flag unhung and you deserve to be shot 25 times through the head but General Santa Anna who thanks you for the kindness you did him asked me if I captured you to spare your life which I will do on one condition & that is that you will give me your word of honor never again to Take up arms against Mexico—I agreed to comply with his condition and he then told me I was free. He then said he contemplated sending the other 54 Prisoners to Mexico and asked me if I thought they would be able to walk there. I said they were most of them dear friends of mine and all of them good people and it would hurt me very much to see them have to walk all of the way to Mexico I told him he did not have to walk from Fort Bend to Sanjacinto and I thought if the prisoners had to go to Mexico they had better be sent on horseback or in wagons and not be made to foot it At the End of a week he sent Martinez again to my house saying that he wanted to see me. When I came to his quarters he offered me a seat which I took and then he asked me if I still remembered his sparing my life I told him I did—He said now tell me candidly if you think I am running any risk by staying in San Antonio—I told him that he had now been in San Antonio 10 days and in 3 or 4 days more he would have to fight if he staid—He asked me how I knew this and why I thought so—I said General Vasques came here and was in quet possession of the town for 12 days but at the end of the 12th he had to fly as fast as his legs could carry him back to Mexico and I expect it would be very prudent for you to begin to think about following his illustrious example. He asked me if I could not be mistaken in my opinions—I told perhaps I could be mistaken but my belief was very firm that it would not be very long the Brave Bull would run from the cowboys who would be trying to pen him—

Bull said cain I rely on your word Manchaca I told him other people relied on it and it might be very wise in him to do so in time—

He then said I will give you a pass port through my lines pickets and guards or into my quarters to pass you any hour day or night and if you learn any thing of importance please come and inform me—I assented took the pass port and left his presence—On the 15th day after Bulls arrival in San Antonio a Mexican named Brunovisso came into town from the San Jose Mission and came to my house and inquired for me—He told me that on his way to town he was stopped by Col Hays and 2 of his men who caught his bridle rein just as he was on the point of fording the river and lead his horse into the timber thicket at the side of the ford and asked him if I was alive and in town. Brunovisso Said he believed so as I was seen the week before—Hays then told Brunovisso he would let him go on provided he promised as soon as he got into town and tell me to go out to him as he wanted me to see him tell General Bull good morning with his rifles next morning—

I went and communicated all this to Bull & told him if he was going to leave town he had the best opportunity he ever would have of leaving—

He said can I rely on this information as being true—(he was a very suspicious Frenchman) and I said if you wait until to morrow morning you will find out whether Col Hays will greet you or not—

I then left Bull and went back to my house

Sure enough next morning early 10 or 15 Rangers with Red Shirts rode into town by the Alamo street—

Bull then a corps of 250 dragoons quartered in the Alamo who saw them and blew their bugle to get ready to attack them—At the same time Bull who was with his infantry on the Plazas gave orders for them to form and he marched them with his dragoons towards the Salado

There Bulls Ball began and a hot fight ensued—Bull sent 60 men to the front to commence the attack and they were every last one killed by Hay's men About this time 50 Americans under a Texan captain Dawson came up to join the main body of Hays command but they with their leader were all cut off and killed by the Dragoons who surrounded them out flanked them and then cut them to pieces—Bull stubbornly fought all day long losing his men like sheep and gaining no advantage over Hays—At 4 oclock he began to send his wounded who were very numerous in to San Antonio and at dark commenced to retreat himself with the survivors of his army to San Antonio—Next day he made preparations about evacuating—He sent for me and had further conversation in relation to the American prisoners—He said he had heard that the 13 lawyers and private citizens were gentlemen but that the remainder were vagabonds and thieves—I told him I believed them all to be gentlemen. he then said they should all in that case be permitted to ride when taken to Mexico—The prisoners gave me a letter to take to Col Hays which said they were treated well by Bull and if he fell in with any of his men asking that they be treated well—I got a horse from a merchant of this place a Mr Jacks and I took the letter to Hays who was then on the Salado with his men—He was much rejoiced to see me alive and well and Hays then read his letter—

He next moved his men to the San Pedro Springs and waited there for Bull to Evacuate which he did at 3 oclock in the evening—

For several days Hays permitted no one but my self and one of his young men named Clay Davis to go into town. Recruits now began to pour into Hay's army and at the end of 3 days after they first camped at the San Pedro Springs—he had 2500 in his ranks—A Court Martial was now called by Hayes & his officers

CHAPTER 14
GENERAL ANTONIO MANCHACA COMMANDER IN CHIEF OF THE ARMY OF THE REPUBLIC OF TEXAS

This Court Martial while I was at home was in session—

While I was being down at home 5 members a committee sent by the court rode up to my door & the chairman handed me a commission which gave me the rank and title of the Chief Commander of the Texas forces—

I was full of gratitude and it hurt me this time to be again forced to decline the honors that had been given to me unsought for—I however bade the chairman take back the commission to the court give it my heart felt thanks and deep regrets and tell the members of the tribunal that my only reason for declining was that I had given my parole of honor never more to take up arms against Mexico. That this parole was given to General Bull on the condition that he would spare my life and I could not violate it—

The Texas army was for some time without a chief commander and before they had elected one they followed Bull who had retreated slowly and attacked him but their attack was ineffectual in asmuch as there was but little discipline or harmony of action in the engagement and The Texans had to fall back after killing a few of Bulls men & losing some of their own and they came here on a retreat leaving the enemy retreating himself in the opposite direction

After the return of the Texans to San Antonio General Burleson came in and then they called a court Martial which was composed of some of

the officers besides General Burleson and Some Civilians among them myself and Messrs Barnes (already mentioned) & Terrel 2 attorneys. We were
members of the court By invitation from General Burleson who courteously requested us participate in the deliberations of the court—

CHAPTER 14TH
"SHALL WE BURN SAN ANTONIO?"

The main question which was under discussion was what should we do
with San Antonio it was so far from other cities of the Republic of Texas
was then a perfect hot bed of Mexican Spies and always the point first
attacked and easiest captured by the Mexicans—These serious drawbacks
were all exhausted by Col Terrel the attorney of Eastern Texas who strongly
advocated burning the town and he was the first to address the court—He
said that the families who lived here could be permitted to go to other
cities of Texas or to Mexico those who preferred the latter Government—

General Burleson after Terrell finished introduced me to the court as a
man in whose opinion he had as much confidence as in the opinion of any
general in his Army and requested me to present my views to the Court I
said I did not like to Speak English for fear of making them laughs at my
pronunciation & I asked Barnes to interpret for me while I spoke in Castillian and I made them a short speech bitterly opposing the sacrifice of
San Antonio to the flames—I said I had an aged mother here who would
be among the people who would be left destitute by the burning of the
town and I said for my self I did not care so much—I moreover asked if
San Antonio was burned who would give the money to support the people
who would be left penniless paupers, until they could go some where else
& earn a livelihood—There were too a great many very old people here
who could not well be moved—

Barnes then slipped a little note in my hand asking me to give way to
him and let him make a speech in behalf of saving San Antonio and I gratified his request—

Barnes was a beautiful speaker and a much more eloquent man than I
and at the clusion of his warm and impetuous speech there was not a dry
eye except his own in the whole court and when General Burleson took
the vote on the question <u>San Antonio was saved</u>!!!

CHAPTER 15
THE MEXICAN WAR WITH THE US COMMENCES

It was some time in April 1845 when Col Harney left San Antonio with 400 Cavalry to meet the U.S. General Taylor (a la Zach) at Corpus Christi where he was with 1500 Regular US troops which he had brought from New Orleans by sea—

Taylor however intending to push on into Mexico ordered Harney not to come to Corpus Christi but to march his cavalry via Presidio Del Rio Grande and Join him some where close to Monterey—

Taylor won a victorious Battle at a lane near Matamoras called Point Isabelle in which entirely destroyed the command of the Mexican Romollo La Vega and captured him—

Taylor passed on to Monterey and and here was joined by Harney who came with his Cavalry from San Antonio. Soon After the Mexican campaign opened in Earnest and all of the battles, described already in the history which is written of the Mexican War, were fought among the most bloody of all Buena Vista—

In 1816 Some laboring men were plowing in a field, which is now the Site of the "Vance Hotel kept by Captain Tobin and owned by the Vance Brothers, and these laborers were fired on by the Indians and 6 were killed: I believe there were 16 Indians, who made the attack From that time to the present the city has grown in size wealth & prosperity the lot which is on the Main street that was formerly sold in 1808 in the time of Governor Cordero for $60 about 300 yards long by 100 wide could not to day be bought for $60,000.00/100

CHAPTER 16
A HISTORY OF THE SETTLEMENT AND INHABITANTS OF SAN ANTONIO

The first Settlers who came here were 16 families of Spanish decendents from the Canary Isles who reached here in 1735—Among them was my Great Grand Father Don Pedro Acon y Frillo and Old Captain Manchaca and his wife. My great grand father had a grant for all of the land for his colony to settle given to him by Barron de Pegnia Flora the Representative of the King of Spain and they chose this part of the country to locate

The had with them the following other families of Castillian descent viz: The Arochas, Delagdo's, Grenado's, Galvanos, Traviesso's, Rodriguez Fernandes, Lealles, Cassanovas, Sepado's, Coubrero's—Calbijo's and Saucedo's They camped on the west side of the San Pedro River in that portion of San Antonio facetiously called "Chihuahua" and were joined by the following mentioned families who shortly thereafter came in from Mexico; viz Perez, Florez Garcias, Cardenas, Gonzales Montez, Sambranas and Sylvas, and intended to commence building the town there—The Indians, who lived in the holes and on the rocky bluff on the banks of the San Antonio River near its head where the large rock quaries where most of the rock used for building purposes is now obtained for the construction of houses in San Antonio, how ever were very troublesome and continually harrassed them so that they were compelled to move on the Eastern side of the San Pedro between that stream and the San Antonio River—

CHAPTER 17TH
THE FIRST HOUSE BUILT IN SAN ANTONIO

These colonists commenced building then like beavers, Making adobe houses—

The School master, whose name I can not recollect, succeeded in finishing his house which is a house now on Flores Street still Standing and is on the Northern Extension of that street about 400 yards north of the Military Plaza and at the present time of writing is occupied by Madam (signora) Antonio Cardenas a lady very nearly of my own age (a little over 76 years.)

The Mexican & Canary Settlers next laid off the Military and Main Plazas and built their residences around them Old Captain Manchacas house is also standing and is Situated on the Corner of Flores and Rio Grande Streets—and is occupied by Marianno Rodriguez—On the N. E. Corner of the Same Streets directly opposite old Captain Manchacas house on the East was Old Angel Navarros house—Angel Navarro was the father of young Antonio Navarro who became a Col in the service of the Army of the Texas Republic—

Next to Manchaca on the westward lived Martianna Hymenis—

Adjoining her place on the west ward was Ignacio Lucera's place which is owned by T T Tell the Attorney—Still next was the residence of José Manchaca who was sent by Salsedo a prisoner to Mexico & died in Chihuahua in prison at the End of a 10 years confinement—Jacob Lane Esq now owns his property and also that adjoining it on the west were Manuel Nunez place was—

Next to Nunez Place and where the Catholic Padres are now domiciliated apposite the old court house & Jail on the north Side of the Military Plaza was Francisco Arocha's place.

I will now take the Western Side of the Military Plaza in rotation—

on the north west corner Just in the rear of the City Jail now Stands the old house of Salvador Rodrigues—which is at present owned by the heirs of the late Ignacio Perez—

Just to his right on the south was the residence of Lewis Manchaca old capt Felix Manchacas brother and also a brother of Don José Manchaca

Right next to him lived old José Flores de Abrégo.

Ignacio del los Santos lived next to him on the South west corner of the Military Plaza—

I now take up the South side of the Military Plaza—

On the west opposite Del los Santos where the Monte Pio (pawn broker's) Shop is was Romillio Perez place—Next to him lived Placido Hernandez. Old Don Pedro Traviesso lived next door to him. Next to him on the South east corner of the Military Plaza lived Francisco Traviesso.

Opposite him on the East Side of Flores at the Corner of Ruiz Street (the Street running on the South boundary of the 2 Plazas Military and Main) was the property of Don Pedro Flores whose heirs now own the property—Adjoining Flores on Ruiz Street Viciente Carbrero owned the locality which is now occupied by the Office of the San Antonio and bounded on the East by the ditch which runs along the west side of the main Plaza—On his right hand adjoining was Manuel Salinas—

Next to Salinas and where the "Central Hotel" kept by Mr Baker stands was old Clementé Delgados residence Next to him on the South side of the Main Plaza lived Thomas Delgado—

Where the livery Stable next to Bakers Central Hotel is situated is the old site of Bartollo Seguins residence who was the Great Grand Father of my captain Seguin so often before mentioned in connection with the Texas Service and the Campaign against Santa Anna—

Next to old Seguin lived Patricio Rodriguez whose Place formed the South East corner of the Main Plaza—

Where Frenches large Stone building the present US Head quarters of this division stands was the property of Francisco Rodriguez.

We now take up the places opposite the Main Plaza on the Eastern Side. Opposite Francisco Rodriguez on the N E Corner of Ruiz & Soledad Street was the property of Francisco Chavis which extends to the Next Corner or to Calavasa (now Market) Street.

On the N.E. Cor of Calavasa & Soledad Streets, stood the old Spanish Calaboose or prison—

Next to the Callaboose or Soledad St where Willie Adams the Government Transfer Contractor has his office was the Old "Corporation House" Next on the right stood The Governors Mansion, the residence of all the old Spanish Governors— (The first whom I recollect to have seen was old Don Antonio Corderro the first one mentioned in my narrative)—Next to the Governors Mansion and at the South East Corner of Commerce (Main) & Saladad Streets was the residence of the family of Granados—Directly opposite them on the N-E Corner of Commerce and Soladad Sts was the Property of Old Manuel Barrera which is now owned by Mr Maverick an occupied as a clothing Store by some Israelites—

Now we come to the North side of the Main Plaza—

On the N.W Corner of Commerce & Saladad where Jack Harrises bar room is stood the residence of Don Thomass Arocha. The property is owned now jointly I believe by Messers Sweet & Sam Smith—

Next to the Corner was Vicente Traviesso property now owned by Mrs. Elliott—Next to Traviesso lived Don Sîmón Arocha a very wealthy and influential Citizen of the old first Community of San Antonio who owned the remainder of the Property facing the Main Plaza on the North including the North East Corner of Main & Acequia Streets—

Opposite on the west on the N W corner of Main (Commerce or Rio Grande) & Acequia Street which is also now owned by Mr Maverick stood the residence Remundo Diaz—Next to Diaz to the west ward or Rio Grande St Fragosa Galvans premises, and next to him Antonio Navarro who lived next to his father Angel Navarro whose residence has already been mentioned

We now take the west side of Main Plaza—

On the N W Corner of the Plaza was the place of Don Francisco Parrera His place is now owned by an aged Mexican widow Donna Trinidad Soto— Next to Him and where the Auction Mart of Mr Frost is located, and already mentioned and the identical spot where David Crocket met James Bowie when he first came into San Antonio from Tennessee—was Don Torrébio Fuentes—domicile in the rear of these two properties and comprising the property in that locality at present owned by Mr. F. Guilbeau was the Property then owned by Signora Tia Chonita—

Next is the Catholic Church which will be here after more fully described—Oposite the South side of the Church on the corner of the small street and facing the Main Plaza and extending to a depth of about ¼ of the

FIGURE 10

The Veramendi Palace, home of the family into which James Bowie married and site of Ben
Milam's death during the Texans' storming of Bexar on 7 December 1835, was among the major
buildings from the Spanish colonial era lost to modernity. The central part of San Antonio that
Menchaca describes in the last part of his recollections has largely been replaced by the city's modern
downtown. "Veramendi Palace," 81–500, Photograph Collection, courtesy of the
University of Texas at San Antonio Libraries Special Collections.

square opposite to the South Side of the Church was the property of Francisco Gallan Next to him and where the "Plaza House" kept by Eugen Deit-
rich Esq stands lived old Don Ignacio Flores who owned the whole square
(with the exception of Gallans cor) facing the Main Plaz on Acequai street
next to Gallans facing ruiz Street facing Military Plaza on Flores Street and
the Catholic Church on the little Street on its South

Mr Veramendi the former President of the Government of Chihuahua
and who became the father in lawe of the Celebrated Hero of the Alamo
James Bowie had a residence in San Antonio situated on Saladad Street
immediately opposite the Post Office — which was the house which is now
used a confectionary and which very recently caught fire and was slightly
injured on the inside —

Houston Street where the Iron Bridge which now spans the San Antonio
and running in front of Sappingtons Stable was not at that laid of and is to

me a modern street—Next however to Veramendi and up to where Houston Street now crosses Soladad was Don Francis Armangual—Adjoining him was the property the lady Yficiaca Rodriguez—

Beyond her and where the property I now live in is situated and where the old mill in its rear on the river bank formerly stood and where Bowie Gave his Grand Ball on the eve of reciving the fatal tidings of Santa Annas Approach stood the residence of Marcos Sepada.

Where the livery stable on the same side of the Street as the post office & opposite diagonaly to the N W of the New Court house on Saladad street is located was Manuel Delgados place On the North East corner of Acequia and (new) Houston Sts was the residence Francisco Casanovas place—next to him and including the corner of Abraje Street—the proper of the widow of Don Antonio Galvan—Don Pedro Sambrano owned the property adjoining Angel Navarro on Flores Street extending from next to the N E Corner of Rio Grande & Flores Sts up to where the Church now built on corner of Houston and Flores Streets Stands, beyond & adjoining him on the north on Flores Street, was Don Mariano Rodriguez—Apposite and adjoining Felix Manchacas place Manuel Verban & next to Verban lived Francisco Montes,

On Main Street where the Banking house of John Twohig Esq Stands—was the residence of Old Antonio Baccha who died of a sunstroke while on the rode to Labahia during the time of the difficulties & hostilities which were going on between Salsedo and Manchaca and Gutiérres—in 1812—Waccine Lealles owne the whole of the property fronting on Alamo St Alemada St or the powder House road—facing the Menger hotel—and facing Bowie Street. Some of which property is now owned by our fellow citizen H Grenet Esq—

I have now mentioned the names and localities of all of the prominent and influential citizens of San Antonio that I can recollect at present and I will now say some thing about the Old Catholic Spanish Missions which are such prominen historical land marks that all who take an interest in historical topics and the sites of celebrated historical land marks should pay them all a visit and study their history closely—I am only able to give a megre and unextensive general outline and sketch of their history but I suppose the Catholic Father Superior here could furnish all of the details necessary—to any who desire to be fully informed in regard to their history.

CHAPTER 18TH
THE MISSIONS & CHURCHES

My parents and the old citizens who were here during my boy hood have informed that the Missions were all of them built by the Indian Christian converts under the immediate Supervision of the Priests (missionaries who came here to convert and civilize them)

The catholic church in the city facing Main Plaza was built in the years 1745 and 1846 having been completed in the latter & commenced in the former year. It was then called the church of San Fernando De Austria.

All but that old wall still standing in the rear and where the alter and vestry is was burned accidently by a boy on the 14 of Nov 182 and repairs were commenced on it in 1829 and they were finished in 1830—

In the year 1873 it was enlarged considerably and now its dimensions are much greater than formerly—

The Alamo

The property the present site of the alamo and the buildings connected with it formerly belonged to 2 brothers named Alexandro & Vicente Gortarri who either presented or sold it to the Catholic Missionaries (the former more likely)

It was built several years after The Church on the Plaza and during 1750 or 1760 and used as a missionary church for the conversion of the Indians until it was occupied by the Mexicans in 1835 Just the preceding year to the time when the Texans used it, Bowie Crock and Travis used it for their Barracks until they were massacred there in March 1836—

After it became the scene of this Horrible massacre no one used it for any purpose what ever and it was shrined and visited only with a sort of dread by all until 1847 when the US Government procured it from the Catholic church church as a store house and Quarter masters department and has been used as such ever since up to the present time—It was first called the mission of San Antonio Valero but both it and the other church on the Plaza were called San Antonio De Bexar—

The Conception Mission was built in 1766. The San Juan in 1765—The De—Spada in 1769 and the San José in 1771—

The 3 first mentioned were first built and with out devoting as much care time or labor to their construction as the last, They are all made in a mavelously solid and substantial manner when you consider the quali-fications of the builders who were Indians who never knew what it was to build a house of any character before and who either lived in caves in the rock or in the open air without any shelter save the friendly shade of a neighboring oak tree—

The Capital of these missions was the last (San José)

It seems that the Missionaries succeeded in converted a very powerful chief and his tribe to Christianity and he took up his residence with them at the Sanjosé Mission as the ruler of the whole tribe and the 5 missions namely Alamo, Conception, San Juan De Spada & San José—

I was told that he dressed as georgeously as a peacock with gold & silver all over him and wore an <u>admirals</u> hat and a Spanish red capâ or cape & cloak

He was very celebrated (among his tribe) as a great man, and a mighty ruler and was esteemed feared and respected by them and he made them very useful building missions and doing other <u>light</u> work of a similar character when ever he required it—

How long this civilization & christianity in the tribe lasted is a matter of history which I am unable to delinieate but as the successors of this tribe did not evince much of either I fear that like in almost all other instances the Efforts to Christanize and civilize "<u>Lo</u> the poor Indian" was a complete failure—

The Alameda—

Corderro the first Governor alluded to in this Narrative as having Cleared away the timber from the river to the 'powder House' hill—in cutting the timber out by the property owned by Leallis found a great many Alamedas or Cotton wood trees and hence the street got its name Alameda or the street of cotton wood trees—the Alamo also derived its name from the same source—

Out Beyond Lealles place on the right hand side of the Alameda road the Old Spanish Governors used to have a sort of park where they went and attended fandangos and other dances, and this Alameda park became a very popular public resort for amusement especially on Sunday long before the park was made at the Springs at the head of the San Pedro (which is a modern resort very popular just at present)

The First Buffaloes Ever sent to Europe are sent from San Antonio

One of the Old Spanish descendants a settler from the Canary Islands when he came here captured some Buffaloes which were then very plentiful and ranged in large herds around San Antonio & he took them over to Spain in the year 1760 and presented them to the King of Spain—who was much pleased with the interesting and odd present—The Monarch to show his appreciation of the gift asked Carbreo to name the reward he desired But the latter was too modest to request any thing beyond enough money to pay his passage back to San Antonio from the European Continent and would not have asked that unless he had spent all of his means in taking the present to his Sovereign—

The King granted his moderate request and conferred on him also the rank of a lieutenant in the Spanish army and gave him his Comississio—

Corbrero returned to San Antonio and gave up his hunting proclivities & became an industrious citizen—

An Old Legend

It was related to me in my youth as a very old legend at that time that many years before a missionary Padre named Marfil with a small band of Christians were crossing the plains and vast prairies Between Nacodoches and San Antonio which at that time completely filled with bands of hostile & nefarious Indians.

One day the illustrious Padre and his followers were resting in the after noon of a very sultry day under a friendly & also shady oak—and one of his adherents exclaim "See Padre! we shall all be killed there is a large band of Savages coming to murder us!" The venerable Padre raised his eyes & looked and said my brother I see nothing but a herd of peacible deer grazing on the Plain.

And Lo! wonderful to behold! in the twinkling of a bed post the savages were transmogrified into deer.

Another Legend

It is also said either of the same or another Padre that he also with his band of Pilgrims had been for several days travelling without any water to drink and they were very nearly perishing of thirst when they came to a grape vine that grew on the spot where the head spring of the San Marcos River is located (which however was not a river at that time) & they commenced to eat the grapes that grew on it and the then said their Prayers when the Padre Pulled up the grape vine by the roots and out burst the water from the base of the hill and that was the origin of the River—

Mollie Moore the Texas poetess however who was born on banks of that beautiful stream near its romantic head forgot in her beautiful poem describing it to insert this legend or was ignorant of it—

Had she done so in her sublime verse the poem would have been much more charming than it is—

BIBLIOGRAPHY

MANUSCRIPT COLLECTIONS

Archdiocese of San Antonio Chancery, San Antonio
    San Fernando Cathedral Archives (cited as SF)
Archivo General de Indias, Seville, Spain
    Audiencia de Guadalajara
Archivo General de la Nación, Mexico City, Mexico
    Provincias Internas (cited as PI)
Bexar County Clerk's Office, San Antonio
    Spanish Archives (cited as BCSA)
Briscoe Center for American History, University of Texas at Austin
    Archivo del Gobierno, Saltillo, transcripts
    Bexar Archives (cited as BA)
    Journals of the San Antonio City Council
    Menchaca, Antonio, Collection (and accession record)
    Nacogdoches Archives Transcripts (cited as NAT)
    San Antonio WPA Records
    Texas Veterans Association Papers
Catholic Archives of Texas, Austin
Daughters of the Republic of Texas Library, San Antonio
    Neuendorff Family Papers
Texas General Land Office, Austin
    County Map Collection
    Court of Claims Files
Texas State Library and Archives Commission, Austin
    Memorials and Petitions

PERIODICALS

Alamo Express (San Antonio)
Austin American-Statesman
Indianola Weekly Bulletin
Northern Standard (Clarksville)
Passing Show (San Antonio)
San Antonio Daily Herald
San Antonio Express
San Antonio Herald
Telegraph and Texas Register (Columbia, Houston)
Texas Sentinel (Austin)
Western Texas (San Antonio)

ONLINE SOURCES

Texas State Historical Association. *The Handbook of Texas Online*. http://www.tshaonline
    .org/handbook (cited as *HOT*).
Ancestry.com. RootsWeb. http://www.rootsweb.ancestry.com.

PUBLISHED PRIMARY AND SECONDARY SOURCES

Alamán, Lucas. *Historia de México desde los primeros movimientos que prepararon su indepen-
    dencia hasta la época presente*. 5 vols. 1852; facsimile ed., Mexico City, Mexico: Fondo
    de Cultura Económica, 1985.
Almaráz, Félix D., Jr. *Tragic Cavalier: Governor Manuel Salcedo of Texas, 1808-1813*. Austin:
    University of Texas Press, 1971.
Anderson, Gary Clayton. *The Indian Southwest, 1580-1830: Ethnogenesis and Reinvention*.
    Norman: University of Oklahoma Press, 1999.
Ashford, Gerald. *Spanish Texas: Yesterday and Today*. Austin: Jenkins Publishing, 1971.
Bacarisse, Charles A. "The Union of Coahuila and Texas." *Southwestern Historical Quar-
    terly* 61 (January 1958): 341–349.
Barnes, Charles Merritt. *Combats and Conquests of Immortal Heroes: Sung in Song and Told in
    Story*. San Antonio: Guessaz and Ferlet, 1910.
Barton, Henry W. *Texas Volunteers in the Mexican War*. Waco: Texian Press, 1970.
Benavides, Adán. "Sacred Space, Profane Reality: The Politics of Building a Church in
    Eighteenth-Century Texas." *Southwestern Historical Quarterly* 107 (July 2003): 1–33.
Bostick, Sion R. "Reminiscences of Sion R. Bostick." *Quarterly of the Texas State Historical
    Association* 5 (October 1901): 85–96.
Broussard, Ray F. "San Antonio during the Texas Republic: A City in Transition." *South-
    western Studies* 5 (1967): 17–21.

Brown, John Henry. *History of Texas*. 2 vols. St. Louis: L. E. Daniell, 1892–1893.

Busto, Rudy V. *King Tiger: The Religious Vision of Reies López Tijerina*. Albuquerque: University of New Mexico Press, 2005.

Camarillo, Albert. *Chicanos in a Changing Society: From Mexican Pueblos to American Barrios in Santa Barbara and Southern California, 1848-1930*. 1979. Reprint, Dallas: Southern Methodist University Press, 2005.

Carlson, Paul. *The Plains Indians*. College Station: Texas A&M University Press, 1998.

Carpenter, V. K., comp. *The State of Texas Federal Population Schedules Seventh Census of the United States, 1850*. Huntsville, AR: Century Enterprises, 1969.

Castañeda, Carlos E. *Our Catholic Heritage in Texas, 1519-1936*. 7 vols. Austin: Von Boeckmann-Jones, 1936–1958.

Chabot, Frederick C. *The Perote Prisoners: Being the Diary of James L. Truehart, Printed for the First Time Together with an Historical Introduction*. San Antonio: Naylor, 1934.

———. *With the Makers of San Antonio*. San Antonio: Artes Gráficas, 1937.

Chipman, Donald A. *Spanish Texas, 1519-1821*. Austin: University of Texas Press, 1992.

Crimm, Carolina Castillo. *De León: A Tejano Family History*. Austin: University of Texas Press, 2003.

Crisp, James Ernest. "Anglo-Texan Attitudes toward the Mexican, 1821–1845." Ph.D. diss., Yale University, 1976.

Day, James M., ed. "Texas Letters and Documents." *Texana* 5 (Spring 1967): 81–84.

De León, Arnoldo. *The Tejano Community, 1836-1900*. Albuquerque, 1982. Reprint, Dallas: Southern Methodist University Press, 1997.

———. *They Called Them Greasers: Anglo Attitudes toward Mexicans in Texas, 1821-1900*. Austin: University of Texas Press, 1983.

De Zavala, Adina. *History and Legends of the Alamo and Other Missions in and around San Antonio*. 1917. Reprint, Houston: Arte Público Press, 1996.

Dimmick, Gregg J. *Sea of Mud: The Retreat of the Mexican Army after San Jacinto, An Archeological Investigation*. Austin: Texas State Historical Association, 2004.

Dobie, J. Frank, ed. *Legends of Texas*. Publications of the Texas Folk-Lore Society, no. 3, 2nd ed. Austin: Texas Folk-Lore Society, 1924.

Downs, Fane. "The History of Mexicans in Texas, 1820–1845." Ph.D. diss., Texas Tech University, 1970.

Edwards, Lester C. *The Life of Sam Houston: The Hunter, Patriot, and Statesman of Texas*. New York: G. G. Evans, 1860.

Filisola, Vicente. *Memorias para la historia de la Guerra de Tejas*. 2 vols. Mexico City, Mexico: R. Rafael, 1848–1849.

Foote, Henry Stuart. *Texas and the Texans; Or, Advance of the Anglo-Americans to the South-West*. 2 vols. Philadelphia: Thomas Cowperthwait, 1841. Reprint, Austin, TX: Steck, 1935.

Fowler, Will. *Santa Anna of Mexico*. Lincoln: University of Nebraska Press, 2007.

Garrett, Julia K. *Green Flag over Texas: The Last Years of Spain in Texas*. 1939. Reprint, Austin: Pemberton Press, 1969.

Gómez, Laura E. *Manifest Destinies: The Making of the Mexican American Race.* New York: New York University Press, 2007.

Griswold del Castillo, Richard. *The Los Angeles Barrio, 1850–1890: A Social History.* Berkeley: University of California Press, 1979.

Hämäläinen, Pekka. *The Comanche Empire.* New Haven, CT: Yale University Press, 2008.

Hansen, Todd, ed. *The Alamo Reader: A Study in History.* Mechanicsburg, PA: Stackpole Books, 2003.

Hardin, Stephen L. "Efficient in the Cause." In *Tejano Journey, 1770–1850,* edited by Gerald E. Poyo. Austin: University of Texas Press, 1996.

———. *Texian Iliad: A Military History of the Texas Revolution, 1835–1836.* Austin: University of Texas Press, 1994.

Henderson, Harry McCorry. "The Magee-Gutiérrez Expedition." *Southwestern Historical Quarterly* 55 (July 1951): 43–61.

Henson, Margaret Swett. *Lorenzo de Zavala: The Pragmatic Idealist.* Fort Worth: Texas Christian University Press, 1996.

Houston, Sam. *The Writings of Sam Houston, 1813–1863,* edited by Amelia W. Williams and Eugene C. Barker. 8 vols. Austin: University of Texas Press, 1938–1943.

James, Marquis. *The Raven: A Biography of Sam Houston.* Indianapolis: Bobbs-Merrill, 1929.

Jenkins, John Holmes, comp. *The Papers of the Texas Revolution, 1835–1836.* 10 vols. Austin, TX: Presidial Press, 1973.

Knight, Larry. "The Cart War: Defining American in San Antonio in the 1850s." *Southwestern Historical Quarterly* 109 (January 2006): 319–336.

Kuykendall, J. H., comp. "Reminiscences of Early Texans: A Collection from the Austin Papers." *Quarterly of the Texas State Historical Association* 6 (January 1903): 311–330.

Labadie, N. D. "San Jacinto Campaign." *The Texas Almanac for 1859.* N.p., 1859.

Lamar, Mirabeau Buonaparte. *The Papers of Mirabeau Buonaparte Lamar,* edited by Charles Adams Gulick Jr. and Katherine Elliott. 6 vols. Austin: Von Boeckmann-Jones, 1973.

Laws of the Republic of Texas Passed the First Session of Third Congress. Houston: Intelligencer Office, 1839.

Linenthal, Edward Tabor. *Sacred Ground: Americans and Their Battlefields.* Urbana: University of Illinois Press, 1991.

Linn, John J. *Reminiscences of Fifty Years in Texas.* New York, 1883. Reprint, Austin: State House, 1986.

Littlejohn, E. G. "The Holy Spring of Father Margil at Nacogdoches." In *Legends of Texas,* edited by J. Frank Dobie. Austin: Texas Folk-Lore Society, 1924.

Matovina, Timothy. *Tejano Religion and Ethnicity: San Antonio, 1821–1860.* Austin: University of Texas Press, 1995.

———, ed. *The Alamo Remembered: Tejano Accounts and Perspectives.* Austin: University of Texas Press, 1995.

Maverick, Mary A. *Memoirs of Mary A. Maverick,* edited by Rena Maverick Green. San Antonio: Alamo, 1921.

Maverick, Samuel. *Samuel Maverick, Texan: 1803-1870. A Collection of Letters, Journals, and Memoirs*, edited by Rena Maverick Green. San Antonio: privately printed, 1952.

McGraw, A. Joachim, John W. Clark Jr., and Elizabeth A. Robbins, eds. *A Texas Legacy, the Old San Antonio Road and the Caminos Reales: A Tricentennial History, 1691-1991*. Austin: Texas State Department of Highways and Public Transportation, Highway Design Division, 1998.

Menchaca, Antonio. *Memoirs*, edited by Frederick C. Chabot. San Antonio: Yanaguana Society, 1937.

———. "The Memoirs of Captain Menchaca: Being an Unpublished Manuscript Detailing Events in San Antonio from 1807 to the Battle of San Jacinto," edited and annotated by James Pearson Newcomb Sr. *The Passing Show: A Weekly Journal of Public Interest*, vol. 1, no. 32 (22 June 1907), no. 33 (29 June 1907), no. 34 (6 July 1907), no. 35 (12 July 1907), no. 36 (20 July 1907), and no. 37 (29 July 1907).

Montejano, David. *Anglos and Mexicans in the Making of Texas, 1836-1986*. Austin: University of Texas Press, 1986.

Mooney & Morrison's General Directory of the City of San Antonio, for 1877-1878. Galveston: Galveston News, 1877.

Nance, Joseph Milton. *After San Jacinto: The Texas-Mexican Frontier, 1836-1841*. Austin: University of Texas Press, 1963.

———. *Attack and Counter-Attack: The Texas-Mexican Frontier, 1842*. Austin: University of Texas Press, 1964.

———, ed. and trans. "Brigadier General Adrián Woll's Report of His Expedition into Texas in 1842." *Southwestern Historical Quarterly* 58 (April 1955): 523-552.

Navarro, José Antonio. *Apuntes históricos interesantes de San Antonio de Béxar escritos por el C. Dn. José Antonio Navarro, en noviembre de 1853. Y publicados por varios de sus amigos*. San Antonio: privately printed, 1869.

———. *Defending Mexican Valor in Texas: José Antonio Navarro's Historical Writings, 1853-1857*, edited by David R. McDonald and Timothy Matovina. Austin: State House, 1995.

Peña, José Enrique de la. *With Santa Anna in Texas: A Personal Narrative of the Revolution*, translated by Carmen Perry. Exp. ed. College Station: Texas A&M University Press, 1997.

Rippy, J. Fred. "Border Troubles along the Rio Grande, 1848–1860." *Southwestern Historical Quarterly* 23 (October 1919): 91–111.

Rodríguez, J[osé] M[aría]. *Rodríguez Memoirs of Early Texas*. San Antonio: Passing Show Printing, 1913. Reprint, San Antonio: Standard, 1961.

Sánchez, Rosaura. *Telling Identities: The Californio Testimonios*. Minneapolis: University of Minnesota Press, 1994.

Schwarz, Ted. *Forgotten Battlefield of the First Texas Revolution: The Battle of Medina, August 18, 1813*, edited by Robert Thonhoff. Austin: Eakin Press, 1985.

Seguín, Juan N. *Personal Memoirs of John N. Seguín from the Year 1834 to the Retreat of General Woll from the City of San Antonio in 1842*. San Antonio: Ledger Book and Job Office, 1858.

———. *A Revolution Remembered: The Memoirs and Selected Correspondence of Juan N. Seguín*, edited by Jesús F. de la Teja. Austin: State House, 1991; 2nd ed., Austin: Texas State Historical Association, 2002.

Teja, Jesús F. de la. "Rebellion on the Frontier." In *Tejano Journey, 1770–1850*, edited by Gerald E. Poyo. Austin: University of Texas Press, 1996.

———. *San Antonio de Béxar: A Community on New Spain's Northern Frontier*. Albuquerque: University of New Mexico Press, 1995.

———. "Why Urbano and María Trinidad Can't Get Married: Social Relations in Late Colonial San Antonio." *Southwestern Historical Quarterly* 112 (October 2008): 121–146.

———, ed. *Tejano Leadership in Mexican and Revolutionary Texas*. College Station: Texas A&M University Press, 2010.

Teja, Jesús F. de la, and John Wheat. "Béxar: Profile of a Tejano Community, 1820–1832." *Southwestern Historical Quarterly* 89 (July 1985): 7–34.

Weber, David J. *The Spanish Frontier in North America*. New Haven, CT: Yale University Press, 1992.

Weddle, Robert S. *The San Sabá Mission: Spanish Pivot in Texas*. Austin: University of Texas Press, 1964.

White, Gifford. *1830 Citizens of Texas*. Austin: Eakin, 1983.

———, ed. *The 1840 Census of the Republic of Texas*. Austin: Pemberton Press, 1966.

Winkler, E. W., ed. "The Bexar and Dawson Prisoners." *Quarterly of the Texas State Historical Association* 13 (April 1910): 292–324.

Winters, J. W. *True Veterans of Texas: An Authentic Account of the Battle of San Jacinto*. Pearsall: Pearsall Leader Printers, n.d.

Wright, S. J. *San Antonio de Béxar: Historical, Traditional, Legendary*. Austin: Morgan, 1916.

INDEX

Page numbers shown in **bold** indicate figures or illustrations.

Lightning Source UK Ltd.
Milton Keynes UK
UKHW011941160922
408955UK00011B/247